The Loblolly Book

The Loblolly Book

Water Witching, Wild Hog Hunting, Home Remedies,
Grandma's Moral Tales, and Other Affairs of Plain Texas Living

Edited by Thad Sitton

Photo of Ed Bell by Dee Azadian.
Photographs in "Water Witching" Chapter by John Suhrstedt.

Ted Hinton interview in Bonnie and Clyde used by permission of HOUSTON CHRONICLE.

Copyright © 1983 by Thad Sitton, ed. All rights including reproduction by photographic or electronic process and translation into other languages are fully reserved under the International Copyright Union, the Universal Copyright Convention, and the Pan-American Copyright Convention. Reproduction or use of this book in whole or in part in any manner without written permission of the publisher is strictly prohibited.

Texas Monthly Press, Inc.
P.O. Box 1569
Austin, Texas 78767

   B C D E F G H

ISBN 0-932012-28-0

Library of Congress Cataloging in Publication Data Main entry under title:
The Loblolly book.

　1. Texas—Social life and customs—Addresses, essays, lectures. 2. Folklore—Texas—Addresses, essays, lectures. 3. Handicraft—Texas—Addresses, essays, lectures. 4. Texas—Biography—Addresses, essays, lectures. I. Sitton, Thad, 1941-
F391.L82 1983   306'.09764   83-14471
ISBN 0-932012-28-0

Book design by Jim Darilek and Kathi Branson

Contents

Acknowledgments 1
Introduction 3
Wild Hog Hunting on the Sabine 7
Sheriff Corbett Akins: Bloodhounds and Bootleggers 19
Folks Who Knew Bonnie and Clyde 47
Sunbonnets 73
Feed Sacks 77
Cooking Up a Batch of Lye Soap 81
Grandmother's Home Remedies 85
Faith Healing 111
Coming to Texas: Two Settlement Tales 117
Courtship, Wedding, Shivaree 127
Death Lore 135
Country Epitaphs 143
Hant Stories 151
Ed Bell: Truths and Windy Tales 157
Pure, Raw Bee Honey 171
Mules Remembered 177
Grandma's Moral Tales 187
Witching for Water (and Oil) 193
Jack Pate: "I'd Rather Be a Cowboy than Anything" 203
From Skip-Rope Rhymes to Sacred Harp 211
Fifty Country Proverbs 231
Monroe Brannon 235
Student Contributors 247

Acknowledgments

The editor would like to thank the following individuals for sharing their memories: Dr. F. E. Abernethy, Corbett Akins, Brandy Anderson, Mrs. Hatti Ball, Mrs. Mildred Beheler, Ed Bell, Charlene Berryman, Monroe Brannon, Isaac Brown, Grace Burns, Perry Cartwright, D. D. Chadwick, Leon Choate, R. E. Choate, Charles Christian, Mable Clark, Mrs. Pearl Collins, Gus Davis, Mrs. Myrtle Davis, LeRoy De Loney, Mrs. De Steiguer, Mrs. Hiram Dry, Linnie DuBose, Alex Duncan, Raybon Ford, James Garrison, Mrs. Delores Graves, Ernest Graves, Mrs. Greer Griffith, Max Haddick, Jim Hammars, Matt Hancock, Leo Covington Hanna, Odell Hardin, Tom Havard, Luther Helm, Ted Hinton, Mrs. Katie Holt, Robin Hooper, Mrs. Doris House, Mr. and Mrs. Odell Hudson, Mrs. J. W. Hudson, Mrs. Faye Humber, Lizzie Jeffress, Lucille Johnson, Dennis Jones, Kelly Jones, Mrs. Jack Kelly, Pete Kennedy, Mrs. W. T. Koonce, George Kright, Clara Evelyn Latham, Floy H. Latham, Mrs. Elma Lawhorn, Leon Lewis, Beverly Lyons, Rudolph Marshall, Conway McMillian, Jim Milford, Lester Patton Miller, William Moore, Leo Muckleroy, Ernest Murphy, Mrs. Nancy Parker, Copeland Pass, Jack Pate, William Pate, B. A. Patterson, Mrs. Ollie Prince, Bobby Reider, Opal Vaughn Rhodes, Teresa Ritter, Mrs. Billie Robinson, Callie Robinson, Hall Rousseau, Alvin J. Schkade, Carl Schkade, Rev. A. W. Smith, John Wesley Smith, "Mama" Jewell Smith, Theresa Smith, Mr. Snelson, Ellen Starkey, Lox Tinkle, John Tyson, Herman Venson, F. David Waldrop, Waymon Walker, Earlie Webb, Opella Weir, Sybil Whiddon, U. H. Wilson, Marvin Wolfe, Ronnie Wolfe, Mrs. Odell Youngblood, Mrs. Ruby Youngblood, and Mrs. Sandra Youngblood.

Introduction

The Loblolly Book is about Texas people, folklore, folk crafts, and folk history. The materials in this book were produced as the result of a unique experiment in Texas education, an experiment that has far from run its course. The articles in *The Loblolly Book* are drawn from previously published issues of the student journals *Loblolly* (Gary High School, Gary, Texas), *Old Timer* (Albany High School, Albany, Texas), *Chinquapin* (Douglass School, Douglass, Texas), *The Plum Creek Press* (Lockhart Intermediate School, Lockhart, Texas), and *Black Gold* (Carthage Junior College, Carthage, Texas).

It all began with *Foxfire* in Rabun Gap, Georgia. As Lincoln King told me, "I had taught at Gary a year and a half when at Christmas of 1972 my wife got a copy of the first *Foxfire* book. I grabbed the book and went all through it over Christmas vacation. As I read, I thought that, if these kids can do it, Texas kids can do it, too. I went back to school and got tentative clearance. Nobody, including myself, knew exactly what we were trying to do."

In the beginning, neither did teacher Eliot Wigginton of *Foxfire*. Frustrated with the educational status quo (his students had set his desk on fire!), Wigginton walked into class one day and proposed the publication of some kind of national magazine. Just what this meant was worked out in the months that followed. Students selected the name "Foxfire" for their project, and in the spring of 1967 Wigginton and his classes at Rabun Gap/Nacoochee School in rural north Georgia began publishing a magazine of community oral history, folklore, and folklife. Wigginton served as project adviser, but the students themselves did the work. With tape recorders and cameras in hand, they field-collected the raw materials for their journal from the living repositories of the "old mountain culture"—in many cases their own grandparents and great-grandparents. Then they transcribed and edited their field data into articles with titles like "Moonshining as a Fine Art," "Snake Lore," and "Building a Log Cabin." It worked like a charm. Student motivation was high, community acceptance of the magazine was excellent, and *Foxfire* was launched.

An anthology of student articles from *Foxfire* was published by Doubleday in 1972 as *The Foxfire Book*. Since then, over two hundred classroom teachers have reacted as did Lincoln King in 1972, who thought, "If those kids can do it, our kids can do it, too." In one way or another, this happened at Albany for teacher Winfred Waller, at Douglass for Pauline Toumlin, and at Lockhart for Barbara Crouch.

For other teachers and students, *The Foxfire Book* became a sort of gauntlet thrown—an implicit challenge to try to replicate the *Foxfire* pattern in their schools, with materials drawn from their distinctive regional folk cultures. Again and again they have done so, often with great success. All that is necessary (as one teacher told me) is "an arm and a leg, blood, sweat, and tears." This is no exaggeration. Getting out a quarterly or biannual magazine while performing the usual complement of Sisyphean tasks associated with classroom teaching *is* an enterprise little short of heroic.

This is an editorial point of view, of course. The students and teachers whose personal blood, sweat, and tears have produced the twenty-eight issues of *Loblolly,* the fifteen issues of *Chinquapin,* the nine issues of *Old Timer,* and the eight issues of *The Plum Creek Press* do not, so far as I know, view themselves as heroic. But they should, students and teachers alike, because production of the oral history/folklore magazine based upon fieldwork in the home community can be a most difficult task, given the standard operating procedures of many public secondary schools. It is a rare enterprise that allows students out into the community during school hours to converse with flesh-and-blood citizens and to learn from them.

Wherever it takes root, the "Foxfire magazine" is fueled by pride in the regional folk culture, by a sense of place and of community. It is therefore not surprising that the idea has done well in Texas, where the sense of regional and cultural distinctiveness runs deep and strong. *Loblolly* and *Chinquapin* have their roots in the piney woods of deep East Texas; *The Plum Creek Press* hails from Caldwell County, where a mix of East and Central Texas traditions prevails; and *Old Timer* is West Texas, born and bred.

Other student magazines, still in formative stages, offer great promise for the future. *Those Comforting Hills* (Comfort, Texas) and *Hidden Memories* (Burton, Texas) operate in communities where Tex-German traditions are strong, and in El Paso, *Sombras Del Pasado* [Shadows of the Past] is beginning to tap the rich folkways of Hispanic Texas.

Texas is a land of regional traditions and numerous ethnic cultures, many of which still retain a strong measure of vitality in the rapidly urbanizing society of 1983. It seems fertile ground for other applications of the Foxfire idea. Both *Loblolly* and *Old Timer* have been helped by their involvement in the Texas Historical Association's "Junior Historian" program, and it is very possible that the junior historians will give birth to additional publishing programs.

According to Lincoln King of *Loblolly,* "What we've been trying to do with the magazine is to discover, collect, and preserve the local and regional history of East Texas. While the students are doing this, they discover much, much more about themselves, their own roots, heritage, and culture." Some of the projects (notably *Chinquapin* and *Old Timer*) make sophisticated use of documentary sources in their studies of local history, but most magazines rely heavily on oral history, recording their community history from those who experienced it firsthand. In a recurrent pattern, testimony so recorded is transcribed directly from the interview tapes and presented verbatim in the magazine, "with the bark on."

In Texas, as elsewhere in the United States, this fresh approach to the recording of local history has achieved strong community acceptance. Each of the Texas magazines is a celebration of regional culture and home community and a successful attempt to present that community with something it seems to really need—a body of "popular" history to help it remember, and better understand, its collective past. Academic historians have rarely provided this grass-roots history, and local historical and genealogical societies (where they exist at all) have seldom produced works that explored the contributions of *all* segments of their communities. The magazines are filling a significant void and doing real work.

At *Loblolly, Old Timer, Chinquapin, The Plum Creek Press,* and other Texas projects, students go out into their communities to document and preserve aspects of traditional history that yet survive in the memories of living men and women. This is not the "big picture" history of the academicians, or accounts of the doings of a political elite, but the grass-roots patterns of daily life in early twentieth-century Texas. Students are working the fertile ground that lies between the formal disciplines of folklore and social history to produce articles on topics as colorful and various as wild hog hunting, death customs, play-parties, and the musical traditions of sacred harp.

These vanishing aspects of Texas tradition are rarely recorded in documentary sources, and so they often pass into oblivion along with the memories that knew them as the intimate, unremarkable, repetitive patterns of daily life. And it is a kind of paradox that while political history may often seem much the same from one era to the next, the humble details of daily life—changing as they do—come to seem quite exotic. Younger readers will have much to learn in this book from living men and women who tell of a time when household soap was made in big black pots in the yard, when underwear was often crafted from feed sacks, when bacon was pursued in the river bottoms at considerable risk to life and limb, and when getting married was a good deal more hazardous than at present!

Perhaps if we are old enough, many of our own grandparents may have told us much of this. But if they didn't, now, thanks to these students and teachers, we have the collective grandparents of *The Loblolly Book.*

Sometimes the elements of social history and folklore recorded by the journals seem of genuine scholarly interest. Pork was the mainstay of the nineteenth-century diet, at least in East Texas, but the running of feral hogs in the bottoms and the annual hunt, using dogs to mark, castrate, and slaughter them have rarely been described in detail. Here, from *Loblolly,* is "Wild Hog Hunting on the Sabine." Likewise, turn-of-the-century Texas ran on mule power, but historians of the future will look in vain for scholarly treatises on the raising, training, and use of mules, as well as other mule lore. "Mules Remembered" is the detailed recollections of men who spent much of their working life in association with the quixotic animal. And the epic "Folks Who Knew Bonnie and Clyde" is a fascinating exploration of the varieties of folk memory about Bonnie Parker and Clyde Barrow, the flamboyant East Texas "Depression bandits" of the 1930's.

This mixed bag of social history and folklore is precisely that portion of our collective past most likely to be lost to future generations. Americans of the twenty-first century should be appropriately grateful to these students and teachers who had the energy and good sense to preserve late nineteenth- and early twentieth-century oral tradition before it was too late. As C. L. Sonnichsen admonished, "The grass roots historian must do his work before the night cometh, in which no man can work."

On porches and in front parlors, these students have sat in for many of us—those who never quite found the time for tape-recorded interviews with *their* grandparents—for the ones of us who waited a little too long. Here are some of what we might have recorded: "the magnificent hunting tales, the ghost stories that kept a thousand children sleepless, the intricate tricks of self-sufficiency acquired through years of trial and error, the eloquent and haunting stories of suffering and sharing and building and healing and planting and harvesting...."

To further echo my predecessor, Eliot Wigginton, "The contents of this book need little introduction; they stand on their own as helpful instructions and enjoyable reading." This testimony comes from the Texas grass roots, collected by Texas schoolchildren from the generations of their grandparents and great-grandparents. Its themes are individuality, self-reliance, pride, humor, and a certain propensity for violence. It is the authentic voice of a Texas that is passing away.

Thad Sitton

Wild Hog Hunting on the Sabine

In the nineteenth and early twentieth century, pork, not beef, was the mainstay of the rural East Texas diet. Much of this pork was obtained from razorback hogs that were left to fend for themselves in the hardwood bottoms for most of the year. Periodically, in an operation that was a cross between roundup and hunt, the wild hogs were tracked down by their owners for purposes of marking and butchering. In the late winter of 1975, *Loblolly* followed Waymon Walker, a man who still runs hogs in the old way, on his yearly hunt in the Sabine bottoms—a most exciting way to get one's bacon!

—Loblolly

Waymon Walker

I was raised here on this place. My daddy ran hogs and turned them loose in the river bottom that way. A lot of times when I ran short of hogs, I'd go to the sale where they was a-sellin' these wild hogs and buy me a bunch. I've done this a number of times during my life. I'd take them back here next to the road and mark their ears and turn them loose. You know, we got it so each animal on the range had a mark, an earmark. I've raised them all my life and handled them that way.

Like I said, I was born right here on this tract of land. It belonged to my daddy and mother. The only time I was away from here for any length of time was when I went to World War II.

I have what we call woods hogs. They make their own living by eating acorns through the acorn season, which starts from fall to usually way up into spring before they play out. That's when they get fat from acorns and hickory nuts, so we kill them then.

In the summer, they usually just eat herbs. They also live on different kinds of soft roots that's in the low places. If the water goes dry in the ponds, they catch the fish out of them, crawfish and other kinds. That's the way they make their living, but they have a hard time through the summer.

I imagine if I counted all the pigs, I'd have somewhere around 150 to 160 head. I don't know exactly myself.

I've got two different marks, one that my brothers use. We have those marks recorded in the records over there at the Recorder's Office in Carthage. My mark is a split in the right ear and a fallow fork in the left.

If you're handling hogs in the woods in the summertime, they'll spread out. They'll spread out over the woods in groups of three or four looking for something to eat. When there's plenty to eat, there may be thirty head in a bunch of hogs. When the sows are grown pigs, they get ready to bring pigs. They'll stop in a thicket somewhere to bring pigs and bunch together. They'll quit the main old bunch to start a bunch of their own. In winter there may be just two sows and pigs staying together, or there may be, say, eight or nine sows in one bunch. We have to take some of them sows, three or four, when they get fat, to make sausage out of them. When you have so many sows in one bunch, they will leave to go way up the river, even crossing the river on you. They got to look over such a wide territory in a day's time, for each one of them is trying to find something to eat. It's easier for just a few in a bunch, say fifteen or twenty, to find something to eat than a bunch of thirty-five to forty. They'll move so far and move around on you so much, until they're hard to tend to when you have so many in one bunch.

The pigs live to about seven or eight years old. I imagine hogs at that age would be about as old as a person of seventy-five or eighty years. We usually kill the boars when they're no older than three years.

It depends on the high water, when maybe a lot of pigs drown, as to how many I kill in a year. In a good year I'll get seventy-five or eighty. It depends on the acorns, too. A lot of my pigs die when the sows wean them in the summertime when there's not much for them to eat.

I have had trouble with people getting my hogs every once in a while. That's to be expected in anything. I caught people doing it. After that, we'd kinda just have a little round over it, and I'd let them go. I guess anything a person has got, there will always be somebody after it. I don't mind so much when they get my boars, but it really hurts when they get my sows.

A year and a half or so ago, I got my leg broken, so now I give one of my brothers a share of the hogs for helping me out with them. We ride together when the water's down wherever we can to care and keep an eye on those hogs.

We train dogs, starting out using hound dogs that will trail. Any kind of a dog won't do, you gotta have a hound dog. You need a hound to follow the hogs to find their tracks. He has to find out where they rooted in these old ponds. You can always find one sloughing around. If you run a bunch of hogs out of the thicket, you usually sic the dogs on them, barking at them and teaching them what you want them to do. They'll pick it up within themselves. I'll take about a year to get a dog trained where he'll bay hogs to separate one off from the others. You know he's trained by the words I say to him. I holler at mine when they're baying a bunch of hogs. They do this by trailing them or taking them someplace. When there's a change in their voice, from a long ways off, they've found the hogs. Usually it's a different bark. In training them you gotta teach them what you want them to do. Then, if they won't do that, get a limb and rap them a few times. If they don't come out when you bay a bunch of hogs, holler for your dogs to come out. Call "Come out, come out," like that. If he doesn't, he'll come out every time when he's being strapped. Let him know, though, what you're giving him a whipping about.

I've got a red hound out there now that's my trail dog. I've had him cut twice this winter by the hogs. My grandfather once had one old dog that got too close to a hog—like to have torn him all to pieces!

My horse is just as well trained as the dogs. When I shoot an old boar down in the woods, I use the horse to drag him out. And the horse doesn't get scared. I killed one that weighed about 275 pounds yesterday, and I dragged him out on the rope around the horn of the saddle. And he's broken also to work with a harness on. He works the fields for me on all my crops. He's part of my regular Depression rig for farming I have here.

I have a horn that I use to call my dogs, especially when they run off and I want them to come back. When my brother and I are in different places in the woods, I blow my horn to let him know where I'm at. If I blow three long blows, that's a call blow. He knows then that I want him to come over to where I'm at. I strap my horn to my saddle.

We killed two hogs on Saturday. We killed them after we rounded them up with the dogs. The ones we killed are the fat hogs. Kill them with a rifle. We got us a rope there about the size of a well rope. We'll loop a rope around his head and tie it around the horn of the saddle. Then we drag him out of the swamps to a road where we can get him in our truck.

We bring him in, then, and build fires around the pots. We have pine out of the woods, enough to heat the water in the two washpots out there. After we get the water, we build a fire around the pots. It depends on whether the hog had a good bit of age on it, like 200 or 250 pounds. It takes a hotter temperature to scald a hog like that than a 100- or 125-pound hog. You have to have hot water fixed just right so you can scald the hog. At the same time, if it's too hot, it will set the hair on him. This is when the hair will scald and won't come out. The way I can tell when the water is right is to just run my fingers through it right quick to see if it's hot enough. Then we cut the leaders in the back legs, so we can put these sticks in there, the "gambling sticks." Together, all of us catches the back legs and the front legs so we can hang him up. That takes a pretty good effort to hang up one that weighs over 200 pounds. With some more hot water out of this washpot, we pour it over the hog to get all the loose hair off. Getting the hair off him is called scraping the hog down.

The sticks that you use in their legs to hang them up are made of different lengths. Of course the big hogs have to have a longer stick than the small hogs. Say you're killing a 100-pound hog, why, it don't take a stick over sixteen inches long to spread his legs apart. They're called gambling sticks, any kind of green sticks about the size of a fifty-cent piece wide. You can make some maybe two feet long for bigger hogs.

We cut his throat, then we start up there between his back legs and come right down his stomach with our knives. We take his entrails out and then wash him out with cold water from the hydrant. We let him hang there on the pole to drain until we finish scraping another hog, or for about a half hour. When we take the entrails out, we save the liver because we like it. He's got a gall on his liver so we take a knife to cut that off and then rinse the liver.

After the hog has drained good, we lay him on that bench with him laying straight on his back. You start off by taking his head off. Then, by cutting on each side of his backbone, you will be able to take the backbone out. Also, take the ribs out of the middlings, and then cut the fat off the middlings. The middlings are cut off, leaving the shoulder and ham.

From the shoulders to the back to where his shoulder bone meets, we call a knuckle joint. This is where we cut it off and leave the leg in one piece. The other piece we call a square shoulder. That's the way we cut the hog up. With the ax we chop all up and down the backbone, four to five inches apart. You can cut any length you want for cooking.

After cutting the hog, we lay it out in the smokehouse. If you got a couple of hogs, sprinkle about ten pounds of salt on them. Let it lay there to get the animal heat out. We put about twenty more pounds when we salt it down the next day.

You have to let it stay in the smokehouse for twenty-one days or longer, then you can take it out. I put water in them washpots and scald the meat to take the salt off. Then you get some kind of string, punch some holes in the meat, and hang it in the smokehouse. Put in there an old tub with some old oak bark—that will put taste in the meat. Cut you a little green hickory and sassafras, about the size of your leg and about a foot long. Split them open with an ax to make you some sticks of wood, and put that hickory and sassafras in that oak bark. It will start a smoke in there so strong that you can't put your head in. Have a tub of water setting by the smokehouse. You can put some water on the wood to keep the fire from blazing up. Leave it smoking about four or five hours. About a week after, let it air out good. Then smoke it again until you've done that about four times. That meat won't weigh but about a half of what it weighed when it was green. When it is finished, you can take it somewhere to get it sliced and put it in your deep freeze.

Waymon Walker beginning the hunt

Dogs baying a big sow

The Loblolly Book

Hog and dogs fight it out

Kelly Walker starting to tie up the sow

Wild Hog Hunting on the Sabine

Putting the dragline Around the Jaws

An unhappy sow

The Loblolly Book

Dragging the sow to a clear spot on the river bottom

Waymon Walker dragging the sow to the slaughter

The Loblolly Book

Kelly Walker tries to catch boar with rope loop

Fight in the briar patch

The boar, now a barrow, gets his ears marked

Man, dog, and struggling hog

The Loblolly Book

Waymon Walker calls in the dogs

Sheriff Corbett Akins: Bloodhounds and Bootleggers

Corbett Akins is a past sheriff of Panola County and is well known and loved not only in this area, but all over Texas. Mr. Akins has proved to be a wealth of information on everything from making fiddles to running bloodhounds to finding moonshine stills.

During part of the time that he was sheriff of Panola County, he wrote a weekly article for the *Panola Watchman* about the adventures and mishaps of the sheriff and his fellow officers. It is from these articles that *Loblolly* got the information for the second part of the Corbett Akins story.

Thanks to Mrs. Doris House for use of the *Watchman* microfilms from February to November 1951, the source of these selections from "The Sheriff's Column" by Corbett Akins.

—Loblolly

Corbett Akins
I was born in Panola County, East Texas, seven miles west of Beckville, Texas, on Friday morning, October the twenty-first, 1892. When I was born, my mother and daddy named me Clifford. I went by the name of Clifford for six months, but after six months Jim Corbett and John L. Sullivan had a fight, and Jim Corbett whipped John L. Sullivan. My daddy came in from the field one day, saw me jumping and a-bouncing on the bed, and says, "We gonna call that boy Jim Corbett." And I been named Jim Corbett ever since. I was raised on the farm, lived with my mother and my daddy, and plowed an old mule till I was twenty-one years of age. My daddy always told me, "Son, when you get to be twenty-one years old you can leave home."

I went to lots of places when I was a kid with my daddy, and we went to sacred harp conventions. He was a teacher of the sacred harp, and finally taught me to sing. I would get up and lead a song. I didn't have shoes to wear to singings and my daddy finally bought me a pair of brogans. People don't know what they are now. They're a little shoe that looks like a slipper, but they are hard and have a brass buckle on them. He tried to make me wear them, but we had to walk two or three miles to the school or church. So I'd put them under my arm and when we got there I'd put them on.

I never knew what it was to ride to school. One school was about two miles, the other was about three. We'd walk every morning. We took our lunch in a tin bucket or syrup bucket. About all we'd have would be a packed sweet potato, a boiled egg, a piece of bacon or ham, and a biscuit. I recall one day we were all eating dinner and there was a young lady that had some syrup in a snuff bottle. She took that syrup around back of a boy and poured it on the top of his head.

At lunchtime me and my brother had a spring where we put our lunch because we had buttermilk. I recall an old bunch of hogs found out where our milk was. So we decided to kill the hogs. We beat up some glass real fine and put it in some biscuits and we fed them to the hogs. Instead of killing them, it just made them fatter. So we had to move our refrigerator. There was always something going on.

I went to school at Brooks Schoolhouse, which was just a country school. We didn't have no heaters, other than just old wooden heaters, and the schoolhouse was made out of one- by twelve-inch plane. I stayed in that school the biggest part of my school days, but my daddy wanted to educate me, so he sent me to Beckville. I went to school in Beckville and what you call graduated. Those days, they didn't have no diplomas or nothing, just when you made a certain grade and you graduated. I made that grade and the biggest trouble I had was algebra, and a fellow who takes algebra oughta be killed anyhow. Well, after staying in the school at Beckville, I graduated, and I thought I was a smart boy. I went back out there on the farm and begin to farm again.

In October Papa put me in the field, breaking land with an old mule by the name of Pat. Old Pat was a long-eared mule and every time she stepped forward her ears would go with her. I came in one evening most near dead. I looked at my daddy, and I says, "Well, Daddy, I'm gonna leave home tomorrow." He said, "Son, don't do that. I'll need you around the farm. Somebody's got to milk the cows and help your mama."

When I was a small boy, we'd kill our hogs in the fall of the year and hang the meat in the smokehouse. It was our job to see that the hickory fire was burning in the smokehouse to dry the meat. We also had to cook the lard. We would take the fat part of the hog, chop it up, and place it in a pot to boil it. After letting it cool, we'd dip the lard off. The part that was left was the cracklins. We put the cracklins in a tub and took it to the smokehouse. While they were warm, we would place them in a small jar. After placing the cracklins in the jar, we pressed them to get the lard that was left.

My brother and I were looking after the smokehouse to make sure the fire kept burning. My mother left that afternoon to help a neighbor quilt. She told us not to let the fire go out. My papa had gone to Carthage to be on the jury. Before he left that morning, I heard him tell my mother that it might be one or two o'clock that night before he got back. He had to ride the thirteen miles on a mule.

Horace and I got all the cracklins squeezed out into the cracklin jars. We had vented up the fire. We were sitting there like two little boys playing and having fun. I picked up this small, greasy churn that we had had the cracklins in. When he turned around I put that churn over his head. I was not thinking about any trouble. Naturally, he reached up and tried to get the churn off his head, but he couldn't. After he worked a good while, I tried to get it off. I pulled on that churn until I gave out.

About six o'clock my mother came in; she wanted to know where Horace was. "My brother," I says, "he's in the smokehouse with a churn on his head." She went out to the smokehouse and brought my brother Horace out. She worked with that till way in the night and stretched his neck as long as a crane but never did get it off. So after that she brought Horace into the house and put us to bed, and I wanna tell ya it is a job to sleep with a fellow with a churn on his head. He rolled and tumbled and beat the bed!

In the late hours, near two or three o'clock, my daddy came in. And my mother called my father, says, "Lee," which was my father's name, "Lee, Horace has got a churn on his head." But anyhow, we got him out of the bed and set him on the old bench. We didn't have many chairs those days; most all we had was just benches, or stools you might call them. Well, he worked and worked and he couldn't get it off. So after a while he decided that there had to be something done. I remember quite well when he told my mother to go to the tool box and get his hammer to bust it off. She says, "Lee, don't do that, that will kill him." We lived so far in the country, we didn't, couldn't, get to no doctor or nothing. But after she told him that will kill Horace, he says, "Well, he's gonna die anyhow so, get me the hammer." I remember quite well he got the hammer, hit the side of that churn, and busted it. And you know, my brother's ears looked like two bananas. They'd done turned blue and swollen. After that, Papa took him to town the next day to see if there's anything to be done for swollen ears. And Doctor Hornsburger, which was several miles from our home, said to take him on back, and said, "Nothing you can do except just feed him some peas and clabber and buttermilk and collards."

Another time, we had two steers that we had been working to a small wagon. We made a yoke out of a limb and hooked it to those yearlings to take the wagon. Then we'd go hickory-nut hunting. One day the yearlings got scared and ran away. It tore up our wagon, and one of them broke the yoke and got away. We didn't know how we was gonna get our wagon back to the house.

I finally suggested to Horace, "You just put your head in that yoke." We cut a limb and made another yoke. "You hold up that side and you and the other yearling will pull the wagon home." Well, on the way home, we met a dog who had had somebody tie a tin can to his tail. It was full of rocks. That dog came out of the woods and passed by us, making all that fuss. When he did, the yearling ran away with my brother in that yoke. The yearling like to have killed Horace, being that he was on the ground and being dragged.

I guess if the yoke hadn't broke it would have pulled his head off. We finally got the wagon back to the house. My brother was skinned all over. In them days, we had nothing to put on a skinned place but turpentine and coal oil. Mother pulled that shirttail off Horace and poured that turpentine and coal oil on them skinned places. It took us another week to catch him. Horace had a rough time of it.

Where did I go after I left home? Well, after I plowed that old mule all day and was completely exhausted, I told my daddy I was gonna leave. He tried to get me to stay. Well, the next morning I got up. I didn't have any clothes. I remember I picked cotton, eighty cents a hundred, one of the best cotton pickers ever hit Panola County. I picked 627 pounds one day. So I bought me a pair of trousers, and a shirt or two. I had them in a suitcase that was large enough to carry a half a bale of cotton. We got in the wagon and went to Beckville. When we got to Beckville, my daddy went to the bank and borrowed thirty dollars and he gave me three ten-dollar bills, which left three dollars for interest.

I left there going west to get rich. I went to Jefferson, Texas. I had an uncle living over there, and after spending the night there, I went to Jefferson and got me a job. They was building a new courthouse. They was paying me three dollars a day, and they gave me the job of rolling cement up a platform up to the second story. And about eleven o'clock I couldn't make it to the top and an old fellow helped me and I slipped and dumped that load of cement in my lap. Well, I left there, and to this date Marion County, Jefferson, Texas, owes me a dollar and a half for a hard half-day's labor.

But I went on down to the railroad and decided that I must do something. I remember mighty well I was standing on the side of the railroad track, and I heard this old engine coming. And if a boy has never heard a locomotive snort under steam and coal, they don't know what's in life. But a boxcar came by and I grabbed it, and I rode that freight train into Longview, on into Fort Worth. And when I got to Fort Worth I decided to go further.

Corbett Akins

I caught a freight train out of there and I remember mighty well I was lonesome, hungry. But I rode that freight train into Wichita, Kansas. I remember quite well before getting into Wichita I was hungry and cold, and I had one twenty-five-cent piece. I walked up in town and saw a big carnival. I watched a man pitching balls. You got three balls for a dime, and I caught the trick of pitching balls, got three balls in the bucket, you got a dollar. I stood right there and when I quit pitching balls I had six dollars. The man that was operating the carnival refused to let me pitch anymore. I remember the sheriff of that county mighty well. I didn't know him at that time, but he walked up to me and said, "What's the matter, son?" I says, "That man won't let me pitch anymore." He told him, says, "You let him pitch or close it up." Well, he closed it up.

So I went on back down into the freight yards, and it was cold, and I got in the inside of a thrashing machine which had a tray or sifter in the bottom, and I slept there that night.

The next morning I caught a freight train and went into El Reno, Oklahoma. After I got into El Reno, Oklahoma, I grabbed what they call the Fast Flyer, a passenger train. I'd ridden that train eight or ten miles, and I thought I was safe, but in those days the fire in the boilers was coals, and I was in the first blind. If you don't know what a blind is, it's where the coach is coupled, leaves a door and a partition there. But after staying in there awhile, the fire got to flying just about to burn me up. The blind opened up on me. And when it did I saw a brakeman there, and if I was to see him today I'd kill him. That guy began to kick me, and I went down on the tenders, if you know what a tender is, that's a rod that goes down on a coal chute. And when I got down as far as I could go, this brakeman or whoever he was crawled on down there and stomped my hands off, down through the sunflowers I went.

When I hit the ground I didn't have many clothes left; they were torn all to pieces. But I went into Hobo Town. Hobo Town is where all the hoboes meet. I can recall mighty well I went up there, even smelled something cooking. It smelled good, it was good. I stood around there like a big crane in a tadpole pond. And one old man, whiskers look like Santa Claus, says, "Son, are you hungry?" I told him, yes, I was hungry, and they fed me. Well, after they fed me I was still going to Hutchinson, Kansas. And this was on Saturday.

Sunday morning I caught a work train out of Wichita, Kansas, and going to Hutchinson, Kansas, and I had ridden this train ten or twelve miles and the brakeman kicked me off, out on the bald plains in the prairies in Kansas. Well, the night came. I saw a haystack where they'd thrashed wheat. This haystack was larger than any kind of courthouse. I knew I had to stay somewhere because the wind was blowing. I crawled up on this haystack and when I did, there was enough owls flew out of the top of that haystack to make a poultry yard. But, anyway, I spread that hay out in the top of this haystack, laid down, and slept. I went on my way and I stopped off at a little town. I went walking into this little town. I remember quite well there was a bunch of women with tambourines, one little guitar, and I can recall the song mighty well. They were singing: "Oh, where is my boy tonight/Once as new as the morning dew/Oh, where is my boy tonight?"

Well, that brought me back to home; I wanted to come back to them collards and turnip greens. But I decided to go further. And after getting up, I had to walk seven or eight miles from that little town. I couldn't catch a train. And if you never been hungry in your life you don't know what it is to be hungry. I can recall some little old pump station, water tank, and one old man there that run a store, only store in the place. And I'd call him a Santa Claus if I could see him today. When I walked into the store he looked at me, course I was dirty and ragged, he says, "What's your troubles, son?" I says, "I'm hungry." He says, "Son, I haven't got a thing here to eat but some cheese and crackers." Well, that sounded like a big preaching dinner to me. He cut off a chunk of cheese, and those days they had what they call them old cheese racks and a big lever that you could cut off any amount. Well, he cut me off a slice of that and dropped it in a sixteen-pound paper sack. When he dropped that into that sack, he filled it full of crackers out of a barrel. In them days there wasn't no crackers in boxes or nothing; they come out of a barrel. He give it to me and said, "Son, when you go out the back door there's a big sack there full of onions; you get you an onion and go out there to the windmill back of the store." Now that was one wonderful meal.

So I went on after eating that Thanksgiving dinner into Hutchinson, Kansas, on out of Elkhart, Kansas, all up through that country. Rode a freight train days and nights, and don't ever do it, boys. Life is just what you make it. And I remember an old man way out there in Kansas. I was broke. I had gone on and met a man named Stride. He was a thirty-second-degree Mason. And I told him, "I'm broke. I'm hungry." And that man fed me. I got me a little ol' job at Hutchinson, hamburger joint. And I made quite a bit of money out of it.

In those days western Kansas, southwestern Kansas, was giving away land to anybody who wanted to file on it. But I got ahold of an old Model-T car and I went to Springfield, Colorado. When I got there, there wasn't no land to be filed on. An old man had built a shack there, what we would call a cotton house in this country. And he had it fenced, part of it. He says, "I'll sell you my releasement here for two hundred dollars." And I had the money. A releasement is where somebody had filed and they gonna turn it back to the government. I filed, and I bought 160 acres of land. But I had to live on this land three years and cultivate or plow up 8 acres each and every year for three years. So I moved into this shack, I got me an old mule and a big horse and what you call a mustang. I went out there to the camp one evening, and I said to myself, "My God, why do you want to get in this place?" When I stopped the team I started to get out on the left-hand side, was in a covered wagon, if you know what a covered wagon is, a singletree, and a doubletree. But I stepped on the doubletree to step out on the left-hand side, and when I did I saw two big rattlesnakes. Well, I crawled over on the other side and got out, unhitched my team. I had brought with me what they call a breaking plow, and after staying there and resting up I decided I would break my 8 acres of land.

I began to plow. I hadn't been there over two hours till there was a little yellow cloud came up above me. I didn't think nothing about it, but just kept a-plowing. There wasn't but a few minutes when we had a 'lectrical storm, and hail fell so fast and so hard that I turned one horse a-loose, [and] a mule, I believe, a-loose. It got to hailing so hard till I crawled up under this mare and stuck my head out between her front legs. Hail was thick on the ground. Well, after a while it begin to lightning just so fast, storm just "*whomp, whomp,*" I left that mare, and I was trying to get back to the shack.

Now, a lot of people don't believe it if I was to tell you, you folks here, you wouldn't believe I jumped lightning for half a mile. But that lightning would hit that hail, you know, and glide on the top of it. I finally got back to my shack. The next day I didn't have a horse, I didn't have a mule, and I didn't have a mustang. But I got to looking, and I finally found my mare, but my real plow horse I didn't find him for about two or three weeks, and he was dead.

Well, that left me with that mare and that mustang. I didn't know what to do, but I stayed around the cabin there a day or two and shot rabbits with my .22, which is about all I had to eat. I went on back then and tried to plow a little more and build some fence. Woke up one morning after I'd spent the day in Springfield. Somebody had stole all of my fence, my post, and everything I had.

So that was pretty disheartening. My neighbor Old Man Johnson came down and said, "You fixing to leave, aren't you?" I said, "Yes, I'm gonna leave." He said, "Well, I got a daughter that'll be here tomorrow. She has TB and wants to come out here on this high climate." He says, "I'll give you two hundred dollars for your releasement." I was glad to get it. We got into the old Ford car and went to Lamar, Colorado, and when I filed off, he filed on. That Springfield, Colorado, today is a pretty nice town. And 160 acres of land that I had filed on is completely covered with gas wells. It's a rich piece of territory. If I'd a-stayed there, probably I'd a-been a millionaire.

I left Colorado and caught a freight train one Sunday evening to Wichita, Kansas, and I rode what they call the bumpers. That's where the two cars come together like this; I rode astraddle of that for fifty-five miles to a water station. Then I got off to find a place to get in a car because you can't hardly ride in them bumpers, they a-flopping so. I got a job in Elkhart, Kansas, for the Johnson Machine Company. I worked for a Mr. Johnson about four or five months, saved up a little money, and decided I'd come home. I caught the train coming back east, and after riding the bumpers for about fifty-five miles, the train stopped at a water tank. I decided it would be better riding into Fort Worth in a boxcar and did so.

Well, I then went on down to the depot, the main depot at Fort Worth, and a freight yard fixing to take a train to come back. The conductor asked for my ticket. I told him, "Mister, I done give you my ticket." He says, "No, you haven't." I says, "I know I have." He says, "I'm gonna have to put you off the train." I says, "Well, put me off." He turned around, give me that little old slip he stuck in my hat, and I went on into Terrell, Texas. I was really a bum.

After making it into Terrell, Texas, I stayed with my uncle, Charley Magnum, a few days. I decided I wanted to come home. So I came down here and stayed with my daddy quite a while, got me a job as an automobile mechanic in Beckville, Texas, and learned to be a pretty good automobile mechanic.

In 1926 I got a job with the Snap-on Ranch Company. I was steel manager for Snap-on Ranch Company for quite a while. I had the states of Louisiana, Texas, Mississippi, and Oklahoma. And at that time the company was paying me $75 a week and expenses; that was big money then. Well, I stayed with that job until I got tired of it.

Then I came back home. Had me a brand new automobile, money in my pockets, and met up with a little old girl by the name of La Rue Chadwick. Well, she liked that automobile more than she did me, but when the car wore out she liked me more than she did the automobile. So I courted that old gal, and we finally married the first day of May, 1928. In 1930 we moved here to Carthage, bought this little home and that old filling station, and I went in the garage business. We paid $1750 for two acres of land, house, and filling station.

I was elected constable in 1937. I ran a garage and filling station. I voted each and every year, and on this particular year I got an idea to run for constable. So I decided I would go out and get votes. I ran a gristmill, and if I found somebody hungry I would give them a package of meal. I recall one time it was about three A.M., and this man woke me up and wanted me to ground some corn. So I got up and grounded it for him and when we got through he asked me if I was going to take any toll. I said my toll was when he fed that meal to his babies. So that man, all the time I was running, he would vote for me.

Another way was, I had a portable light plant, and I would carry it around in the old buggy I had, and made it to all the box suppers. There was a box supper at least once or twice a week then. I'd get there early, back my hoppy up to the door, run some wires into the church, and when the people got there I had it lit up like the streets of New York. And that was quite a comment to me because people were bragging about me. I heard two of my opponents as they came in the door. When the two came in the door and saw those three hundred-watt light bulbs a-burning, one said to the other, "Hell, we might as well go on home, Corbett's got this thing lit up to where we couldn't see anybody, much less get a vote." So they left.

I made a number of speeches during my years as constable. One time, I was running against a man, out of town, and he would distribute pamphlets, etcetera, to every mailbox in the county. I found one of them and walked up to his car and he slapped me in the face. When he slapped me, that made me nearly as mad as a possum. I pulled him out of the car and took my pistol and pistol-whipped him till he couldn't get up. They got a rumor started that Corbett Akins wouldn't do for sheriff anymore. He pistol-whipped a man till the blood run in his boots. When it come to my time to speak that night, I got up there and told the people and said, "I am proud to tell you that if you fellers knew the history of that man, you'd have whipped him a little harder." The man that I whipped was carrying that filthy, funny stuff to each and every mailbox and home in the county. And I told the people there that this same man is the man that I arrested for stealing hogs, a man that was in jail shortly after he was living with another woman. I said, "If you people want to vote against me because I hit the man, just go ahead."

And I made many votes by taking off warts; that's a gift to me. When I was eight years old, on Christmas Eve, my mother gave me and my brother a dogwood broom and told us to sweep the yard. And she said, "If you don't, Santa Claus ain't gonna come see you." So we swept a little bit. But then, me and my brother walked about two miles down to some hickory-nut trees. We knew there were lots of hickory nuts there. So we went into the woods picking them up. I recall quite well when I was bent over I saw an old man coming with whiskers down almost to his navel. Of course, the first thing I thought of was what Mama said: "If you don't sweep the yard, Santa ain't gonna come see you." So it scared me, and I started to run off. This old man got ahold of me and said, "Son, don't be scared. I'm not gonna hurt you. I see you got a wart there on your thumb." I only had one wart on me, on my thumb. He rubbed that wart and looked at me and said, "Son, when you get to be twenty-one years old, you can take off warts." And from then on I could take a wart off anybody: man, mule, horse, cow, hog, or dog. I've been called from my home to take them off horses and cows. I've never failed, and I've tried everything except a toad frog. I never thought about taking them off of them. So that got me lots of votes.

During my ten years in office, I recall speeches I made. I had a voice like a bugle and a mouth like a dishpan, but I got the job done. One Saturday before the election day, they were telling my opponents and they were telling me that the bootleggers and the gamblers were paying me. They knew it wasn't so. But in my speech I told the people that all the things they said weren't true. I said, "Even if it was true, there are two people who wouldn't vote against me just as sure as my name is Corbett Akins, and I want you to see those people." I said, "Mama, stand up!" She stood up with gray hair down to her shoulders, and I said, "That's one of them. I want the other one to stand up." I said, "Daddy, will you rise?" My daddy, about eighty years old, was there with tears in his eyes. He said, "What my son is telling you folks is true. He *did not* accept any money from the bootleggers or gamblers." It was my [first] election, and I had five opponents. And I beat every one of them the first election.

I was elected constable first of the year, I believe in 1938. And Carthage at that time was beginning to lease land and [had] a little oil boom, and it was pretty rough. I had a deputy and a night watchman. So in February, after being in office six or seven weeks, they was having trouble at a café north side of the square. The owner had had trouble with the law and run the law away. I passed by one day, and he said, "Constable, don't you come over here. You won't last either." I says, "I'm elected by the people and if you violate the law and I come after you, I gonna get you or get part of you." He says, "Naw, you won't."

I never thought much more about it. In a few days I was sitting in my office one night, and I heard an awful commotion over there. I saw this man pick up a broom and knock a waitress completely off the stool with it, hit her side the head. Well, she run out of there, came to my office. I made her stay in my office. I told her not to go back over there. After a while I said, "You go over there on that corner and you stay there. When the bus comes you go back to San Augustine," and she went over there.

While she was waiting on the corner, I saw the café owner get in his automobile, go get his wife, and bring her back to the café. Well, when he brought her there, she saw this woman. She came out of that café with a six-inch butcher knife, and she went over and made a dive for this little waitress. And when she did, she finally caught her, and they clinched. They was just standing in the street, and the wife was hacking her over the head. I left the office, and by the time I got out there, the café owner had come out of this café with a .44-40 pistol. As I walked up, he was standing there and telling everybody to stand back. I came up there to where he was guarding his wife and this woman with his pistol. I called him by name, and I says, "Drop your pistol." Well, he didn't drop the pistol. I had my gun on him. Instead of dropping his pistol he backed back to his place of business. Opened his door, screen door, with his left elbow, and when I stepped up on the sidewalk I saw him when he raised the pistol. I heard the click of it, single action, double action, but when it clicked the last time I was up on the sidewalk. My pistol fired four times, and he went down in the door. When he did, his brother was sitting back on a stool at the back of the café. He placed his pistol up on his wrist, took dead aim, and when the gun fired he shot a hole right though the top of my cowboy hat. When he did that, I fired at him. He went down under a table, pulled hisself up on the door, and shot at the night watchman running down the street. I had shot four times at the café owner in the door, shot one time at the brother on the stool, and shot one time when he went under the table. My gun when it snapped, *"bling."* I didn't know what the trouble was. But after it was all over, I knew I had an empty gun. The café owner was carried to Shreveport, and he died shortly after he got over there.

In my days before I ever expected to be an officer, I knew there was a number of stills in Panola County. I didn't know what whiskey looked like or tasted like, but I'd heard about it. The only thing I knew about, coming off the farm, was walking around a churn and dasher and churning and making butter, or going out to the cow pen and milking an old cow. But when I become of age I heard about corn liquor. I heard my daddy talk about people making it. So, after I became the sheriff of Panola County, I knew that I had to do right, because I had a boy, and a wife, and the people throughout Panola County that voted for me. I was determined to do what was right or die, and I have done that from that day to this. Here are some of my tales of moonshiners.

Stills are often located by smoke, but I also located them with my bloodhounds, which trail the party from their home to the place they make the whiskey. Most stills are hidden underground. This is done by digging a pit, covering the pit with logs and dirt and planting bushes on top of it, and leaving a place of entrance with a door with a bush nailed to it—this is where you pull the bush and the door comes open and you go down into the still, which is all camouflaged.

They are also found by tracks which you notice goes all in one direction. And there will be another trail leading from the still. They never walk back and forth in the same trail. When you find a trail like that, you can rest assured there is something. And after you get near the still you will notice the treetops, brush in piles, and logs are moved. You can tell there is a still close by the way the leaves and grass are mashed down. If it looks like there is a lot of traffic in one spot you can rest assured that there is a still nearby. But they could be anywhere.

I was an old expert whiskey-still catcher. I got eighteen while I was sheriff and constable. Out here north, northwest of town, there was one that been operating there ever since I was a boy, and I knew it was there. So one evening I decided I'd go look for it. I took my .22 automatic rifle, got my car, got up here close to Rock Hill. I run into this young feller name of Gab Williams. He says, "Where you going?" I says, "I'm going squirrel hunting; come and go with me." Well, I knew I wasn't going a-squirrel hunting. But I was a-going up there to search, walk around, and see if I could see it.

Well, when I got up there, where I wanted to go, there was a field that had been plowed with a two-horse plow, and it was just as smooth as this floor except plow ridges. And right out in the middle of that field there was a pine bush. I never thought a thing about it, but I walked in around and directly I seen a man come out from under that bush. So I told this kid, I said, "Come on, let's go see what's over there." Went over there and it was this pine bush which was about four foot in diameter and maybe five foot high. And when I got there I could see tracks all around it. I got ahold of this pine bush, and when I did, I pulled the door open. When I pulled the door open, I knew I'd found the still. I throwed this door back and I went down in it and it was a still twelve feet square. I got down in the clay and below it was one eight foot square. I got down in there and there was a thirty-foot well, clay and all, well rope, and a bucket! I believe there was five or seven barrels of mash and all kind of buckets and things down in there. After I got through checking, this old boy that went with me, he was scared to death after he found out what it was.

So I decided to get out of that place. There was a five-gallon jug, it was a jug made like the old Texas water jug, little mouth with a handle on it. It was a five-gallon and it was full of whiskey. Well, I got that thing and I started out with it. This old boy helped me up with it. When I started out that hole, there was three men standing in four foot of me, just standing there. Man, I didn't know what to do! I went back down in the still. I had read about stills being dynamited with people down in there and being killed when you come out. There I was twenty miles away from home; didn't nobody know where me and this boy was, and it worried me. I went on back down in the still, and I set there until the sun begin to make a yellow beam at the treetops, just about dark. I decided I'd come out of there. I took my hat and put it on my rifle barrel, and I stuck that hat out first, 'cause I figured if he was gonna shoot me I figured he'd shoot the hat and I'd be all right. But then nothing happened, and I crawled on up. I told old Jake, I said, "Give me that five-gallon jug." Well, we came out of that thing, and I walked about two hundred yards, and there was four men run up to me just like they was fixing to grab me. I didn't know what to do. It was my intention to shoot at them but I didn't. The gun done fired, and I can hear that wire now as them four men were hitting the barbwire fence down there. That wire going *"wheep, whap, whap."* Well, that was the end of that. I got that five gallons of whiskey, got in my car, and came back to the office, got some deputies, went back out there. It was late when we got there, lost lots of time. When we got there, wasn't a well bucket, there wasn't a rope, wasn't a can, there wasn't a bit of mash, wasn't nothing in it. They had come back there and destroyed it while I was gone. But I had an idea who they was, so I called the revenue men the next day. We went out there and got their fingerprints off of some of those old cans and things and classified them, found out who they belonged to.

But that's a wonderful history for any sheriff or any constable or any officer: don't never go by yourself anywhere. After those experiences, I learned me that any officer who goes alone is foolish. The state of Texas made a wonderful move when they put a man with a partner. If you get killed, you just get killed, but where there's two you're not as likely to.

In 1939 me and the liquor control board had information at that time that there was a man who was making whiskey on Dr. Daniels' farm on Brushey Creek below Gary. Me and a constable went down there one day and we located the still. After locating the still, we came back to Carthage and got in contact with the alcoholic unit in Tyler. They sent a man down here to help me apprehend the one that was making the whiskey in the Gary community. We went in there about eleven o'clock at night, and it was cold, way below zero. We stayed in there and waited but we had already checked the still. There was a copper still with a big cooker and a number of feet of coil that went into a barrel of water used to condense the steam from the still to make whiskey. We knew that they would be there before the daylight hours because there was five barrels of mash. We had checked the mash, and you knew in checking mash after the mash had settled that the water turns blue. It had to be cooked because if you didn't it would spoil.

Well, we stayed there for those few hours and until about four o'clock. As the sun broke through the treetops, we heard the crisp footsteps of someone coming. And, you know, at that time of night and when it was zero weather, you could hear the leaves breaking. We knew that someone was coming and then we saw a husky man coming into the still. He went in and checked all the barrels of mash. After he checked those barrels of mash, he came out near me. I was almost snoring; I had been up all that night. After he didn't see anybody there, he went back to the five barrels of mash, checked the still, and saw that everything was all right. Then he looked down at the ground and walked around and walked out to a small bush, took his pocketknife out of his pocket, opened it up, and cut off a limb. When he cut the limb off, he took it and trimmed it up nicely. Then he raised it up on top of his shoe sole. He measured from the heel of his shoe to the end of his toe. He went down and took that stick he had made. He went and measured the track he had seen around the still. When he did, he saw the measurements on that stick didn't suit the measurement of the track he had in the still. After measuring that track, he got up and stood and looked all around. He went back to the spring that was furnishing the water for the still. He knelt down upon his knees and took a big drink of that water and spit it out of his mouth.

Bob Regan, the revenue man, told me, "Corbett, I think we ought to watch that man because he's fixing to leave here." Well, the whiskey cooker walked down near the still, which included a fifty-five–gallon drum. This fifty-five–gallon drum was his cooker. He had already went in the woods and picked up a bunch of limbs and started a fire under the cooker. So he got the fire going and everything was cooking well. He then took this limb he had measured his footsteps [with] and again went down near the still. He laid this switch on this measurement by his track. When he got up after measuring that track he looked all around again. He wasn't satisfied. He walked over to the barrel and raised the lid on one barrel. There wasn't but this one barrel of the five that was closed. And after he walked up to this, he reached down in the barrel and pulled out a possum that had gone down in that mash and drowned. But still he kept walking and looking. He walked over to barrel number four which was within ten feet of me. And when he did, he reached in that barrel and stirred on top of that mash. When that mash is ready it is always settled, and he took out of the top of that mash, which was blue and swimming, and you could see very readily that there was something wrong. He reached over in this barrel, which was within ten feet in front of me, and pulled out a rat that had fallen in the mash. And I said to myself, "My God, how can a man drink that whiskey with possum in it and with a rat in it." Well, he pitched that rat out, and he stood up and still wasn't satisfied. He went back over near the big still which was the fifty-five–gallon drum, and for a last time he measured that track. When he did, he raised straight up and shook his head, and Mr. Regan said, "Well, Corbett, he is fixing to leave." When he did, he took through the woods and was gone.

We both took off after him. We ran him about a half of a mile or better. We went around the hills chasing him. On the other hill we saw a shack which was on the bluff that crosses Brushey Creek. He went into this shack. When we got up to this shack, there was his wife and two kids. His wife said, "My gosh, what do you want?" We told her we was after the moonshiner. She said, "Don't bother that man 'cause he is just trying to feed us chillins." I said, "Well, how does he feed you?" She said, "He takes the whiskey and sells it to the people around here." We arrested him anyway and took him on up to Gary and then brought him to Carthage and put him in jail. He immediately made his bond and was released by the judge. After that, about thirty days, the court was called, and I went before the judge and told him this was a poor man with a little wife and two kids. I told him the whiskey he was making and selling in Gary was to feed his family. The judge told me he was going to turn this party back to me and let him go on back to Brushey Creek. He was not to make any more whiskey, but to get him a plow and a mule and plant him some corn and plant him some cotton and make him a living. And he did.

If you want to be a perfect moonshiner, you have got to know your stuff. The best is to take wooden barrels, not metallic barrels, and take those wooden barrels and be sure they are clean. It's best to build a fire in those barrels and clean them out. After you do that, if you want to make a good grade of whiskey: First, put about four or five gallons of water in this barrel; second, take a hundred pound of corn chop and pour into this water and let it set about twenty-four hours, until that barrel of corn chop is swelled and fermented good. When you do that, go to your store and get about fifty pounds of sugar and pour into the chops. Mix it completely, and then finish filling your barrel, a fifty-five–gallon barrel, up to the top about six inches from the rim. And when you do that get you about eight or ten yeast cakes and drop into this barrel and then stir it all completely and forget about it. In about four days come back to this barrel and completely stir it up and add about five pounds of sugar. That five pounds of sugar to fifty-five gallons will be one fifth of the barrel. In about three or four days this barrel will ferment on top. Dip that off and throw it out. If you ain't got no chickens, take that home to your hogs. In two or three weeks you will come back and you will see it has fermented perfectly.

When you look into that barrel, you will see it looks exactly like the blue sky in heaven. When it gets blue and hard, you take a teacup and you take about a mouthful and rinse your mouth out with it. You don't have to swallow it. If it tastes bitter, wait just a few days and then come back and get your still ready. After you have got your still ready, you take all that blue top and put it in this cooking barrel and you start you a fire under the cooking barrel. It begins to get it to boil and going out through the copper still. Then you begin to make whiskey. But when you get down to the bottom, be sure you know what you are doing, because when you get to the bottom that's what the ol' whiskey maker calls white lightning. You save the bottom stuff, just cut your still off, pour into your fifty-five–gallon drum a hundred pounds of chops and fifty pounds of sugar, and fill it up with water and let it ferment again. And then you get the second run of whiskey, and the second run is better than the best. I could take you boys down in the bottom and make whiskey and make a fortune.

Well, I was elected sheriff in the summer of 1942, and I served as sheriff till '52, ten years, sheriff of Panola County. At that time Panola County was a rough, tough place. Gas and oil boom, biggest gas-oil boom ever known in the world was at Henderson, thirty miles west of us. I was sheriff during those times, and I know all the help I had was one deputy and one night watchman and nobody else.

But I had a pack of bloodhounds. I had sixteen of the best bloodhounds that ever hit the earth. And a-many a night I heard them trailing a man, and when they hit a man he's gonna have to take a tree, 'cause they'll kill him. I had two old hounds called Nip and Tuck, and lot of people say, well, dogs can't talk. But dogs can talk, 'cause old Tuck would hit that trail, and you'd hear him just as plain at one or two o'clock at night say, "How o-o-o-old is he?" And Old Nip would say, "21, 22, 21, 22, 21, 22." Had another old dog called Old Doc, cost me $368 when he was a puppy. He could trail any track 100 to 120 hours old. He came from England. Now Old Doc, whenever he hit a man's trail out there—and he would bark for nothing but a man's trail—he was just like a big old gobbler. You could hear him holler just as plain. You knew he was fixing to get gone.

And I had one old dog named Rock, he was a wonderful dog. He'd trail with a pack all night, but when the party he was chasing crossed a foot log, Rock was the only dog that wouldn't cross. Old Rock would sit down on that log and beg just as pitiful as if you was whopping him with a limer. But when you got there Old Rock would go on across. That was his instinct; he wanted to wait there and show the sheriff which way he'd gone.

I know one night we was up here at Kilgore. I had my pack of hounds, and a man had attacked a woman up there. She had rode the bus a mile west of Longview and then had to walk about as far from here to the square. And this man attacked her before she got home. He cut her throat

Corbett Akins and Father

from ear to ear. Noble Crawford called me, and I went up there and put them hounds on that track. We ran that track, I guess, three hours, and we heard the dogs bay. We stayed pretty close, for some had horses, and when they bayed we all rushed up there and they were in a pen. A man had made a pen up there for some pet deer. High fence, had on top of it three barbwires. And when we got there, this man knew we was fixing to catch him; he went over that fence, and when he did a barb caught a piece of the jumper and tore out a piece about two or three inches long. We got that off. Well, we got them dogs through that fence, and we went over there several miles, and they bayed again. When we got there, there was a woman sitting in there churning. We ask her where her husband was because them deputies knew who it was when we got to this house. She said, "He's not here, hadn't been here tonight." The boys was a-shining lights under the house, and they had a brick chimney, and you know how a brick chimney is built—it is hollered out under there. Well, in the hollered place under this fireplace, there was a tub. One of the deputies went under there and drug it out, and in this tub was a pair of striped overalls and a striped jumper, and they was just as bloody as they could be. So we took the clothes and this man ran out of there and run into another deputy's hands and we caught him.

The Loblolly Book

One time, we were called to Jasper County from Carthage. We were called there after two fugitives escaped from Jasper one night about eight o'clock. We went to Jasper and stayed all night. The next morning we ate breakfast and then got together with the sheriff and his posse. We turned the dogs loose about eight. The track was twenty hours old, and we ran that track from eight that morning to four that afternoon for a total distance of sixteen miles. The dogs led us to the Neches River where the suspects had throwed a gun into the water. One old dog went into the water and came back. We then went into the water and came out with the gun. We left there and in a short while jumped the two fugitives; that was about two-thirty in the afternoon. We run them until about three-thirty, when I saw them come out of a river bottom in an old field. They crossed the field with the dogs close behind them. And they ran into an old house or shack, and the dogs went in behind them. When the fugitives came out, one was carrying a pump shotgun. About that time I arrived at the house with some of the other officers, and so did a man riding a horse. I told him I wanted the horse, and I threw my gun on him and made him get down. I told my deputy, Acie Henigan, to get on it and stay with the dogs. He did, and the dogs crowded the fugitives so close that they throwed the box of shells away and the shotgun. But Henigan and the dogs stayed with them. A little after four that afternoon, the dogs bayed the two fugitives in a pond of water. They were standing in the water neck-deep, and Old Doc, the old mean dog which was a full-blood bloodhound, had swam out into the pond. He put his front feet upon one man's shoulder with his hind feet on the man's legs, and was standing there barking in the man's face. Old Nip and Trouble, they were swimming around them, and I could hear them old dogs talking. I can hear them now, Old Nip would say, "H-o-o-o-ld it," and Trouble would say, "21, 22, 21, 22."

Another troublesome race I had was on New Year's Eve. I got a report that two men were in the woods standing behind a tarpaulin formed in the shape of a tent. Also parked by this tarpaulin was a Chevrolet sedan. So after getting the report, I got in my car and drove out into those woods to investigate. When I did, they saw my car and took off. I radioed back to the office and told the deputies to bring the bloodhounds. They brought out Old Nip and Tuck, Doc, Hitler (a mean type), and Trouble. That was somewhere after the noon hour when we turned the dogs loose. We run those thugs all the evening through the woods near Keatchie, Louisiana. We never could catch them because of so many fences. The dogs tailed but stayed on the men's trail. The men jumped from one net wire fence to another, and the dogs couldn't stay with them. But we run those dogs all that evening and all that night, a total of better than sixteen hours. At seven o'clock the next morning it was awful cold, and I decided the best thing to do was to call off the hunt. But while we were standing there, boys came by with a book satchel and I asked them, "Have you seen two men down there in the woods, one with a red shirt on?" They say, "Yessa, captain, they over there in the woods about a mile and half beside the trail." I told my deputies to stay there, I would go over there and see what I could do. Well, I borrowed a horse from a man at this house and asked the old woman, did she have an old stocking I could borrow. She went into the house and got an old-timey stocking and gave it to me. Well, I tied a knot in it and placed it over my head, placed my raincoat around my neck, and got astraddle of this old horse.

Well, I rode that trail for about a mile and a half. I saw a log heap afire. And I also saw two men a-laying on the ground near the fire. When I saw the men, I then looked and saw five head of cattle grazing out on the edge of the trail. I got around these cattle, drove them to the trail, and began to holler and yell at them. And I drove those cattle right close by those two men, within twenty foot of them. When I got near to the men, I jumped off the horse and threw my gun on them and made them lay down. I walked in between them and handcuffed the inside hands. After I had apprehended them one of them looked at me and said, "If we knowed that you was the sheriff you would be a dead S.O.B. now. We thought you was some farmer driving his cows up." Both of those thugs were escaped from the Huntsville pen where they were serving life terms for murder.

I got behind those two men with my gun and marched them that mile or mile and a half where the other officers were. We loaded them into cars and took them to town and placed them in jail. We called the sheriff in Rockwall County. He had warrants for them because they had burglarized a place in Rockwall. He took those two prisoners to Rockwall and placed them in jail. That night they sawed out of their cell and got loose again. And if they were ever apprehended I never knowed about it.

In this race for the two murderers, I had my prize dog, Old Doc, which I got from England. He was a full-blood registered bloodhound. I paid $368 for him when he arrived in Shreveport and got off the plane. Nip and Tuck were two prize dogs; both were registered. I got them out of New York State. The other dogs I raised myself. But Nip, Tuck, and Doc were my prize dogs.

I was called to Gilmer, Texas, by the sheriff there on a Thursday night. He asked me if I could be there the next morning at five o'clock with my bloodhounds to help catch a man suspected of cattle rustling. I told them I would, and the next morning, around five or six o'clock, I was in the woods with my dogs and the sheriff. He stated that a man had been coming in there every Thursday night for a number of Thursdays, and he had an automobile and a trailer that held three cows. He would get in that river bottom and catch his load.

When we got there that morning and turned the dogs loose, it wasn't long before they hit the trail. They stayed on that trail thirty minutes to an hour until they came to an old car body. That was where the cow thieves had cooked breakfast and had slept under that old car body. We went on down the trail a little further, and I could hear that the dogs had treed something. I got within about a hundred yards of them. Then I heard a terrible commotion, and I saw a man get up and start running. The dogs had tore all of his clothes off him. What had happened was that he had climbed a tree, and the wind was blowing awful hard. He had got so far up in the top, the top broke out, and when it broke he fell down in the middle of those dogs who'd got him. They ran about a mile, about four or five dogs on his heels. Well, after a while they treed him again down on the river bottom. This time they treed him up a tree about eight or ten inches in diameter. This tree didn't have any limbs on it until about twenty feet up. The dogs had cowed him so much that he had climbed up that tree about twenty-five feet. I could hear him a-hollering as I got nearer, "Come here, come here." When I came to the tree I seen him up there, and this tree was bending way over. I said, "Come down." He said, "Not until you tie those dogs and then I'll come down." Well, after he got on the ground I was a-talking to him, and he was chewed up pretty bad because all my dogs loved meat.

We directed that man up the trail to his car and trailer, and in there he had two head of cattle. He hadn't got the third on yet. The sheriff turned the cattle back into the bottom and carried the man into Gilmer. The sheriff found out the man's name and that his boy had been helping him. In all the commotion the boy had hit the road and had caught a ride and gone back home. The sheriff got a warrant and brought him back to jail. They were tried in the Gilmer court and sentenced to five years in Huntsville pen.

"THE SHERIFF'S COLUMN"
(From the *Panola Watchman*, 1951)

Thursday, February 8, 1951

I believe in years past, there had been a tendency to overlook opportunities for dogs to be used with an advantageous solution of various crimes. Modern high speed communication, paved roads, etc. have curtailed their use. But despite these changed conditions, it is believed that cases solved with great difficulty or even remaining unsolved, could have been cleared readily if bloodhounds had been promptly and properly used. This applies to the country territory. Bloodhounds, with their highly developed sense of smell, are invaluable in following a trail. Various wood tracks cannot be followed by night. Even when footprints can be seen, the officers may be confused by the tracks of other individuals. The bloodhounds follow the distinctive scent of the one person as readily as if it were marked with a colored thread. In weeds or brush, he may get the scent from the vegetation when ground conditions are unfavorable for tracking. In other words, the bloodhounds can be used successfully whenever an individual travels on foot, and as long as he continues on foot.

Corbett Akins and hound

Auto Use: Even when an automobile is used to leave the scene of the crime, bloodhounds can be used up to the point where the car was entered. If the car is located soon thereafter, the trail can be followed from the car to any other point as long as the party followed is traveling on foot. Often the trail leads to a suspect who finds it difficult to deny the bloodhounds identification.

Thursday, February 15, 1951

The Bloodhounds Lead Sheriff: Recently, I took my dogs to a skirt of woods where two thugs were camped and parked a stolen automobile. After following the trail in a cross country manner for three or four miles, I took my dogs back a mile to a point where someone said they had seen the two thugs cross the road. This party insisted that the law-breakers had gone in different directions from that which had been followed by the dogs. Upon reaching the place indicated by the informer, the dogs followed the tracks for a short distance then doubled back and followed the trail originally taken.

Bloodhounds follow the scent of the person and not his visible tracks. For this reason, in following a fresh trail under favorable conditions, they may travel as much as 100 feet to the right or left of the trail. Where the fugitive changes directions, they may overrun visible tracks and pick up the trail some distance ahead where he resumes the original direction of travel. Some experiences might lead some to believe that bloodhounds are not reliable. A trained bloodhound is absolutely reliable in following a given scent as long as it is possible for any animal to follow it. On this mentioned race, Ol' Frank, my start dog, was clubbed or kicked, and two weeks later, I heard him talking to the Master of Dog Heaven. He made a whining noise when he saw me, and seemed to say, "It is finished." He is now buried in Panola County jail yard, a marker at his grave. Any unsatisfactory results are due to an untrained dog, unfavorable conditions for tracking, or inexperience on the part of the person handling the dog. I've found from experience that the best results are obtained when dogs are turned loose and not restricted to a leash. The chief objective to this is that you want to be mounted on horseback in order to stay with the dogs. East Texas fences are many, so I mostly take it on foot.

From Experience: Experience has also shown that the best results are obtained by working two dogs at a time. One dog may be used, but, as a trail is sometimes lost and has to be picked up again, two dogs are faster than one. When more than two dogs are used, I find that there is more confusion, and more difficulty in keeping the dogs at work. Contrary to popular belief, a bloodhound gets a certain scent and follows only the one scent, regardless of how many other persons may have been at the place where the trailing started. For example, if bloodhounds are used to track two men who have fled from an abandoned auto, the dogs may follow the trail of only one of the two men. If the two separate, the dogs will stay on the trail of the one they were originally following. It is possible, however, that each dog may follow the scent of a different man. In that case, the dogs will go in different directions when the trail of the two men separate. If two fugitives are being sought, but the dogs pick up the trail of only one, they will not trail the second man until the memory of the first man has been forgotten by them.

Take Up Scent: I estimate it will take a bloodhound two or three hours to forget a scent sufficiently to take up a second trail. For this reason, when I answer a call, I take all dogs. Two of which are immediately put to work, while the others are held in reserve so as to be available if it becomes necessary to trail another person. Bloodhounds have a highly developed sense of smell, and can be trained to trail either animals or persons. Contrary to some people's belief, bloodhounds are not blood-thirsty. They can be trained to attack or not to attack; however, great care must be exercised in order to keep them confined, lest they in some way might harm children or other persons. In trailing felons, it is best to have a dog that will catch. There is a sure cinch that a fugitive will take a tree or if he gets into an auto, there's a chance for a road block and then cause the apprehension of the wanted party or parties.

Up to 70 Hours: I believe a good bloodhound could pick up a scent up to 70 hours after the person trailed has left the place. The damper the weather, the longer the scent can be picked up. Even in rainy weather, a trail can be picked up so long as the water has not washed over all the tracks. Where only a part of the tracks have been covered by water, the bloodhound can still be able to follow the trail. In East Texas, the hot dry weather makes it very difficult for a dog to pick up a trail.

When bloodhounds follow a trail to the bank of a stream they will work along the bank until they are convinced that the party crossed the stream. After crossing the stream, the dogs will work along the bank until they are able to pick up the other trail on that side of the stream.

Where Used: When bloodhounds are used, all persons should be kept away from the place where the dogs are to pick up the trail. This may consist of some article dropped by the persons to be trailed. A handkerchief, purse, etc. The seat cushion of an abandoned automobile, a footprint left under a window by a burglar or peeping-tom. Speaking of peeping-toms, my dogs were the cause of the arrest and conviction of six peepers in 1947, and 21 criminals in East Texas the same year. If any other person sits in an auto, picks up the dropped article, or walks in the footprint, the bloodhounds will not find one scent, but a mixture of two or more. It is absolutely necessary that the dogs be given the initial scent, from some article which is only the one distinctive scent.

Thereafter, the dogs will be able to pick out and follow that scent, even though it may be a bit at times mingled with others. Any place where a person walks or sits, or any garment worn by an individual for any period of time, will contain the distinctive scent of that person. The longer the garment is worn, however, the better the dogs will be able to pick up the scent, as the bloodhounds rely solely on smell for trailing. Leather readily retains a scent and after the shoes have been worn a few times, it is possible for a bloodhound to continue the trail made by shoes even on a paved street. Rubber boots or shoes do not interfere much with trailing.

Bloodhounds will work for anyone and no great skill is necessary in order to use them. Each dog has his or her own peculiarities and will work better when these are taken into consideration. For example, some dogs may require firm handling, while a more sensitive dog would be inclined to cower when spoken to in a rough manner. For this reason, it is desirable that dogs of the same nature be worked together. Like all dogs, bloodhounds like nothing better than a hunting trip. In order to keep them in good condition, it is necessary that dogs with two or three years experience should be worked at least once each week. Dogs of less experience should be worked more often. Daily, if possible. The dogs enjoy even practice runs. They soon learn to distinguish between trips of practice and real chase. As for the dogs themselves, I have found that the female dog is steadier.

Thursday, March 1, 1951

This week we issued receipts to the bootleggers for the 100 bottles of liquor, but they won't be getting it back. All of the liquor confiscated goes directly to the State Liquor Control Board and they will be happy to hear that we have a big supply for them. I still believe that the Good Book says that the way of the transgressor is hard.

We got another pistol packer. The Judge was nice to him; just $100 in cost and 30 days in jail. So the people will be safe that long. The driver is the party that cut one car half into, and wrecked his own. But at that, he crawled out of the flying steel and wanted to whip the man that hit him.

Thursday, March 8, 1951

Spring Is Here: Folks, spring must be here from the number of underworld characters at work hereabouts and over the state. Don't be taken in when some stranger comes to your house to borrow an article. Be sure you know them. If not, you stand a chance of losing your silverware, fur coat, etc.

Drunk Drivers: We had another drunk driver this week, after I'd already started writing this, and he was a tough one. I had to knock him loose from a pocket knife. Tried to stop him several times, but he said he was going home. He was going south, but his home is in Marshall. Must have gotten a little turned around.

Thursday, March 29, 1951

Gypsy Women: Monday, we picked up two Gypsy women. We received a report from the west part of the county to be on the lookout for them. We found in their possession a ham, two quilt tops, a blow torch, and a mattress. Keep me posted on such characters. They are vags and I don't permit them to stop in this county.

Thursday, April 5, 1951

Find Still: Tuesday, March 28, we found the big boy moved in and set up house keeping about four miles west of Beckville. After several days searching, we discovered the largest still ever set up in Panola County. I led the search, and was abley assisted by Travis Gentry, Constable of Beckville. Plenty of whiskey and equipment. This mash was boiled off with a 200 gallon butane set up. We found seven Mexicans, (wetbacks) but they could "no savvy." They'll be deported to Old Mexico. The white man in charge was released to federal authorities in Tyler.

Marijuana: Last week we caught a car load of people. Four men and one woman from Port Arthur with a car load of marijuana. After chase they were caught and turned over to the Federals.

I took a draw off of one of the marijuana cigarettes. A new graveyard would be too good for a human who would deliberately and habitually smoke rot like that. I always liked to try anything. I did, but no more.

There are times when a law enforcer has to try everything to catch a violator. I went in on a still one time and helped cook up a batch until I caught the entire crew. I also once slipped into a dice game with about 20 whites and several Negroes shooting crap. But I was recognized when I started to fade the party next to me. At that, the Negroes got away, and from the rate they were running, they probably ended up in a new land.

Thursday, April 12, 1951

Saturday night a man that believes in law enforcement called me and said, while driving along the road, a small girl walking with a limp excitedly rushed to his car and cried, "Please do something, my Daddy has nearly killed me, and is beating my mother to death!"

When reported to me, I rushed out to the place. Folks, there were six crying frightened babies cowering under beds and other places trying to hide. The wife was hidden in the dark. We saw the husband hurriedly dash across to a light and put it out. We went on into the house and nothing was to be seen but a tell-tale bottle of old man Seagram 7, with the contents almost gone. But we knew daddy was there.

Constable Johnny Roberts of DeBerry peered into a closet and shouted "Come out of there!" I looked closer and saw a man's foot that was not quite hidden among the old clothes.

He spent the night in the County Bastille. Next day, the wife reported in and said she couldn't support the six babies and herself, so Judge Pierce fined him $25. The man shed a few tears and said he'd quit drinking a number of times and now he was quitting again. Judge sprayed a little brown mule tobacco, (the Judge always cogitates best when he has a good chew) and told the man he had better straighten up. He said he planned to stop these wife beatings. He further told him that a man's wife and babies are the only real bouquet he has. Why some men want to mistreat and destroy such beautiful flowers is something he couldn't understand.

Thursday, July 19, 1951

Last weekend, we got a call to come to Jefferson and bring the dogs. After checking, we found that it was a violator that we wanted in this county. He had been picked up by the Cass County officers and placed in jail, but had made his escape. We took up the trail from an old barn where he had slept. After six hours of running, my dogs got so hot, they could not bark and I couldn't whistle. I saw the escaped man run out of the woods. Someone came through a country road in a pickup, and the fugitive jumped in and stole a ride, making his getaway. He had no shirt, no hat, no shoes, and just a pair of his trousers left on. These boys that have been to the pen know how to take off.

One old sore spot of Carthage is gone. The place we have had so much trouble with. I call it Bootlegging and Bay Rum Alley. It was a nest of old tourist cabins, a hideout for 'leggers. I bought them and had them moved out of town. I'm a little old to be a Boy Scout, but I feel like I did a good deed by taking care of this sore spot. If you can't catch them, destroy their nest is a good policy to follow, I think.

Cussing Fight: Last Thursday, we had a call to the west end of the county. I found there had been a cussing fight involving two women and a man. The man was brought into court and paid a fine. He said he lost his temper. Also lost his money—the J.P. helped him count it, so it will be safe now.

Thursday, August 2, 1951

Another Call: Got a call Tuesday night from a 15-year-old boy who said he wanted to sleep in the jail. Said he couldn't stay at home. I had checked on him before, and found he had a good home, but was afraid of work. I told him I would be up there in a few minutes with a good hickory elm switch and see if he couldn't outrun me home. I further told him, I was going to warm his britches if I found him in town after dark. Well, he evidently took me at my word, and his mother may have a good boy now.

Thursday, August 9, 1951

Rough Sabbath: Sunday morning started out rough. We had a call to a fishing camp on the river. On investigation we found that the owner had been robbed and knocked in the head. He now has two black eyes, and so far we haven't found the guilty party. We did find a bunch that had been drinking that old green beer which sometimes causes black eyes as well as headaches.

Thursday, September 13, 1951
This weekend was very quiet. A few were given the once over, but the man we checked for bootlegging and the one we have had a number of reports on were caught, and a case filed. We had spent lots of time lately, slow trailing the subject. I am sure the people on North 59 Highway wondered why we stayed near one place for so long. The man we caught said we had ruined him. I hope our County Judge can let him know that whiskey traffic doesn't pay.

These old timers are hard to catch as they know the law so they carry two pints and sell it, then they go get two more. The law says they must have in their possession more than a quart to make a case. A constable made a raid on two places and found them within the law. The city police are trying to help with the apprehension of liquor violators.

Criticism: I suggest that these who are criticizing the sheriff read Proverbs 6:16-19 and Proverbs 10:18. I have been criticized about punch boards, marble tables, etc., but the new law says they're out.

Thursday, September 20, 1951
This week my deputies and I spent the week in trying to hem up a whiskey maker. We lost about two nights of sleep doing so. The second night, I got two men to go to the suspect's house and try to make a buy. He said it would take him some time to go and get it. He went back into the house and came out to the men with a shot gun in his hand. The men asked him what he was going to do with that gun. He replied that it might come in handy. It wasn't any trouble for me to hide and not be seen. I was in the middle with a big deputy on each side. We did have a fuss about getting behind a tree.

I stayed there waiting for the return of the two men that were going to make a buy. In the late hours, we left. I found out the man with the gun let the undercover men see the sunrise. They said they prayed for each other. Now you folks can see some of our work isn't fun.

Travis Gentry, Constable at Beckville, rolled up part of Tatum and placed a drunk in jail. Later we got a call to the jail and the man said someone had robbed him. He said he had his money in the cuff of his trousers and a jail mate had relieved him of it. After a little work, we got his money back for him, but it wasn't enough to pay his fine. But with a few days of rest in our nice county hotel, he paid out. You see, after a conviction, the one in jail gets $3.00 credit on his fine per day. So if you run out of a job, the county will give you a bed and two meals and credit you with $3.00

for each day in the county hotel. Another nice thing is nobody can get in to harm you and you can't fall out of your room and get hurt and there is a fellow on duty with a pistol to protect you. So the next time you violate the law, it's yours for free.

Thursday, October 25, 1951
   Wild Man: A wild man reported to be in the river bottom. The caller said he was eating huckleberries like a goat eating leaves. Will report more next week. Ol' Doc will tell me the way he has gone.

Folks Who Knew Bonnie and Clyde

You can get much farther with a kind word and a gun than you can with a kind word alone.
— Al Capone

Loblolly's pursuit of the story of Bonnie Parker and Clyde Barrow extended over a period of six months. It took its student journalists to many parts of East Texas for interviews, and they corresponded with other people in places much farther away.

Loblolly found that Bonnie and Clyde still hold a fascination for many people. Some the students spoke to were very careful in what they said for fear of hurting persons still living whose lives were touched by the pair in the early 1930's. They discovered that people still hold widely differing views on the two outlaws. These included a first cousin of Clyde, others who had met or seen them (or thought they had), and still others who remembered the impact Bonnie and Clyde had upon the area.

After a lapse of half a century, fact and legend seem hopelessly intertwined in people's memories of Bonnie and Clyde. Some identified C. W. Moss as the one who betrayed Bonnie and Clyde into the ambush that resulted in their deaths, but this was only the Hollywood name used in the movie. Actually, it was Henry Methvin who cooperated with the law in return for a pardon. Some people defended the pair and gave them a Robin Hood personality, justifying their crimes as a result of being forced into an outlaw life. Other persons remembered them as a sorry pair of murderers who got what they deserved.

Bonnie Parker

There were conflicting stories, such as who pulled the trigger during their various murders. Clyde told his cousin that he had personally never shot anyone, but Floyd Hamilton (gunman Raymond Hamilton's brother) was quoted in a paper as saying that Clyde had admitted to killing ten people. *Loblolly* came to the conclusion that a lot of the truth involving Bonnie and Clyde will never be known. In some cases, readers will have to decide for themselves which of the following material is fact and which is legend.

—*Loblolly*

Clyde Barrow

Leon Lewis

Clyde styled himself after Pretty Boy Floyd and the others up in the East Coast area. He was like a Robin Hood. He stole from the rich and gave it away. It was during the worst of the Depression, when most had no money at all. The banks seemed to be just holding the money. Clyde didn't steal for personal gain. That's why he could appear in a lot of places and not fear being turned in to the law. He wasn't the usual outlaw. He also appreciated a fine automobile. There wasn't a sheriff's car that could catch him.

Max Haddick

My recollections of seeing Bonnie and Clyde are not of great importance, but I did see them. I can't recall the exact date, as it was way back in the 1930's and I have difficulty remembering things that happened yesterday.

I was a newspaper delivery boy in Mexia, Texas, when Bonnie and Clyde came through. They kidnapped a woman just outside of Mexia and made her ride with them down to somewhere around Conroe. They released her unharmed, but scared the bejabbers out of her.

I was on Milam Street about an hour before sundown. The car Bonnie and Clyde used was a Model-A Ford touring car. They stopped near me, and Clyde got out and walked around the car. I think he was checking his tires, but I did not carry on any conversation with him. In fact, I didn't have the slightest idea who it was until much later.

I was quite close and did get a good look at both of them. Bonnie was a mess. They had, I believe, been sleeping out along the Trinity River and living like animals. Both their faces were welted with mosquito bites, and they were very dirty. Clyde was wearing a suit, but it was a total mess.

He kicked at the tires and then jumped back into the car and said something like, "Let's get out of here" and took off. I never saw them again.

Opal Vaughn Rhodes

Clyde Barrow lived with my uncle Jeff and aunt Edda Weathersbee near Payne Spring close to Eustace, Texas. It was on their ranch when he was a young boy. I don't know how long he stayed with them. They had no children of their own, and he became thought of as one of the family. He was a quiet and a good boy from what they said. I never knew him.

My uncle Pink Vaughn (Aunt Edda's half brother) was a member of the Texas Rangers. He went out to Uncle Jeff's place one time looking for Clyde when Clyde was on the run from the law. Uncle Jeff and Aunt Edda told Uncle Pink to get out and never come back again. After Clyde got killed, I heard that he had hid out at Uncle Jeff's place some. So, Clyde touched and divided my family.

Leo Covington Hanna

I lived at Martinsville. I met them in the country anyway. He came to Martinsville several times before he was a fugitive, and he was a very Christian boy. He grew up in a Christian family, and he was nice-looking. He came to our parties when he was a fugitive, and I dated him. We would pair off at the parties, that was my way home. If the parties was close to my house he would walk me home. If it was too far of a walk we would ride that Model-T Ford. It was the one that he had all his running gear in, and that he did all his running from the law in. He was a very good driver.

The first two visits, he was in trouble, and he would come there and hide out until it kind of blowed over. So he stayed there, and he was just the nicest guy, most delightful person you could know. The first time that they really got in trouble was when he first robbed the bank in Dallas, and this girl who is Bonnie Parker was in on the robbery. She was doing the driving. And he went into the bank with a gun and held the bank up. He went out and got away and started running.

I knew them after that. They would come down to our neighborhood and hide out awhile. And then she would go to the parties, and then they would practice with their rifles or their guns. One time Bonnie was out practicing with their guns, and Bonnie almost shot her toe off.

They came over to Shelby County to a cave about seven miles south of Center in the Shorts Community. And one or the other would go into Center and get supplies and go back. There was a gang of five, and they all stayed in the cave until the law got too close. Then at some gas station, the law talked to a little guy that squealed on them. So Bonnie and Clyde thought the law was getting too close.

I am seventy-three years old. If Clyde were alive today, he would be about seventy-three or seventy-five years old. Bonnie was younger than Clyde. They went for about five years without getting caught. When they got shot up, they said that they had just lots of money. When they were in the gang of five, they had two cars. Bonnie and Clyde rode in one car, and the other three rode in the other car. She was for sure pregnant when killed. We were of the opinion that they were all married. Her baby was due later in the spring. Clyde went to church in our community, and so did Bonnie. It was the First Baptist Church.

R. E. Choate
Henry Rich shaved him once, and I was working there in the barbershop at that time. There was no way to prove that it was Clyde, but we saw them so much in the papers that anyone would have known them. About ten o'clock that morning he came, and Mr. Rich shaved him. And while he was shaving him, there was a woman in the car outside, and Clyde kept raising up and looking out through a big glass window at her all the time.

She was in a Ford with a V-8 engine. Those were the cars they stole because they were the only ones at that time that had the V-8 in them. After Clyde left we all got to kidding Mr. Rich about Clyde raising up and looking out. We asked if he wasn't nervous. He said, "No, I had the razor; if he tried anything I would just cut his head off."

Corbett Akins
In the 1930's I was operating a filling station on Highway 59 here in Carthage next to my home. About two-thirty one afternoon, a Ford automobile drove up to my station and stopped. A man and a woman were in the Ford. The man got out and went into the shop and looked around. The woman stayed in the car with a blanket over her lap. I sold them eleven gallons of gas and they took off.

I found out after they left, it was Clyde Barrow and Bonnie Parker. As

I understood, the car at my station had been stolen and was later found abandoned down near Tenaha. From there, they got into another car and went to Louisiana. And when they got there, they stayed a few days. They had something to do with an ex-convict over there. They were killed in Louisiana shortly after that. It was then that I realized I had faced Bonnie Parker and Clyde Barrow.

I remember how Bonnie looked that day. She was a small woman and had a narrow freckle face. She had almost red hair. Clyde was about five feet eight inches tall with broad shoulders.

They didn't create any trouble that day in Carthage. They just paid me for the gas and took off. And that night, I heard a report that they were jumped in Tenaha and abandoned the car. When the stolen car was found, there was a .38 automatic Colt pistol which was traced back to Bonnie and Clyde.

I do remember that they acted kind of strange, though, at the station. Before he got out of the car, he looked all up and down the road, looked in the station. I could tell he wanted to do something besides kill a man 'cause he didn't stay in the back long. In fact, the business he had in the station was to use the restroom in back.

Bonnie stayed in the car, she never did move. But she watched the road, she watched the shop, and watched me. If I had known it was Bonnie Parker sitting there, I'm pretty sure I would have had a bowel movement.

When I saw them that day, though, they were nice-looking people, respectable looking. Clyde talked to me and seemed very pleasant. He didn't say anything out of the way, just paid me for the gas and left. I don't recall the price of gasoline, but it wasn't a dollar a gallon.

Ernest Graves

Well, the first time that I met Bonnie and Clyde was in Gary. They had a lot of friends in Timpson, and when they went through these parts, they would just drive up and spend the night with the relatives or their friends. On this side of Lake Murvaul there is the road that you turn off on to go to the lake, but then it was dirt. Bonnie and Clyde was coming up that hill and got stuck. So I went and got Levi Koonce and his wagon and team out there. We pulled them out of there and left and went on toward Clayton. They told us who they were, that they were Bonnie and Clyde. The way that they paid us was a fifth of whiskey or a quart of whiskey. I want to think of a man they called Red Tate, or something like that. They stayed with him.

Before this Clyde had broke out of the pen. Bonnie was with him, and they had got away from the dogs trailing them. It was just too cold for the dogs to travel, the cold water and ice was something, so the dogs lost them. They would get out and always come back here to Timpson or Center. Matter of fact, Clyde still has some kinfolks around here somewhere.

One day Bonnie and Clyde seen me, and I did not know them. Clyde walked up to me and said, "I am Clyde and this is Bonnie Parker, shake our hands." On the old Clayton road, beside the road, there was a watering hole and a sand embankment where we sat and I personally drunk whiskey with Bonnie and Clyde. Whiskey was two dollars a gallon, almost fifty cents a swallow. In my opinion I don't believe that they would have shot you if you left them alone. But they did not want them alive, and they did not want them to give up. They wanted them dead.

William Pate

There was an old man that lived on the Banks farm. Bonnie and Clyde would come and stay there. The man that owned the Banks farm was an Old Man Fuller. I saw Bonnie and Clyde come to Timpson one time. Clyde, he got out of the car and walked around the square. Bonnie never even got out of the car. Clyde got out of the car and went to the bank and looked at the bank and came back and got into the car and they left. He looked like he was six feet tall. Bonnie was a little bitty thing, and she looked like she weighed about one hundred pounds. She had redlike hair. If you ever saw Bonnie and Clyde in Timpson, you knew not to tell anyone that they had been seen there. One time Daddy and I went to Timpson, and we saw them come through, and we went up close enough to see the guns. They were laying behind the seat in an old '34 Ford. When it come down to really good driving, Clyde could drive that '34 Ford.

C. W. Moss's daddy is the one who turned them in. C. W. ran around with them, and he helped rob some of the banks, but he never did do much of the hard work. Bonnie always sat in the car and waited on Clyde with a gun, or stayed and watched the car. C. W. did most of the driving while Bonnie and Clyde did most of the dangerous work. But when it come time to recognize them, we could recognize them because everybody stood back. Well, the first time that I seen them I thought that I would be afraid of them, and I was not really scared of them.

Buck, Clyde's brother, was shot in Louisiana somewhere. But when Buck was shot, it did not kill him on the spot. He lived about one hour after he was shot. Buck's wife, so to be called, she was the one that was always scared. Every time they went to rob a bank, she went to bawling and squalling.

Conway McMillian

This area was down the river from Shelby County, over and down the river from Logansport. Bonnie and Clyde would go and come there; they might stay a week, four or five days, or longer. Then they would blow out like the wind. The reason they had such good cover was everyone would help them because they more or less worshiped them and would help them.

One time I went to their hideout. I didn't know they were there, or I wouldn't have gone there. But they were back in the house. I didn't fool around. I got on 'cause I had rather not tangle up with them.

They killed several law officers. They killed one out at Grapevine, Texas, a highway patrolman, just for stopping the car for something minor, like to check driver's license. They didn't know what he was stopping them for. So they killed him.

I am sure that I saw them because they were around Logansport too much for me not to have seen them. But I never knew if I saw them.

At the same time, though they were heroes, people still feared them and wouldn't cross them. They knew as long as they didn't cross them, they would get along with them. Yes, they helped the people they stayed with. They were generous of them because they'd rather have a place to stay than money. It was somewhere to stay while things cooled off. I did know one person that they stayed with. I've been to his house for business reasons several times. One time I went and Bonnie and Clyde were there. I didn't see them, but I could tell they were there by the way the people acted and what they said. I didn't linger because I didn't want to see them.

B. A. Patterson

Well, I know that his parents lived down here. It was not too far down this road I live on here. I heard there was some woman up in the East and he was hid out up there one day. He saw this woman over a rub board washing. He went down there and asked her for something to eat. She cooked a nice dinner for him. Some time later he went back through there, and he gave her a washing machine. The way it was, they robbed from the rich and gave to the poor. I saw Clyde when he was a kid, but I can't remember what he looked like. They used to live on the same farm we lived on. There was a big plantation between Garrison and Martinsville, and we lived on it, too.

I don't think they did anything wrong around here. But Bonnie did smoke cigars.

John Tyson

I have to go back in history about forty years. I believe it was 1933 or 1934 that the Bonnie and Clyde story popped up. At the time, I was going to school at the college at Marshall, Texas, which is now East Texas Baptist College. And to get home on any weekend from school was a matter of hitchhiking, 'cause there wasn't any other way for poor folks to travel back and forth to school.

This, of course, was about the time that Bonnie and Clyde were all over the country doing bad things. They were really famous in this part of East Texas for the simple reason, down in the lower part of Shelby County, they had some relatives. I don't remember which one, but I believe it was his relatives that lived below Stockman, in there someplace. And, of course, it was common knowledge in this country that sometimes, when things got pretty warm, they would come down here waiting for things to cool off.

In any case, on a Friday afternoon after school, I was hitchhiking a ride from Marshall to Timpson. And in those days, as you can well imagine, there wasn't much transportation on the road. The good thing about it in those days was that people weren't afraid to death to pick up a kid hitchhiking. And the chance was pretty good if a car came by.

I had gone from the campus, across Marshall, to the south side on what used to be Highway 35. It's now 59. Then this black four-door Ford sedan, kind of like a touring car, pulled up and stopped. And this was the time of the first V-8's that Ford ever came out with. And this was a popular model. Naturally, I was thrilled to death.

I ran up to get in the car, and kind of fumbled with the door. I wasn't used to this model car. When I got in I saw the driver was a woman. Her dress was up over her knees, and a gun was laying between her legs. Right off I was pretty apprehensive about the whole situation. But she insisted that I hop in, which I did. Of course, I regretted it after I got inside. Because when I looked over there, I saw a holster sewed on the left door. And in the holster was another pistol.

Well, by then you can imagine I was looking straight and saying nothing. It hadn't occurred to me who the driver might be. But in any case it was somebody I didn't want to be in the car with. So off down the road we went. And it wasn't long before we were going seventy-five to eighty miles per hour. Since I had never been over fifty miles per hour before, I was nervous.

Nothing was being said by either one of us. And then suddenly she turned to me and said something like, "What's the matter, kid, you scared?" And I could only answer, "Yes." And off down the road we would go.

By then, I looked around further and saw a shotgun and rifle in the back seat. And by now I was trying to think of some way to get out of the deal. Maybe today sophisticated kids wouldn't have been quite so nervous. But for a country boy like me, I was really upset about the whole thing.

I was also trying to figure out who I was with. Naturally, at that time, Bonnie and Clyde were famous and well known in this area. This was the first thing that crossed my mind, that I was riding with the famous Bonnie. I don't really know if it was Bonnie or not. But I put it all together, and I was convinced it was her.

I decided I had all of that I wanted because I started making up these fantasies that if the police stopped the car, I was going to get killed. So when we got outside Tenaha I told her a house we came to was my home. And the girl stopped the car and I got out. I thanked her and off she went. I haven't seen Bonnie since.

Leo Muckleroy

Clyde's mother and my mother were sisters. His mother's name was Cummie and my mother's name was Susie.

Clyde was born right on top of the Swift Hill on Highway 7. There's a lookout, the Highway Department built a lookout, scenic view deal. Right on top of the hill, right there where that place was built, that's where Clyde was born. He was about four years old when they moved from Swift to Dallas.

I believe it all started in Dallas. Clyde was working for some company up there. An old boy that was working in the office wanted Clyde to help him rob this place. He told Clyde, "I'll leave the safe open, leave the money in there, and leave a window unlocked. And you come in and I'll meet you later." And after they got everything set up, Clyde went in that night, and the other fellow wasn't waiting on him. He sat there and sat there and waited awhile. And he got up and took his flashlight and walked over to where the safe was. And just as he stuck his hand out to touch the handle of that safe, why, this old boy had called the law and put them in on him. And they got him for attempted robbery and break-in. That was before he went to the pen. I don't know just how long the sentence was, but he stayed in the pen.

Finally, he got out on parole. For some reason or the other, they revoked his parole and had an order out to pick him up. And that was when he had met Bonnie. He asked her if she'd go with him. Bonnie had all of her papers signed, she was fixing to go into a convent, be a nun. She made the statement, the night, first time she had ever seen him, she knew she didn't want to be a nun. I guess you might say that started it.

Well, after he got really hot, as the law got after him, why, he'd come to our house, hide his car in our barn. I was living about a mile north of Martinsville, towards Garrison. It was just an old rough country road then. I wasn't married. I was just a jugheaded boy about eighteen. He'd stay a week at a time. He stayed there, I guess, on three different visits, and every time, he never stayed over a week. I guess the shortest visit was about four days, and the longest was about six.

He was the most likable kind of an old boy. You never saw him when he wasn't smiling. He was always doing lots of kidding. And if he had fifteen cents and you wanted it, why, you got it all. Every time he ever come there and started to leave, he'd always say to either my daddy or he'd ask my mother, "You need any money?" And they always told him, they probably needed it, but they wouldn't take any. Told him no, they didn't need it, didn't need any money. Said they had plenty to eat and a place to stay. Where nobody was after him, he was just that way. And he always had a little sneaky smile on his face. He was likable. You just couldn't keep from liking him.

Bonnie was very energetic. When my mother went to the kitchen, well, she went with her. She helped her cook. She helped her clean up the kitchen and helped her make the beds, clean up the house. She was an energetic old girl and knew how to do things besides hijack banks and filling stations and stuff.

They were just part of a family. They were nervous, you could tell they was nervous when they got there. By the time they left they seemed to be rested and relaxed. But when they went to bed at night, each one had a gun under their pillow.

My dad didn't know anything about it. In other words, he figured the gun was laying in there somewhere where Clyde could get to in case something come up. But he walked in one morning, I believe it was the second time they were there. He walked in there. Mama had breakfast ready. He went in, and they were still asleep. And he just laid his hand on Clyde's shoulder, and he said, "Breakfast is ready." And when he moved, well, that gun was sticking right in Papa's face. And Clyde said, "Uncle Jim, don't ever do that no more. Just holler, say breakfast is ready." He said, "That will be all that'll be necessary." You know, they were just on edge. That's how nervous they really were.

And they got out and around. Every day, sometimes during the day, he'd go to Martinsville. Old Man Fuller was running the store down there. The old man got a daily paper, and Clyde would ask him, "Can I read your paper?" And he'd say, "You sure can." And he'd take the paper and go in the back, and the old man knew who he was. He'd go back in the back of the store and read the paper. One time he was there, he read that the Barrow gang had robbed a bank in Indiana the day before. Oh, there was a terrible write-up about that.

Clyde come up front—it was really funny to him. He said, "Now, Mr. Fuller, you know that I didn't do this and there wasn't no Barrow gang. It's just me and Bonnie." He said, "You know we wasn't in Indiana, 'cause I was right here yesterday talking to you and reading the paper."

And later years, why, this man that ran the store, Fuller, was elected county judge. But he knew Clyde personally, about everybody around there knew him really.

Everybody that met him liked him. I don't know whether it was respect to the family, or whether they just liked him and didn't want to turn him in. I just don't know, really never did give it a thought.

Clyde's favorite food was fried chicken. And if Mother didn't have any fryers, why, he'd always go up above home about two miles. It was to a woman's house, and she nearly always had three or four fried chickens. And just whatever amount she had, well, that was what he bought. The last time he was in, we went up there. She said, "Yes, sir, I got four fryers." He said, "Well, I want them." She said, "Well, you try to catch them." We caught 'em all but one. And there was one nice rooster in the bunch. Clyde said, "I sure wish we had that one." She told him, "Mr. Clyde, you'll just have to shoot it." He replied, "We'll see if we can." And we drove that chicken around in the yard and finally got it up in the corner of the fence. And he killed that chicken with his pistol. Course, the old woman thought that was the grandest thing in the world, that she got to sell chickens to Mr. Clyde Barrow.

The only shooting I ever saw him do was when he killed the chicken.

Sometimes him and my brother, who was a year or two older than me, they'd walk off down in the woods down there, and you'd hear 'em down there shooting. And nobody thought anything about it. My brother was a bird hunter and a squirrel hunter, and they thought nothing of him shooting.

Clyde always said that Buck loved to shoot, then ask questions later. He said, "We'd rather run than shoot." Course, you know, I asked him, "Just how many have you killed?" And he looked at me just as straight and he never batted an eye, and said, "Honestly, I never killed a man in my life." I said, "Who did all the shooting?" He said, "Well, I'll tell you." He said, "It was Bonnie and Raymond Hamilton and Henry Methvin. Methvin was with us and Raymond Hamilton was with us." And he said, "That was the trigger." He said, "I didn't trust nobody to drive, I done all the driving. They did the triggering, don't you think that they didn't."

Bonnie had a .38 Colt nickel-plated automatic, and he had a .45 automatic, nickel-plated, and a pearl handle on it. It was a beautiful thing. He didn't particularly care for six-guns, said they shoot for a while and then they'd run out of ammunition.

The old house where we used to live is still standing at Martinsville. And, I guess it was the last time they was there, Bonnie and Clyde was cleaning their guns. They were going to leave the next morning. When Bonnie put hers together, she was sitting there pointing it. She had on a pair of sandals and she was sitting there pointing the gun. It looked like she was pointing at her big toe. Clyde said, "That thing might be loaded, you might oughta check it." And she said, "There's no use to check it, it's not loaded." And she pulled the trigger. It was loaded. And that bullet went down between the toe next to her big toe and her other toe, right down between those two toes. It really blistered it, and the bullet went through the floor. I don't imagine anybody in the country would know where the bullet went through the floor other than maybe me. But he, Clyde, was sitting on the edge of the bed with her. He jumped up and said, "My God, you could have killed somebody. Get your stuff, let's go."

In five minutes they were gone, and that was the last time they were ever in our house. When they started to leave, Mama went and told 'em, "Now, Clyde, come back any time you want to." But he told her, "No, we won't be back. The law's liable to come in here; some of y'all might be killed." And he said, "If the law didn't, Bonnie's liable to let her ol' gun go off and kill one of you." And he laughed. He was a joker.

And he told my mother, "Now, we won't be back here anymore because we're afraid. Actually what we're afraid of is maybe sometime the law will find we're here. The laws will come in, and trying to shoot us, they're liable to kill some of y'all. I wouldn't have that happen for nothing in the world." He told Mother just how much he enjoyed coming here, but he wouldn't come back anymore. They were just too hot after him.

So he never came back. I saw him one time after then. The sheriff in

Nacogdoches picked up a boy who stole a car in Dallas. The sheriff over there [Dallas] was a good friend of ours, Carl Buttler. So Sheriff Buttler, since there were no telephones back then, he came out to Martinsville, and he asked me if I'd like to drive the car in. I was about nineteen, I guess, then. He said he'd buy me a bus ticket back home. Course, I jumped at that proposition.

Well, after I got to Dallas, I was standing out front of Clyde's daddy's store. Back then, I always wore an old big hat and a pair of cowboy boots. Course I couldn't ride a stick horse. But anyway, Clyde's daddy, his name was Henry, ran a filling station by the store out in west Dallas. And I was standing there facing their store and talking to Uncle Henry. He then said, "There went Clyde and Bonnie." Course I looked and I didn't see anything. And he told me, "You walk on down the street there." There was a vacant lot there. So I walked on down that street, and when I met them they threw a letter at me. They didn't stop, they both just hollered at me and asked me how I was getting along. And Bonnie said, "We thought you was the law standing up there, or we'd hollered at you when we came by."

I walked on by it, then I turned around, and as I walked back up the street, I picked up the letter and carried it back in. The letter was to his mother telling her where to come meet them. They had their regular meeting place somewhere out in Dallas. So that was about eight-thirty or nine o'clock in the evening. They went to see them; they got back in that night about three-thirty. Before they left, I just begged them to let me go with them. His mother said, "Oh, no." That was the last I seen him living.

And, of course, lots of people have told some long tales, that they had seen them and how ragged and all they dressed. But they didn't. He dressed like a millionaire, and she did, too. That's the reason they parked the car and walked out in the street and nobody knew them. He wore a stickpin in his tie that looked like a hawkeye, a diamond. I don't feel like he bought it, I feel like he got it from some hijack somewhere. The laws either got it or it was shot off of him. Nobody ever knew anything about it. They claimed that he only had between four and five hundred dollars on him. I was told that he had a money belt on and it was loaded.

He was supposed to pull a job over in Minden, Louisiana, or over in that vicinity. It was a setup job. They found that out later. All he had to do was just walk in with a suitcase, and a bag would have ten thousand dollars in it. And then the president of the bank would record so much more than that. It was a way to cover a bank shortage. But they killed him before he got back to pick up the money.

And so, after he didn't get back, bank examiners come in and found how much money was short at the bank. Lots of his jobs were setup jobs.

That was about four or five months before they were killed. The sad thing about the thing was, of course, them getting on the wrong road. They were hoping to get married, and were going to go under an assumed name. He had bought them a place either in Montana or just over in Canada. Last time he was through Dallas, he told his mother he had some important papers to sign and leave with her. They couldn't even find an indelible pencil or fountain pen. And he told her, "I'll be back in two or three days, and you'll have one to sign it." That was when he was killed in Louisiana.

They acted like they was a fool about each other. You know, one time they claimed that Raymond Hamilton was riding with them—Clyde was in the back seat asleep—and Hamilton told Bonnie, "You know what we oughta do? We oughta just shoot him and throw him out and me and you just go on." And she let him know right quick that there wasn't but one man in her life. And that there would never be one after Clyde. But she was a fool about him, and he appeared to be crazy about her.

There's a certain age, these boys and girls, they like the wild side of life. I'm gonna tell you the God's truth. Half the time that all this was going on, if Clyde would have said, "Leo, why don't you go with us?" I expect I'd have gone.

Leo Muckleroy contributed the following poems written by Bonnie Parker.

Outlaws

Billy rode on a pinto horse—
Billy the Kid I mean—
And he met Clyde Barrow riding
In a little gray machine.

Billy drew his bridle rein
And Barrow stopped his car,
And the dead man talked to the living man
Under the morning star.

Billy said to the Barrow boy,
"Is this the way you ride,
In a car that does its ninety per,
Machine guns at each side?

"I only had my pinto horse
And my six-gun tried and true,
I could shoot but they got me,
And some day they will get you!

"For the men who live like you and me
Are playing a losing game,
And the way we shoot, or the way we ride,
Is all about the same.

"And the like of us may never hope
For death to set us free,

For the living are always after you
And the dead are after me."

Then out of the East arose the sound
Of hoof-beats with the dawn
And Billy pulled his rein and said,
"I must be moving on."

And out of the West came the glare of a light
And the drone of a motor's song,
And Barrow set his foot on the gas
And shouted back, "So long!"

So into the East, Clyde Barrow rode,
And Billy, into the West;
The living man who can know no peace
And the dead who can know no rest.

Bonnie Parker's Last Poem

You have read the story of Jesse James,
Of how he lived and died.
If you still are in need of something to read,
Here is the story of Bonnie and Clyde.

Now Bonnie and Clyde are the Barrow gang.
I'm sure you all have read
How they rob and steal,
And how those who squeal,
Are usually found dying or dead.

There are lots of untruths to their write-ups,
They are not so merciless as that;
They hate all the laws,
The stool pigeons, spotters and rats.

They class them as cold-blooded killers,
They say they are heartless and mean,
But I say this with pride
That I once knew Clyde
When he was honest and upright and clean.

But the law fooled around,
Kept tracking him down
And locking him up in a cell,
Till he said to me,
"I will never be free,
So I will meet a few of them in hell."

This road was so dimly lighted,
There was no highway signs to guide,
But they made up their minds
If the roads were all blind
They wouldn't give up till they died.

The road gets dimmer and dimmer,
Sometimes you can hardly see,
Still it's fight, man to man,
And do all you can,
For they know they can never be free.

If they try to act like citizens
And rent them a nice little flat.
About the third night they are invited to fight
By a submachine gun rat-tat-tat.

If a policeman is killed in Dallas
And they have no clues for a guide;
If they can't find a friend
They just wipe the slate clean
And hang it on Bonnie and Clyde.

Two crimes have been done in America
Not accredited to the Barrow mob,
For they had no hand
In the kidnapping demand
Or the Kansas City depot job.

A newsboy once said to his buddy,
"I wish old Clyde would get jumped,
In this awful hard times
We might make a few dimes
If five or six laws got bumped."

The police haven't got the report yet,
Clyde sent a wireless today
Saying, "We have a peace flag of white
We stretch out at night,
We have joined the NRA."

They don't think they are too tough or desperate,
They know the law always wins.
They have been shot at before
But they do not ignore
That death was the wages of sin.

From heartbreaks some people have suffered,
From weariness some people have died,

But take it all in all,
Our troubles are small,
Till we get like Bonnie and Clyde.

Some day they will go down together,
And they will bury them side by side,
To a few it means grief,
To the law it's relief,
But it is death to Bonnie and Clyde.

A newspaper article appeared in 1969 based on an interview with Leo Muckleroy about his knowledge of Bonnie and Clyde. After the article appeared, Muckleroy received a letter from a woman who had been near or on the scene when the two were killed. *Loblolly* believes it has never been made public that anyone else was close to the ambush scene. The letter, in part, is as follows:

Dear Sir:
This is not a crank letter, and it is meant to be an understanding one.
I do not like to open old wounds, yet this one has never exactly healed with me.
You see, I was married and living with my husband, at the time Bonnie and Clyde were killed on a little country road out of or near Arcadia, Louisiana.
I was collecting and making replacements of fruit-trees in and near Arcadia. I was driving a nursery pick-up, and I had a young Negro boy to assist me. He was riding in the back of the pick-up truck.
There was a Negro man who lived down back of the big house, at the dead end of this country road. He lived back in the pasture, and was a hard man to collect from. I was on this road, and was about three-quarters of a mile from town. A man stepped out of the bushes, and told me to turn my truck back to town. I turned around, the road was a sand bed, and drove back as I had come for a quarter of a mile.
He looked like the law. So instead of going on back to town, I drove my pick-up truck off the sandy road in the trees and bushes. I told the little boy to stay in the truck, not get out for any reason, that I would be back soon. He was frightened to death, and wanted to go home.
I kept to the woods, went about one hundred yards, and thought of something I wanted to do. So I went back to the pick-up truck, in the bushes and reached in the glove compartment and got a penny box of matches. The little boy was say-

ing "Lordie lets go home." I told him to shut-up and keep quiet or he might get shot. You see the newspapers had placed Bonnie and Clyde in or near the Arkansas line. And I knew that the law was not there for no reason. And I suspected what it was.

After coming out into the road, down from where the truck was, I walked out into the sandy road with some straw and weeds and some small sticks, all I could find. They were rotten and just smoked mostly. I built a smoke in the center of the dirt road, it only made a small smoke. But I thought anyone seeing it would realize there had been or were people around. It was a small smoke. I could not find anything bigger than some trash to build it with. After doing this I walked back into the woods. I lay on my stomach, facing the dirt road where the smoke was. It burned out and there was only a tiny whisp of smoke coming from the trash. But I waited, I was afraid to walk near the road too many times, as I had been told in an authoritative way to get off that road and back to town. I got tired just lying on my belly and got up and started easing off down the road in the direction the man giving orders went. There was a small creek bed just off the road. I layed down in it facing the highway.

Finally I heard a car after hours of waiting. I could not see it from where I was but it seemed to speed up after passing where the smoke was (if they saw it). I feel they did, for they speeded up and were driving fast. Then after they had gone a ways I heard shots, volleys of shots. I started to where they came from and kept way back into the bushes. I was raised in the Piney woods and was very much at home in the woods, but I was afraid to get too close to the road. First place, I was afraid any movement on my part that Bonnie or Clyde would shoot me, and on the other hand, the law.

I went close enough to where I could hear voices after the shooting, and I listened. I knew then it was Bonnie and Clyde and they were dead. I then broke down and was shaking all over, I crawled to where I could see them on my belly, scared and shook up very bad and near crying. Returning to the truck was the longest distance I ever traveled. I got in the truck still scared I would be seen leaving. And the boy was wringing his hands, and near crying he was so scared, so was I. I could hardly hold the wheel of the pick-up. I knew I only had a short time to get off the road before people would be there. And I would be caught there and there would be questions.

After leaving in the truck, very careful not to race the motor, driving slow until I had gone about a quarter of a mile back toward Arcadia, then I drove that truck as fast as I could. I was very careful to tell that little boy that if he ever said anything about this, they would lock him up for life or even shoot him to keep his trap shut.

Do you know after this, that little boy played sick every time I asked him to go with me on a delivery? He stayed clear of me every day. He would go in the other pick-ups with the men, but never me. I'm sure he never spoke of this. I didn't until now.

Ernest Murphy

I'm originally from Arcadia, Louisiana. That's the parish seat of Bienville Parish. And I was there the day that Bonnie and Clyde were killed. I was over there on May 23, 1934, helping my father on abstract work. An abstractor works on land records, you know. An oil company was leasing land through that part of the state, and I was running down the records in the courthouse.

I was there at the time that they called in to the sheriff's office that Bonnie and Clyde had been killed. They were on their way in to bring the bodies to the morgue in Arcadia. So all the people in the courthouse rushed over to witness the bringing in of the bodies. This was about ten o'clock in the morning. We went over to see the bodies brought in. And they brought the car in, too. It's amazing, but it was still drivable. The Texas Rangers and local lawmen who had been in on the shooting came into town at the same time.

Arcadia was a town of about twenty-five hundred people, but about ten thousand people gathered there. It was kind of a show to see all the people massing around and going through the morgue to see the bodies. They had two doors on the funeral home, and they let the people circle around one side and go out the other after viewing the bodies. There was a continuous stream of people filing through there.

Well, the ambush was kind of a case of hush-hush, and we didn't know anything was going on. It was kept so quiet until it was all over. It was over there at a little place called Sailes where the killing took place. I went over there afterwards to see where it happened. And the layout was on a gravel road. It was an area that was elevated on both sides above the road. That's where the Texas Rangers and sheriff's people were when the killing took place.

There was a Mr. Methvin down in the southern part of the parish, and his son was involved with Bonnie and Clyde. In order for him to get out of his trouble, they told him if he would turn them in, they would let him off.

Bonnie and Clyde were staying at Mr. Methvin's place. It was on this route going down to Sailes. Mr. Methvin was in an old Ford truck, and he had stopped there in the road. This had been arranged as to where he would stop. The lawmen were hidden in the elevated area there above the road. They knew about what time they would be coming along. And when Bonnie and Clyde drove up there, they recognized Mr. Methvin's truck. Mr. Methvin got out of his truck and came over there and told them he had a little truck trouble, and that's why he was stopped. He got back in his truck and gave the watching lawmen a signal. And that's when the officers above opened fire. That's when the killing took place. They didn't try to get them to surrender, because the two of them were riding in that car with guns and ammunition in their laps. They knew they always traveled that way, and didn't want any more lawmen killed by Bonnie and Clyde.

Their families were notified after the killings so they could claim the bodies. I believe they lived somewhere around Dallas. And they turned the bodies over to them.

The car was kept there at the Arcadia Courthouse jail in a fenced area. There was a lady up north somewhere, I believe in Illinois, that the car was stolen from. And she came down to claim it.

People were really relieved because Bonnie and Clyde had been traveling all over this part of the country. They had different license plates they carried along with them through different states. They spent a lot of time in East Texas, too.

I never could figure out why people tried to make heroes out of them. They sure weren't heroes to my thinking.

Ted Hinton

This is the latest version—and perhaps the most authentic—of the final days of Bonnie and Clyde. Primarily, it is the story of Ted Hinton, the last survivor of the six-man ambush team that killed Clyde Barrow and Bonnie Parker on May 23, 1934, on a gravel road in swamp country near Gibsland, Louisiana.

The other five peace officers, including the legendary Frank Hamer, a former Texas Ranger captain, are all now dead. Hinton, seventy-two, lives in his hometown of Dallas. He was twenty-seven years old, a Dallas deputy sheriff, when he joined Hamer in the manhunt for Bonnie and Clyde, whose gang was blamed for fourteen slayings, including nine peace officers, and numerous bank robberies in the Southwest.

Hinton's version of how the outlaws were tracked down is detailed in a deposition, sworn testimony, that *Loblolly* obtained from the *Houston Chronicle*. Hinton's deposition was taken after Frank Hamer's widow sued Warner Brothers Seven Arts, Inc., the filmmakers who produced the movie, *Bonnie and Clyde,* for $1.7 million.

The widow claimed the movie had defamed the character of her late husband, Frank Hamer, by erroneously depicting him as a "vindictive killer from ambush." She also alleged that the scenes showing Bonnie and Clyde capturing Hamer and humiliating him were not true.

Homer's hit squad

During the taking of his deposition, Ted Hinton was asked if the outlaws had ever captured Frank Hamer.

Ted Hinton—Oh, man, no; he ain't never been captured by nobody, except the Good Lord.

Q.—Did Capt. Hamer enjoy talking about the fact that he had killed people in his lifetime?

A.—No, he didn't. [One published report said that Hamer, during his long career as a Texas Ranger, had killed fifty-three men, not counting Mexican bandits. Hamer, in an interview in 1953 with *Houston Chronicle* reporter Don Hinga, did not deny that report.]

Q.—Had he ever mentioned that to you at all?

A.—No. I did hear him say that he had been in a lot of gun battles; he did say that. [Hamer, who stood six feet four and a half inches and weighed 230, told reporter Hinga that he had suffered twenty-three bullet wounds and that he still had sixteen bullets in him. "They can't operate," he said. "To get them out, they'd have to cut me up too much."]

Q. — Posters had been spread all over the United States and everybody knew what they looked like, didn't they?

A. — Yes, a lot of posters had been put out, but some of them wouldn't be correct, like at Joplin, Missouri, when this photographer took a picture and changed it. It showed Bonnie standing in front of the car with a rose in her mouth and a pistol in her hand and one stuck in the belt of her dress. This smart photographer got the picture and changed it, so that instead of having a rose in her mouth, he put a cigar in her mouth and shot it over, and that is what left the idea with everybody that she smoked cigars.

Clyde Barrow missed his calling. He could have been another Johnny Rutherford or A. J. Foyt. Once another officer and I took off after Bonnie and Clyde in a front-wheel-drive Ford, then considered one of the fastest of motorcars. Clyde got away from us in a little Ford V-8 he'd stolen. For one thing we couldn't match his skill at spinning around corners on gravel roads. He was a truly great high-speed driver.

Q. — Tell us how your group knew that Bonnie and Clyde were in Louisiana?

A. — We had come over from somewhere in Arkansas, and we went to Shreveport, and we went to the New Inn Hotel. We called the chief of police and the sheriff to let them know we were there. Later that night we got a call from the chief of police. He said, "There might be something to it or there might not be," but when we got any kind of report we would investigate it. It turned out that a squad of officers had been going down the main street in Shreveport, and there was a restaurant there, and a boy and girl parked there in front of the restaurant in a brown Ford car. We knew that was the last car Clyde had, the one he had stolen from Jess Warner in Topeka; and when it was reported to us that a car of that description had been seen down there at the restaurant, we thought we would go down there and see if we could find out something about it.

I took some pictures of Clyde and Bonnie that I had and of Henry Methvin and Raymond Hamilton and some others.

I talked to the waitress and found out that somebody had been in there and ordered a lot of food [and got up before it was served and walked out without paying]. I showed her these pictures and she said, "Yes, that was the guy [Henry Methvin] that got up and walked out."

So what happened was when the two police went down the street, that's when Clyde and Bonnie took off and left Henry Methvin there in the restaurant; so when he got out of there they had already gone, and we just figured he sauntered off somewhere.

We put two and two together right quick and decided he had gone there to get something for them to eat and then when Bonnie and Clyde took off, Henry knew that something had happened they didn't expect.

Next morning we went down to Gibsland, Louisiana. That is near where Henry Methvin's father lived.

We knew that Clyde was going to get back with Henry Methvin some way, and we figured that to do that he would get getting [sic] in touch with Henry Methvin's father.

We got in contact with the sheriff of that parish, Bienville Parish. The sheriff was Henderson Jordan, and he had a deputy named Presley Oakley, and then we went out on this road toward where Henry Methvin's father lived. We would go out and take a look at it and see if we could figure out which way they may go, because we figured that they would be out looking for Henry somewhere.

We just drove out there that evening and waited.

Q. – Where was that?

A. – About fifteen miles southwest of Gibsland, Louisiana. It was down there in the swamps about four miles from where the Methvins lived. We went down this gravel road and picked a place to stop.

And we stayed there Monday and Tuesday night, and then about four o'clock in the morning [May 23, 1934], this truck was coming; we just figured it was Mr. Methvin's. He was coming this way, he was going east; and we stopped him and pulled his car off to the side and took the right front tire off of it.

Q. – Who was there with you?

A. – Henderson Jordan, the sheriff of that parish; and Presley Oakley, his deputy; Frank Hamer; Manny Gault; Bob Alcorn; and myself.

Q. – Then what happened?

A. – About nine-fifteen that morning we heard something coming down the road. I knew as soon as I heard it that it was Clyde. You could hear, the way he drove an automobile. There didn't anybody else drive one like he did, and I knew it was him when I heard them coming.

Q. – You could tell from the sound of the car who it was?

A. – Yes, because there wasn't anybody else that would drive one like he did.

Q. – Do you mean he drove fast, raced the car?

A. – Yes, he drove like nobody else did at all. And there was this hill back there that he would have to come over; it was about a half a mile from where we had been waiting.

I didn't have any doubt about who it was, and I didn't know whether he might see something and try to turn around, or what, after he come over the top of the hill. And I had it on him, from the time he came over the hill on down there, I had him in my sights until he was down there, out from me. I just kept him in my sights because I was tired of running that boy.

Q. – That is, you kept him in your sights from the time he came over the top of the hill?

A. – Yes; I just kept him in my sights all of the time, and we just all lined up there and waited for them.

He just kept on coming down the road and got down there to where we were; and as soon as he saw Mr. Methvin's truck, he was going to stop and talk to him. Of course Methvin was not out there by the truck; he was back there behind us, and Clyde drove on down there and nearly got the car stopped just almost out there in front of me. And then when Clyde pulled up there and almost stopped, that is when Bob Alcorn raised up and hollered at him.

Q. – What did he say to him?

A. – He told him to halt.

Q. – What happened then?

A. – Well, then Clyde put the car in gear; anyway, he showered down on the car to take off and when he did, we showered down on him. I had a gun loaded, this .30–06. I had twenty [bullets] in it and I run out of ammunition, and then I picked up a shotgun, and after we started firing, the car began to weave and wobble and spin around there like it was out of control.

I don't know whether he was dead then or not, but I know he had been shot up pretty good, and then I took after the car. I was running between Manny Gault, Henderson Jordan, Presley Oakley, and Frank Hamer. All of us had been shooting. And then I took the shotgun, and when it run out of ammunition, I just threw it down and started to using two pistols that I had with me, and I went on down there where the car was.

Bob Alcorn was out in the road running as far as he could, running behind the car and shooting at it. The other four officers were shooting at the car all of the time, and I was running between them and the car and there didn't a damn one of them hit me. They had been shooting all of the time, and with all of that shooting going on there so close, I was deaf as a post for a while after that; I couldn't hear nothing for about a half a day after that.

Anyway, I went on down there after the car, following it along. It went about half a block down that gravel road. Bonnie was leaning up against the door and she like to have fell out. I caught her, and I was just standing there holding her when she died.

Q. — Did you see Bonnie with a gun?

A. — No, her right hand was shot up, but she had a .45 automatic there. It looked like she had it in her hand. There was blood all over it. I imagine that was the one she had in her hand.

Q. — Other parts of her body were badly shot up also, weren't they?

A. — Not too much; just her hand.

Q. — She had been shot about fifty times, hadn't she?

A. — About that.

Q. — How many times had Clyde been shot?

A. — The embalmer said about fifty-four, fifty-five, or fifty-six in him, I believe.

Death car

Q. – Because of the desperate character of these people, there was never any effort just to wound them; you all went out there to kill them, didn't you?

A. – No, if I had thought that he would go with me without it, I would have attempted to do that, but I knew better than that. I knew they would start shooting just as soon as they saw they had got in a trap. They had never been captured like that, and I knew they wouldn't be taken alive from the time they killed the first man. They would start shooting at anybody that came up to them. They were different people to a lot of the others. Some of these big punks like Dillinger and Karpis, they would just give up if they got cornered somewhere, but I knew these people wouldn't. I knew that they would try to shoot their way out if they got caught anywhere.

Q. – Did anybody ever tell you that the two of them would never be taken alive?

A. – Oh yes, his mother told me that lots of times.

Arms

Sunbonnets

Bonnets have been with us in one form or another for several hundred years. The name is from the coarse medieval cloth called bonnet, derived from the Hindu *banot,* from which early hats or hoods were made. Sunbonnets have been associated with the American scene from the beginning —a practical item like the cowboy's hat.

There were, in effect, two basic patterns for the sunbonnet—the "slat" bonnet and "poke" bonnet. Slat bonnets were designed as work bonnets and were most often worn in the fields and gardens. They derived their name from the wooden or cardboard slats inserted in the crown for stiffening. The poke bonnet had, and has, many variations. The origin of its name is unknown, but it was prettier than the functional slat bonnet and could be made very dressy, according to the trim and decorations added to it. Different versions of the poke bonnet were worn for everyday or for social occasions, depending on the fabric and decoration.

These East Texas bonnets were most probably adapted from patterns originating in the Arkansas Ozarks. In the past, they were considered a functional necessity of every woman's or girl's wardrobe. Bonnets provided protection from the hot, blistering sun, and at that time a tan or sun-bleached hair was regarded as highly unfashionable. Bonnets protected the face, hair, and neck, particularly bonnets of the slat variety, which had the effect of blinders.

Here are a few of the things older members of the Gary community have to say about sunbonnets.

—Loblolly

Minnie Grey in poke bonnet

Mrs. Odell Youngblood

In the earlier days you had work bonnets, everyday bonnets, and "Sunday-go-to-meeting" bonnets. They ranged from the very plain and inexpensive material to ruffles, buttons, appliqués, or laces. The Sunday-go-to-meeting bonnets were something to be talked about between women after church, at church dinners, or socials.

My mother used to make a bonnet different to most. It may have been an earlier model. It was made almost like the regular bonnet, but instead of stiffening the brim so it would hold up, it was divided into sections about two inches wide and six inches long. Into these you inserted little slats of cardboard, often cut out of cracker boxes or soapboxes. When you went to wash the bonnet, you slipped these out. After you washed and ironed your bonnet, you slipped them back in.

Little girls wearing bonnets

Mrs. Ruby Youngblood

I've been making bonnets for many years. I wear them to protect my head from the heat when I go out, and to protect my ears and neck from the cold of winter days. I can't go out bareheaded!

I make bonnets out of any kind of prints that are thick enough, "Dan River" or gingham, any kind of design is all right—it doesn't matter. I always cut the brim and the ruffle, then the crown with the tail on it. You'd sew the ruffle to the brim, which has a lining on the inside. After hemming the tail, you would sew a thin strip 'cross the neck and run a little string of material through it. A little hole is cut in the middle and drawn up as tight as you like. Then tie [it] in a knot. Sew the brim and crown together. Then stitch your ties on at the base of your brim and crown. The ties go under your chin to hold the bonnet on your head.

This pattern has been in my family for ever since I can remember, about eighty years. I can make a bonnet in five minutes after I get it cut out, but I would rather take a whipping than to starch and iron bonnets. You are supposed to have the brim real stiff using starch and ironing while it is wet.

My mama always wore one, and I guess I'm like her. I can't stand that wind blowing in my ears!

Feed Sacks

This article was quite simple to research, since almost everyone interviewed knew something about the making of clothing from feed sacks. During the Depression (and long after it, for many) people didn't have the cash in hand to purchase store-bought clothes, and they made do with homemade wearing apparel sewn together from feed sacks. The feed companies were well aware of this and vied with each other to see who could print up the prettiest feed sacks.

Sometimes, of course, the feed companies' natural tendencies to advertise their products placed certain obstacles in the way of the home seamstress.

—Loblolly

Mrs. Greer Griffith

Well, I don't know how to begin to tell you about the making of clothes out of feed sacks. Mostly we used fertilizer sacks. They were rough, but we had to boil them down to get some of the dye out anyway, so this made them softer and easier to wear. So that we wouldn't all look alike, when we went to the store we would buy packages of dye to dye the material, and it would make up to a right-pretty dress. It really didn't matter to us though [about looking alike], since we all had to wear the sacks then. And they could be made up to be just as pretty as things we could buy—except that no one could afford to buy them! I made all of my children's clothes out of feed sacks and plenty of my own.

Mr. and Mrs. Odell Hudson

Well, what do you want me to tell you kids? Times were hard back then, but it really didn't bother you so much because everybody was having a hard time, and you weren't by yourself.

I would make the kids' clothes out of the feed sacks and fertilizer sacks. You couldn't always get all of the dye out of the fertilizer sacks because it was permanent dye, so the sack numbers would stay on. We would just wash and boil them out, and then dye them if we wanted a different color.

We had patterns that we could go by—you could buy them in the store. But I usually got my sister to make them for me. Most people made their own patterns. You children just don't know how good that you have it now and that you should be glad you didn't have to live back in those hard times!

Mrs. Ollie Prince

We used feed sacks for just about everything we made. This included towels, sheets, pillowcases, cup towels, dishrags, quilt linings, and window curtains. For color, like the quilt lining, we dyed it with red oak bark and green walnut. We also used red clay and would boil that, too, to make a dye.

We also made all kinds of underwear for both men and women. We made shirts for men; baby clothes and diapers; dresses, bonnets, and hats; tablecloths and chair cushions. Feed sacks were put to use for just about everything we needed. We didn't have the money to buy cloth or store-made clothes; we were glad to have those feed sacks.

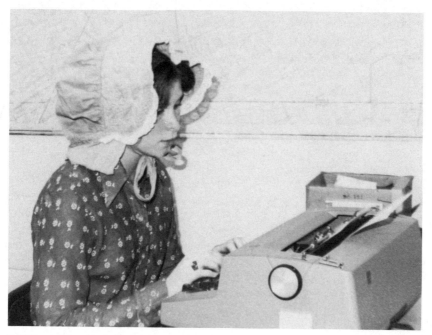

Loblolly student with feedsack bonnet

Monroe Brannon

In 1929, the Depression began with the stock-market crash. In a very short period of time, cotton went from sixteen cents to five cents a pound. People around here just didn't have much money for anything, including clothes.

During that time, people used every batch of cloth that they could find to make garments to wear. Feed stuff came in cloth sacks, such as wheat bran, shorts, and all our flour. Even salt came in cloth sacks. People that had those sacks on hand washed them out and made clothes for their children. I had six children at that time, and there were five in school. We lived in Jasper, and my wife washed out all the cloth sacks that you could possibly find and made the little girls' panties and all of their underclothes.

We made summer pants out of wagon sheets for the men. A wagon sheet was a large white cover of heavy cloth. We'd cut up the wagon sheet to make pants for our boys.

They never could get out all the painting and so on. You'd see a man wearing a shirt made out of fertilizer sack. You could see "8-4-8" across his back! You would see people wearing flour sacks that had different brands of flour on them. All of our children's underwear was made out of the sacks. Anything that was a sack could be used for underwear.

Something funny happened one night. We went to a church meeting and the people all got happy and was a-shouting! We had a flour, Bellwood's Best, and this old lady fell over a bench, and her clothes flew over right across [her] seat. There it said, "48 pounds of Bellwood's Best." That like to have killed us all.

Of course, everybody was about alike in their style of dress; they wore these clothes to work or school. Everybody wore the homemade clothes, and possibly out of the whole bunch there wouldn't be two that hadn't the same kind of pants or shirts. It was a time of make do with what you had, or just go without.

Cooking Up a Batch of Lye Soap

In earlier days, lye made from ashes was an important raw material for the rural housewife and was used to make both lye soap and lye hominy. In both cases, most persons made their own. Some people bought their lye from the store, but Alex Duncan, from the Gary area, tells how his mother made lye directly from ashes from the fireplace. Mrs. Clara Evelyn Latham of Gary and Mrs. Jack Kelly of Douglass give more detailed accounts of the soap-making process; they differ on some of the specifics of how to do it, but they both agree on one crucial point: proper lye soap must be made "by the moon"!

—Chinquapin and Loblolly

Alex Duncan

My mother thought that oak ashes were the best for making lye. We'd split fire-length logs to heat the house. We would clean out the fireplace to collect the ashes. My mother wouldn't use any other type of ashes because she wanted to make pure lye.

To make the lye, we had to build an ash-hopper to go on a prop. The prop was made from a green pine log. We'd level the log off on one side and cut a deep hole and a trench. The ash-hopper was like a low, upside-down house without the floor. It was closed on all four sides with boards extending from the trough at an angle.

We would pack the ashes in the center of it. The vent held water and had to be refilled every once in a while. It took approximately a day for the lye to come out of the ashes. When the trough was filled with lye, we would dip it out into cans or quart jars.

To make her soap, she would make sure that the washpot was perfectly clean—she didn't want any foreign matter in it. Then a fire was built under the half-full pot of lye. Then we'd put in the grease, maybe from ham hocks, fat, or meat skins. She'd stir it with a large paddle. At intervals, she would test the soap by the color it turned when it was cold.

When the soap reached the desired consistency, she would have us rake the fire from under the pot. She left the soap in the pot until it was cold. We would put it in a barrel that we used for washing. When she got ready to wash clothes, she would dip it out with a cup, a dipper, or a gourd. It was easy to dip out, because the soap was never hard. It was a liquid all the time. The soap had a very beautiful color. It was somewhat of a red hue with just a little gold in it. The soap was very good even though she could not cut it into bars like some other people. She didn't like it that way.

Clara Evelyn Latham

I've made lye soap all my life—especially when the kids were little. You used the soap in the kitchen to wash the dishes, the baby's diapers—prettiest white diapers you ever saw hung on a line! Lye soap makes things so white. There's enough lye in it until it cleanses, and that's what it takes to make white. We used it for bathing—bathed in a washtub with water from the well. Used it to wash your hair. Didn't have no dandruff when you used it to wash your hair.

The way I make mine is to put about a gallon or a gallon and a half of water with a can of lye in it. Then chunk in a gallon of cracklins, or whatever meat waste you have. Use a big pot, like outside, to put the water in. Put the water in, then put the lye in, then when the water's warm add the grease. Just let it boil and boil. Then take a teacup and dip some out into a saucer. If it congeals—you know how jelly congeals?—then it's hard enough. You can spread it out and let it dry on a board. Then cut it up and cover it until in the morning!

We never did sell none of our soap. We used that stuff and give away a lot of it. We'd make a washtub full when we'd have to use it all the time. I had five children until I lost our little boy. I had the five to wash for and I didn't have no washing machine. I didn't have no electricity.

Sometimes it makes in just a few minutes. Today I put a little extra water in. Before y'all come it had done started to boil, and I was afraid the pot was gonna dry. That old washpot's a precious old thing. I hardly ever use it, but I love that old pot, just like I do this house.

I don't think the weather has any effect on how it turns out, but my mama never let me make soap unless the moon was full. I did it as long as she lived. She said it never failed when the moon was full. She planted with the moon, too. She happened to be a fine gardener. My mother was a wonderful person. Everything she did nearly worked out perfect!

Mrs. Jack Kelly

I made some [lye soap] three years ago. I bought the lye in a can; I didn't make it. Now, sometimes, I would make my lye. I'd get ashes, take the ashes out of the fireplace, and pour them in a bucket and pour a little water in them. Then I'd let that water just drip through a real thick cloth, and that would be nearly lye. But as a rule I bought my lye, because that was too slow.

I'd cook lard out of hog fat—cooked it out in a big old black pot in the yard and stirred it all the time it was cooking. Well, when it got done and the cracklins got real brown, I put them in a churn, and then I'd put a big cloth over the churn and let that grease drain down into the churn, and then I'd empty the cracklins into an old pan. I'd do that over and over until I got a pot full, all I had to cook. And then I'd take them cracklins and empty them back into the pot and put a can of lye in it. (We'd have to use an old black pot; the lye would eat up anything else. I had my mother's old pot.) And, I would guess, must have been about two gallons of water in it. Lord, it's been so long since then I can't remember!

I put water in it and just stirred it constantly until it began to thicken. And sometimes I'd have to take two cans of lye to eat all the cracklins up. It'd be just real, real thick, and you could hold it up on the paddle, and it'd just drip down like jelly. I'd cover it up overnight with a piece of tin. The next morning I'd go out there with a butcher knife and cut it out in bars. The bars that I wanted to wash the clothes with would be large, and the ones I wanted to wash the dishes would be medium size. And that's all there was, and are, to making soap.

My mama, that's the way she made all of her soap; I had to stay with it. I never will forget when I would say something about making soap to bathe and Jack would say, "We won't have much dinner today." And I'd say, "No, we gonna have peas, cornbread, and chowchow today because I've got to stay out here and stir that soap."

Oh, it would just boil over, just boil over in just a little bit. You'd have to cook it about two or two and a half hours for all that stuff to dissolve. We cooked it on an open fire out in the yard . . . washpot on the two rocks or three rocks, 'cause washpots got three legs. Lorraine Chastain said this morning that they used can lye, but I never used to use it.

I'd cut it in squares and put it in the smokehouse and let it dry. It would get just as hard as a rock. You'd just have to shave it off. You used a big box for it to dry out; you don't want it touching, 'cause it would stick together. Then you'd have to get a knife and cut it apart. So I just left a little space between each bar. If you had it touching one another, you'd have to break the bars up.

We used it to wash with and wash dishes with and take a bath, too, with it. A real greasy spot in the floor—you see, we didn't have any linoleum—I'd take a bar of soap and rub it real, real good, wet it, rub it real good with that bar of soap. Then [I'd] take a broom—have y'all ever seen one of them shuck brooms, it's a big piece of board with a hole bored in it and shucks would be poked through those holes—and that's the way I'd scrub the kitchen and the back porch.

We used to wash our hair in lye soap, and it would just fly, just fly everywhere! We'd put a little bluin' water in it, and that would give it color. And lye soap—gee, I wish I had some now!—it's real good for dandruff. I washed Charles Alton's hair many times in lye soap, and I would tie a towel around him where no soap couldn't get in his eyes.

And Charles Alton would stump his toe and get ground itch, going to the field on his feet, and I'd wash it with lye soap. It would be just as pretty and white as it could be. Sometimes there'd be a little meat skin in the soap, but that didn't make any difference. Mm, Lord, them days, them days!

Grandmother's Home Remedies

Two of *Loblolly*'s good friends are Monroe Brannon and Max Haddick. The former is also a neighbor who spent most of his growing-up years in or around Gary. The latter grew up in Mexia, Texas, and is now Director of Journalism for the Texas University Interscholastic League in Austin. Both had amazing grandmothers who were experts on home remedies and cures. And both of these grandmothers gained most of their curing knowledge from the Indians; Monroe Brannon's from Alabama Indians, and Max Haddick's from the Comanche. Making the discovery of these grandmothers separately, we thought it most appropriate to join them together in one article of *Loblolly*. They never lost a patient, although some of the cures might seem a bit drastic. And they gave to their families much more than just those home remedies, as you will discover here.

—Loblolly

Monroe Brannon's Grandmother, Ann Curb

My great-grandparents, beginning about 1800, and my grandparents on my father's side were all raised in the town of Selma, Alabama. My grandmother was born in 1840, and she and her mother, when she was a girl, assisted the Alabama Indian Reservation, right adjoining them. And they learned all of these old remedies from the Indians. They learned how the Indians used various barks and roots and leaves and berries to cure certain disease. Here is what they learned to use: mullein, horehound, nightshade, may-apple root, snakeroot, sassafras, black-haw roots, pokeroot, peach tree leaves, inner bark of the oak, toothache bark, slippery elm bark, inner bark of pine trees, pine resin, wild cherry tree bark; and the base was usually tallow for making salve and honey for making cough syrups and other medicines. They used homemade vinegar from apples. For a break in the leg or arm, they used clay made up in a dough with vinegar. They would daub that on the limb and let it set for twenty-eight days and break it off. And the leg or arm would be back in place.

They learned practically all the Indians knew. My grandmother went with her mother to the Indian reservation, and those old squaw Indians taught them about those roots and berries and herbs which they used to cure various disease. After my people moved to north Louisiana, my grandmother moved on with us and brought those remedies along and helped my mother raise five boys and five girls. After 1895, she moved with us to Texas, and we went to Dr. Daniels' drugstore for medicine. My grandmother had done all the old Indian remedies. She filled a real need, for we lived too far away to be close to any doctor.

She knew lots of homemade remedies. She used various roots, vines, berries, leaves, and barks of trees to combat the illnesses of our family in the absence of a doctor and out of the need for one. She was more of a pediatrician, or child doctor, although she treated adults. She was helpful with childbirth, too. If one of the babies had the colic, she would go out to the garden and gather catnip leaves. We had some bushes growing in the corner of the garden. The art was to brew those leaves so that you would extract all of the juice and not overheat it. She would brew up a batch of catnip leaves and strain them, then add a little milk. That would really cure a baby of the colic.

With older children, diarrhea was very prevalent in our family. Grandmother would go out and gather about two gallons of peach tree leaves. She would brew it up on the stove just like she did that catnip leaves. That would stop diarrhea. Both catnip and peach tree leaves contained opium. It served the purpose of castoria and paregoric. It contained laudanum.

When we climbed the trees and would get full of poison ivy, we'd break out all over. We would take the grubbing hoe, go out, and get pokeroots. She would cut that up in slices and stew it up in the same manner she did the leaves. You had to be sure you did not overheat it, get it just to a certain temperature to extract the juice from this pokeroot. That would kill the poison. Different poisons will counteract other poisons. Pokeroots would counteract the poison of poison ivy.

If one of us fell out of a tree and sprained our ankle, we took a grubbing hoe, went to the clay pit, and dug up about one or two gallons of red clay dirt. My grandmother would put some vinegar in it and make it into a dough, like biscuit dough. She would encase the ankle and foot in the clay. It would take the swelling out. Now, blood risings were very bad among the kids. They would come on our body most anywhere. They would come on the calf of your leg, and on your back, but mostly on the fleshy part of your rear anatomy. The best remedy for that was a slice of fat meat. She would put that on the sore and it would draw it up to a head. Then she would pick off the top of that sore and remove the core. She would use a homemade salve after that.

For a blood medicine, in the spring we would get the grubbing hoe and go out to a sassafras patch of bushes. They would grow about six or eight feet tall while they were young. We would dig half a bushel or more of the roots. We would wash those roots off real good and cut them into about four-inch lengths, put them in a large pot, and add two or three gallons of water. You could boil that to extract that juice; it was a beautiful amber color. We had to let that cool. It was a great tea, but we also used that as a blood purifier.

My grandmother not only doctored children, she helped older people, too. She helped with the whooping cough, measles, and other diseases. She was a good mother. She was also a devoted Christian and an authority on the scriptures. She passed away October 9, 1913, near Gary. She was laid to rest in the Gary cemetery.

Other Indian medicines were:

Mullein: A plant that grows low on the ground, has broad leaves, and is used for making teas for infants.

Horehound: A vine that grows up on the ground and is good for making tonics.

Nightshade: A vine that grows on the ground. We used this to make salves for poison oak.

May-Apple Root: A root that you boil and get the substance. It acts as a purgative.

Snakeroot: Usually was just worn for its sweet smell. We usually wore it around the neck.

Black-Haw Root: Used as a woman's medicine in place of Cardui.

Red Oak Bark: The inside bark of a red oak was used as an astringent. It was used to control diarrhea.

Toothache Bark: We usually cut that in strips about the size of shoestrings and about four inches long. It was put in a jar with some whiskey and left to set two or three weeks. It was a great blood purifier. We would take it before we went into the fields to pick cotton early in the morning.

Sarsaparilla Bark: The greatest bark we knew of to dig and make sassafras tea. We usually dug a quantity of that in the spring and used it for a blood purifier.

Pine Bark: The inner bark of a pine stewed down properly was our kidney medicine.

Resin: A substance from a pine tree. We would cut out a chip in a pine and let that pocket run full of turpentine. As it got older it was a semihard substance. We used this with pokeroot juice and tallow to make a poison for poison oak and seven-year itch.

Cherry Bark: Wild cherry bark (the inner part) was cut in strips and was put in the stewpot. It was boiled down to a low essence. Honey was then added. It made one of the first cough syrups in the world.

Max Haddick's Grandmother, Molly Bain

You asked for information about Grandma Bain and her cure-alls. You shall have it, but I definitely discourage your using her cures to find surcease from the aches and pains of life. You should take your influenza, bots disease, athlete's foot, and other ailments to a medic, preferably one not schooled in the ancient cures of Comanche Indians.

Now for the miracle cures:

Risings. You probably know these as boils, carbuncles, overgrown pimples, wens, or something else. By any name they are definitely no fun. They begin as a small, red, hard mound somewhere on your anatomy. In my case they tended to dwell in most private places. Other kids got boils in wonderfully conspicuous places, but not me. They could show off their affliction and get sympathy, treatment, and affection. I could never show off without endangering the calm of ladies in the audience.

Treatment—to cure a boil, it had to come to a head. This meant that a small white spot appeared. Under that white spot was a "core," a solid string of something. It had to head out and have the core removed to be cured. To bring it to a head, one took a fresh egg, broke it into a skillet along with a few strips of bacon. While one sloshed the egg to done the top, one took the eggshell and peeled out a bit of the white inner "skin." This skin was applied, wet side down, to the top of the boil. This would draw the boil to a head. Do not laugh. Go get your own egg, secure a bit of this skin, and apply it to a tender area, such as the tip of your nose or the inside of your elbow joint, and wait a moment. It will definitely draw. The boil will head out. You remove the core and dress it with a clean rag, and soon it will be healed. The egg and bacon in the skillet are eaten. It has nothing to do with curing the boil, but Grandma would never waste a thing.

Most boils are brought on by use of old-fashioned soaps that leave a scum of something on the skin. This was a marvelous breeding ground for staph germs, which cause boils. Boils are scarce now because we bathe more often and mostly use bar detergent.

Being Peaked. I never did know what being "peaked" meant, but my grandma did. If I ever sorta hung around the house and was lazy, she would look at me seriously and tell me I was peaked and needed medication. (I looked up "peaked," and it appears that I had a pointed head.) Often on these occasions, she would prepare a horrible mixture of blackstrap molasses, sulfur, and saltpeter. She heated this on her old wood stove. It sent clouds of foul aromas all over the house, causing all us kids to swear that we were in excellent health and were not at all peaked. But she was not to be deterred. When the mess was at its foulest, she gave each of us a heaping tablespoonful. If you are in doubt as to how she got a heaping tablespoonful of a liquid, you have no idea how thick this liquid was. We took it under protest, but we took it. The results were magnificent. We ceased laying around the house. Anytime we thought Grandma was looking, we frisked and frolicked happily to show definitely that we were not at all peaked. Should you find "peaked" in any medicine book, do not send me any information about it. My rigid training as a youth might inspire me to concoct a batch of Grandma's peaked remedy and try it. I am not as strong as I used to be and do not wish to risk this cure again.

Common Cold. You know the symptoms. So did Grandma. To cure a common cold you ate onions. You consumed raw onions, boiled onions, fried onions, fricasseed onions, and drank huge bowls full of onion soup. If the cold persisted, the medication was reinforced with a few chunks of garlic. I am sure that this worked. I recovered from every cold Grandma treated. I feel that the cure may have been in my own breath after her treatment. No one would get close enough to me to reinfect me.

Coughs. Take a quart fruit jar and fill it with rock candy. Add a half cup of honey. Then pour in all the moonshine whiskey you can. Let this steep for a week or two before use. Grandma always kept this cure on hand. When any kid coughs, grab him up and get a scissor hold on his body with your legs. Grab his nose firmly and pull back. This opens his mouth, either to breathe or to yell—or both. When his mouth is open, insert an ounce or two of the cough syrup. Repeat as indicated. If the kid coughed twice in one day, he could get stoned on the cough syrup, but it did seem to ease the tickling in the throat.

Bleeding Cuts. If the bleeding was minor, ignore it. This bleeding cleaned the dirt, twigs, and other stuff out of the cut and promoted healing. If bleeding persisted, go out to the barn and get a big handful of cobwebs. Press the webs to the cut. This definitely stopped the bleeding. It also carried much dirt, dust, and perhaps a few mites and other tiny insects into the wound, causing scarring. I bear some beautiful scars as a result of this treatment, but I did a minimum of bleeding.

Bone Felon on the Heel. I guess the bone felon on the heel was a result of jumping off the buggy shed or other suitable place to jump off. We went barefooted about eleven months of the year. If you landed with a pebble located just right under the heel, it bruised. In a few days you would have a swollen heel that ached and throbbed something awful. The first aid consisted of soaking the entire foot in hot salt water. I do not mean tepid, warm, or very warm. I mean so hot that it took a wonderfully strong Grandma to keep your foot in the foot tub for the first few minutes. Then you sorta got numb and the heat was not so terrible. This caused the felon to get ready. Grandma was the "ready" judge. She would take your foot on her lap and press and prod the afflicted area. I am not sure what criteria she used to determine if the felon was ready, but I do believe it was based mostly on the tone of the youngster's shrieking. When my yells caused the chickens to run to the other side of the yard, it was still "green." When I got to the point that my bellows caused the milk cows (I know it is spelled m-i-l-c-h, but never did see much reason for it) to hoist their tails in the air and run to the south end of the pasture, the felon was ready.

Then Grandma, assisted by Grandpa, Dad, Mom, and a few other able-bodied adults, would put me on the bed, get out Grandpa's straight razor, and proceed to lance the felon. The bed was carefully covered with an old wagon sheet before the victim was installed thereon. With a deft slash of the razor, just a slash, she opened the felon. The results were predictable and the felon now healed.

Nail in the Foot. Barefooted young 'uns seem to be able to find nails with little or no trouble. Nails were rusty and this brought on the danger of blood poisoning. Thusly it was prevented. The foot would first be washed with lye soap and then immersed in kerosene. There was little agony in the process. In fact, it was usually rather pleasant as Grandma would bribe the victim to stay at and soak in the kerosene by offering black-walnut cake, cookies, or fudge. I have set the all-time record for kerosene foot soaking, just because of my delight in her black-walnut goodies.

Thick Blood. As any Indian knows, the blood gets thicker in the wintertime. Have no idea why, but this is true. And, as Grandma knew, it was best to thin it in the springtime. Why, I am not sure, but it had to be done. The only way to accomplish this was to imbibe quantities of sassafras tea. I will not give you the recipe. As good East Texans, you should have learned this from your mom. But you had to drink lots of it.

To assure that we would drink the right dosage, Grandma would give one cookie to each cup of tea consumed. I think I hold a record in consuming sassafras tea and eating cookies.

Thin Blood. At the end of summer, just about time the first frost hits, one must thicken up the blood to prepare for the coming winter. Grandma was not caught short on this, either. One thickened the blood by eating fried pork chops, dumplings, souse meat (hog's head cheese to you big-city folks), and generally increasing the caloric intake. I always loved getting my blood good and thick.

Kidney Trouble. Eat all the watermelon and cantaloupe you can hold. It was not necessary for any adults to hold young 'uns down to administer this therapy. Grandma always diagnosed kidney ailment when the young 'uns headed down the well-beaten path out back to the small essential structure at the far end of our house plot. As us kids were generally well supplied with watermelon, cantaloupe, green peaches, green plums, and other cathartic foods, we often had "kidney trouble." It was well worth it.

Constipation. This was a sad time for any kid. Grandma knew many natural herbs that would alleviate the problem, but had early been converted to a patent medicine known as Black Draught. We were very secretive if afflicted with irregularity, but somehow she knew. When she was sure of her diagnosis, each of the children had to take a drink of Black Draught tea. Her reasoning was that since we all ate at the same table and had the same food, if one of us was constipated, it was very likely that all were. So the dosage was meted out to all. I assure you that it worked.

The Droops. I don't know what the droops are, but most every kid gets them now and then. The symptoms are easy to see. The young 'un just mopes around, not getting into any devilment, never pulling any feathers from the old red rooster's tail, never swiping any watermelons, never getting into any trouble at all. Then it was obvious that that child had the droops. Grandma had a wonderful remedy. She administered copious quantities of pure, undiluted love. She baked favorite cakes, pies, puddings, and such. The droopy one was assigned only very light chores, and nothing was said if those chores were forgotten or poorly done. Grandma just knew that all kids got moody spells and needed some extra attention to get over the droops. Her cure never failed. If I have given you the impression that Grandma was a bit rough on us, forget it. She was so kind and wonderful that we never questioned the wisdom of her medications. She understood children the way few people ever do. She knew what you were thinking ten minutes before you did. If you had trouble of any kind, she was able to fix it up just right. She could make kites, cook, sharpen fishhooks, make a slingshot, mend a rip in the rear end of your overalls without asking any embarrassing questions, and do a thousand things to let a young 'un know that he was someone special to her. I don't know what modern medical science has to say about her remedies, but she raised her thirteen children and a passel of grandkids without losing a one. None of them ever spent a day in jail, sassed a teacher, or backtalked an adult. They all got more fun out of life than you could imagine. She is gone now, but she lives on with me and everyone who ever knew her. I still drink my sassafras tea just so she will know that I am ready for springtime to bust out again. She lived for eighty-eight years, helping everyone who crossed her path, and then just lay down and went to sleep. I suppose she had her share of aches and pains, but I never heard of them. She never complained about anything.

More Home Remedies
In the days before the automobile and all-weather roads, many of the rural areas of East Texas were truly remote. This meant that regular medical attention was often too far away for those who were ill or injured. And, as in so many other aspects of their lives, these early people had to make do and use what was at hand. Turpentine, kerosene, and things found in the fields and woods were put to medical uses.

The result of this was a fantastic amount of medical lore. Some of the remedies were based on sound reasoning and worked. Others were harmless, or useless for the purposes intended. And some were dangerous to the user and certainly worsened his ill, perhaps even fatally. Thus, it is advisable to view these cures with caution.

Still, all things considered, people did an amazing job of doctoring themselves, their families, and their neighbors. And in doing so, they have left us with a rich storehouse of home remedies as a testimonial to their grit and imagination.

Acne

Put buttermilk on face.

Use soap and water, sulfur and grease.

Appendicitis

Rub your side with olive oil and keep it well rubbed.

Apply cold rags to area of pain.

Take mineral oil.

Arthritis

Carry a buckeye in your pocket.

Wear a copper bracelet around arm or leg where it hurts.

Mix gasoline, meal, and salt together, and put it on the area.

Wear a copper bracelet on wrist.

Make a poultice of red clay and vinegar and put it where it hurts.

Get some coal oil out of a lamp, and mix it with liniment and apply.

Mix grapejuice, honey, dried pokeberries, carrot juice, and tomatoes, and put it on.

Mix 3 ounces olive oil, 1 ounce glycerin, 3 ounces powdered senna, 2 ounces powdered charcoal, 1 ounce slippery elm. Add 3 pounds of figs, 1¼ pounds seeded raisins. Grind fruit and add a little of the powdered ingredients at a time. Add olive oil and glycerin. Mix with hand and make into balls about the size of a walnut. Take one in the morning and one at night for a week. Then take one a day for six months.

Asthma

Take spirit of peppermint.

Use a poultice consisting of black pepper and lard.

Put about a tablespoon of Vicks in a small pan of water and boil it. Then rub your chest down and put some under your nose.

Keep a Chihuahua dog around.

Calm nerves.

Take dry leaves and grind into a powder. Then put it in a lid by a fire. Get a piece of cloth and put over your head and the lid and inhale the smoke or odor.

Drink a tea made by boiling a hornet's nest.

Sniff warm salt water.

Sleep on a wooden pillow.

Make a poultice of red clay and vinegar.

Take six drops of spirit of ammonia.

Baldness

Wash your hair with lye soap.

Don't wear a felt hat in summer.

Get some white Vaseline, put it in a pan, turn your fires down low. Rub it in real good and tie your head up. Shampoo your hair the next morning.

Go to the woods, cut a grapevine, and wash hair in sap.

Bleeding

Put the cut in a pan of kerosene or lard right above where it is bleeding, then apply sugar or salt.

Put a pair of scissors down your collar.

Put pine resin on the cut.

Put a dime under your lip, lay on scissors with point pointing toward skull. Apply potash, the black ashes from a fire.

Apply salt on wound.

Place ice on bleeding place.

Cover bleeding place with spider webs.

Put chimney soot on wound.

Mix sugar and soot, and make it into a plaster. Then put it over the wound.

Put a root on cut.

To stop bleeding, pronounce the Biblical verse Ezekiel 16:6 silently three times.

Mix flour and cornstarch together and put on the place.

Put cigarette paper on wound.

Read Ezekiel 16:6 frontwards and backwards.

Put dry powder on [wound] to clog bleeding.

Blood Poisoning

Soak infected area in coal oil.

Take a hot iron and burn place.

Smoke it with a burning wool sack.

Soak it with Epsom salts.

Boils

Take a piece of fat meat or axle grease, and pack it on.

Apply sulfur and rum.

Put [an] Irish potato on it.

Get the yellow of an egg with some salt, and put it on the boil.

Broken Bones

Get some rich splintered slats from stove wood. Then make a real flour paste. Tear long strips off of a sheet. Someone holds the arm or leg, or whatever, while someone else would hold the paste and put it on the broken bone above and below the break. Then put a big piece of material over the paste. Get the slats and put them all the way around the pieces of material. Get the strips of sheet and wrap it tightly around the broken place. Let it stay until you know the bone is knitted back.

Burns

Rub cold butter on burn.

Put butter or lard on, and leave it there for about ten minutes.

Sprinkle soda on burn.

Cover burn with cream.

Put cow dressing, or cow dung, on it.

Apply ice water or ice.

Put aloe vera gel on it.

Burn sweet-gum balls, get the juice, and mix it with Vaseline and put on the burn.

Fix a poultice of salty butter and put on the burns.

Beat an egg in a bowl, add a teaspoon of baking soda in it. Then put it on the burns.

Take roots and boil them in water until it boils down low. Mix the liquid with lard or grease, and place on burns.

Pour weak tea on it.

Canker

Infusion of gold thread, an herb used by Indians.

Chest Congestion

Apply a poultice consisting of axle grease, quinine, mentholatum, and camphorated oil.

Put on Vicks salve and kerosene.

Get a flannel rag and make a stupe for their chest with Vicks salve, coal oil, and tallow.

Make an onion and mustard plaster.

Apply a flannel cloth soaked with tallow and snuff.

Melt some beef tallow and mix a little turpentine into it. Put hog lard in it to keep it from blistering. Then take a woolen cloth large enough to cover the chest. Moisten the cloth in the solution, and place it over your chest. Pull the covers up over you.

Use kerosene, turpentine, sugar, and grease. Mix together, put it in the oven, and get it hot. Then put it on chest.

Get some green peach leaves, turpentine, and Vicks. Mix and cover chest area.

Chicken pox

Take the person out to a chicken house, and let a few chickens fly over him.

Kill a black hen and scald it, then get the water and bathe the person.

Chill

Step across a creek backwards.

Colds

Dirty or used dark stocking worn around neck. Red flannel works, too.

Dry mullein leaves and then smoke them in corncob pipe.

Drink lemon juice and whiskey.

Drink honey and whiskey.

Hog-hoof tea—kill the hog and take his leg and cut his hoof off. Then let it dry out, boil it in some water, and drink the juice.

Take a spoonful of sugar and drop about five drops of turpentine or lamp oil in it and swallow.

Take nine whiffs from a dirty sock.

Take a large lemon and cut it into small pieces. Place in pie dish and cover each slice with a heaping teaspoon of granulated sugar. Place in oven (350°) and bake until a thick syrup (30 to 45 minutes). Take one teaspoon of the syrup.

Heat mustard and put it on a cloth and put it on your chest.

Beat whiskey and eggs together. Take a spoonful every half hour.

Drink catnip, elder blossom, peppermint leaf tea.

Boil Vicks salve in some water and put it under your bed where your head is. Leave it there until your cold goes away.

Mix whiskey, peppermint candy, and honey. Let set overnight so the candy will dissolve. Then take as needed.

Boil mullein leaves, and strain juice and drink it.

Drink a glass of hot lemonade.

Wear an asafetida bag around neck.

Use a mustard plaster.

Colic

Rub Vicks salve on the bottom of a baby's feet.

Give them about one teaspoon of spirits of peppermint.

Give soda or paregoric.

Take a spoonful of castor oil.

Take some Epsom salts in warm water.

Boil pine resin and give a tablespoon of the syrup.

Give soda or vinegar.

Hang garlic around your neck.

Drink onion tea.

Collect asafetida and wear it around neck.

Communicable Diseases

Wear an asafetida amulet around the neck.

Constipation

Take one tablespoon of castor oil or Epsom salts.

Drink Black Draught tea.

Drink prune juice.

Boil inner bark from butternut tree and make a tea.

Eat prunes.

The bark of a peach limb is scraped up. Make a brew of this. Begin with a teaspoonful, and increase if necessary.

Corns

Rub olive oil on them real good.

Put shaving soap in their shoe.

Apply salicylic acid and tallow on corns.

Cough

Gargle with warm salt water and take a teaspoonful of lemon juice and honey together.

Drink salt and lemon, whiskey, and peppermint.

Take honey and alum.

Drink prickly pear syrup.

Fix a cough syrup of honey and Vicks salve.

Take honey, lemon juice, and paregoric.

Chew sugar with moss obtained from north side of a maple tree.

In a teaspoon, fill three-fourths full with sugar, and fill balance with kerosene.

Take honey and soda.

Take a handful of the following: pine buds, sweet-gum buds, holly buds, mullein buds, and wash. Put together and boil. Add honey and piece of alum. Sip as a tea.

Get mullein and sugar and make a syrup out of it. Drink it.

Cramps

Drink milk.

Make a spice tea and drink it hot, one-half cup at a time.

Put heated cloth on.

Turn the sufferer's shoes upside down under the bed.

Tie string around big toe.

Take a swallow of vinegar.

Leg Cramps

Tie some eel skin around leg.

Wear a dime around the ankle on a string.

Croup

Take a wool rag and moisten in Vicks salve and turpentine, add a few drops of coal oil. Heat it and put it on your chest.

Take six drops of turpentine on one teaspoon of sugar.

Mix almond and honey and drink it.

Eat cheese.

Take pine tar and honey.

Rub the throat with skunk oil.

Apply Watkins Liniment.

Mix chestnuts, dried beef, molasses or wine, and eat.

Rub turpentine on your chest and throat.

Take alum.

In a small skillet, heat the following: ¼ cup of tallow, some axle grease, 2 tablespoons of kerosene, 1 teaspoon of turpentine, and any other salve on hand. Cut an old wool rag from pants in the shape of a bib. Dip bib into smoking liquid, and when still hot, slap directly on child's chest.

Get a spoon of sugar with four to five drops of coal oil. Eat it.

Chew tar off a rich pine splinter.

Diarrhea

Eat only burned bread and black coffee.

Take paregoric and castor oil.

Eat egg yolk.

Brown some flour in a skillet and put a little water in it, then drink it.

Mix blackberry root, steeple roots, hard hack, and take as a tea.

Drink a mixture of strawberry blossom, oak bark, sweet leaves, smart weed, and finely grated green apples.

Eat cheese.

Wear asafetida around neck.

Make a tea out of sweet-gum leaves.

Eat green apples.

Take the inside bark of the red oak, put it in a glass of water, drink the water. Do this every hour.

Diabetes

Take sour foods such as lemon juice and sauerkraut.

Dysentery

Boil a tender sweet-gum branch in water and add sugar. Drink it as a tea.

Drink sassafras tea and vinegar.

Earache

Warm mineral oil and put two drops in your ear. Then put a piece of cotton in, too.

Get a piece of a Negro's hair and put it in your ear.

Put wool in your ear.

Blow hot smoke from pipe into ear.

Cook salt and put in a bag and put on ear.

Drop of juice from a "bessie bug" in ear.

Warm castor oil and put a spoonful of it in your ear.

Heat sugar and water, put on a cotton ball, and put in your ear.

Put sweet oil in ear.

Put tobacco juice into the ear.

Eye Ailments

Wash your eye in lukewarm salt water.

Go to the fork in a road and say, "Sty, sty, in my eye; go to the next person who passes by."

Wash out the eye with warm water.

Fever

Bathe in alcohol and ice packs.

Cover up.

Cut long strips of brown paper sack. Soak them in vinegar. Then place strips over the forehead and around your wrist and your ankles.

Drink mullein-root tea, a spoonful of it every three hours.

Drink Black Draught tonic.

Cover up tight and let them sweat. Rub turpentine on person to make them sweat more.

Drink butterweed tea.

Put ice pack in bed, and put feet in a bucket of hot water.

Drink hot water.

Bathe in cold water.

Get some green crabgrass, boil it, and drink the juice.

Flu

Put a few drops of turpentine on sugar, then eat it.

Take Graves Chill Tonic.

Put hot rag on chest.

Rest and drink warm milk.

Freckles

Take buttermilk and rub it on.

Rub face with buttermilk and cornmeal, and put a stocking over face. Wear it all day. It makes the skin white.

Remove them by washing in dew the first day of May.

Put egg whites on them.

Gravel Throat

Get the inside bark of black gum, make a tea, and drink it.

Hay Fever

Get some tobacco and smoke it in a pipe.

Headaches

Rub your temples with Camophophenique.

Drink Black Draught tea.

Rub warm vinegar packs on forehead and back of neck. Apply with brown sack paper.

Tie a tight rag around your head.

Get a cotton string and light it. Blow it out and put it under each nostril and inhale the smoke.

Drink a stiff shot of water mixed with wood ashes.

Take an aspirin, then lay down and put a cold rag over your face.

Hiccups

Hold your breath while you drink nine sips of water.

Drink two teaspoons of vinegar.

Drink honey and sugar.

Take a swallow of water, hold your breath, put your head in a brown paper bag.

Breathe into a paper sack five times.

High Blood Pressure

Eat garlic.

Hives

Take someone whose father died before they were born, and have him blow in the baby's mouth.

Drink onion tea with sugar.

Take an onion and quarter it. Fill it with sulfur and wrap it with a cloth. Put it in ashes until onion is soft. Then take it and squeeze the juice out and drink a teaspoon of it.

Get an onion and bake it. Get the juice from the onion, put a drop of whiskey in it, and then drink it.

Mix saffron roots, sugar, and water, and drink.

Drink mullein tea.

Take a drop of whiskey.

Drink "cucker burr" tea.

Hemorrhoids

Sit in hot water.

Insect Bites

Put chewing tobacco on the bite.

Apply coal oil.

Put soda and tobacco juice on the bite.

Cover bite with sulfur and lard.

Put wet snuff on the bites.

Take seven kinds of grasses and squeeze out the juice. Rub the liquid on the bite or sting.

Rub alcohol on area.

Indigestion

Drink baking soda and water.

Inflamed Finger Joints

Catch a weasel and squeeze it to death.

Insomnia

Take an aspirin or drink hot milk.

Count sheep.

Do fifty push-ups, and then drink one glass of hot milk.

Itch

Put sulfur and grease on it.

Boil red oak bark, put cornmeal in it, and apply where it itches.

Kidney Trouble

Put turpentine on your tongue.

Sip three drops of turpentine and a teaspoon of sugar.

Drink a couple of cups of mineral oil.

Take watermelon seeds and boil them. Make a tea.

Put turpentine on your tongue and navel.

Drink lots of water and lemon juice.

Eat asparagus.

Lice

Use Red Pacific shampoo on head (a salve).

Mix calamine and grease, and rub into hair.

Use lye soap.

Measles

Cover windows. Parch cornmeal and pour water on it. Drink it and go to bed.

Stay quietly in a dark room.

Boil dry corn shucks and make a tea.

Drink hot lemonade or whiskey to make them break out faster.

Mumps

Rub olive oil on your jaws and stay in bed.

Take sardine oil and rub it on your throat.

Tie strands of flax around a girl's neck and around a boy's waist.

Nail in Foot

Soak it in coal oil.

Nail Punctures

Take hot coals; put wool rags over them. When they begin to smoke, hold the puncture over the smoke.

Nausea

Take a hot red-oak coal. Chop it in a cup of cold water. When it stops sizzling, drink the water.

Nerves

Eat celery.

Nosebleed

Put a dime under upper lip.

Put something cold on the back, or pour cold water over the head.

Put a nickel under tongue.

Thread a needle and put it around your neck, and let the needle hang between your shoulders.

Take a cigarette paper and fold four times, and put it between your upper lip and teeth.

Read Ezekiel 16:6, say it three times, and call the person's name.

Put feet in a chair and lay on the floor with a cold cloth over your nose.

Hang an iron pothook around your neck.

Wear a length of red woolen yarn or a piece of nutmeg on a string around neck.

Put cobwebs up your nose.

Pneumonia

Get peach tree leaves and boil them. Mix in meal. Put in a rag and put it on your chest.

Cover chest with a cloth moistened with kerosene and dried mustard.

Mix kerosene, turpentine, and grease. Wet a cloth in that mixture and place on chest.

Cut an onion in half and put on soles of feet.

Drink tea made from a hog hoof.

Put pine needles and turpentine in hot water, and place pans of it around the bed so the person can breathe it.

Poison Ivy

Wash with vinegar.

Rub with jewelweed or sweet fern.

Put buttermilk on it.

Put coffee on it.

Eat poison ivy leaves.

Mix gunpowder and sweet milk together, and rub it on.

Rabies

When they get to where they can't eat, put them in a room and nail them in.

String a needle with black thread, and hang it around neck and never take it off.

Rash

Apply cornstarch.

Bathe in baking soda for a heat rash.

Rub yourself with vinegar.

Brown flour in a skillet and put it on [rash].

Rheumatism

Wear a copper ring or a copper bracelet.

Put 2 pounds of raisins in 1 quart of wine; drink after 48 hours.

Rub the affected parts with the blood of a freshly killed rattlesnake.

Wear a buckeye on a string around neck.

Drink alfalfa tea.

Mix vinegar and kerosene, then rub it where it hurts.

Ringworm

Take iodine and go around the outside of the ring, then paint the inside, and the ring, too.

Take a fig branch, break it, and rub the milk of the branch around the ring.

Burn plain white paper without lines in a plate. Blow ashes away. Use liquid left in plate on ring.

Cut a green walnut and rub it on the ringworm and cover it.

Put kerosene on wound.

Put wet snuff on them.

Snakebite

Take someone with good teeth and make an X on the bite and let him suck the blood out.

Cut the place, suck blood out, then put kerosene on it.

Cut a chicken in half, and lay it on the bite. It draws out the poison.

Get some Old Crow and get the victim to drink a bottle. Then pack ice on the bite.

Tie a cloth above the bite, drain a lot of the blood out. Then put some blue lotion on it.

Soak in coal oil.

Cut a deer heart out and put on bite.

Make a poultice of squash.

Wet place with vinegar, and cake with baking soda.

Sore Throat

Bind the throat with an old silk handkerchief. Keep it bound during the night.

Bind a piece of new beef outside. Sometimes the beef will turn pale or green.

Rub your throat with turpentine, and take honey and almond.

Gargle with warm salt water.

Chew a little piece of asafetida.

Wear gold or amber beads around neck.

Mix sugar and a little turpentine, and sip.

Drink hot salt water and a teaspoon of soda.

Tie a black shoestring loosely around your neck.

Sores

Mix pine resin and sulfur to make a salve to put on sore.

Sprained Ankle

First pour vinegar on it, then get a brown paper sack, and put your foot in it. Then fill sack with red clay.

Boil mullein leaves in vinegar and put on ankle.

Take clay, heat, wet with hot water, and put on ankle.

Stomach Trouble

Mix salt and pepper with vinegar and drink it.

Make some thick flour water and drink it.

Wear asafetida around neck.

Rub turpentine on belly button.

Drink dry tea made of red pepper.

Sunburn

Apply a can of cream or white vinegar.

Thrash [or *Thrush*]

Take someone who hasn't seen their father, and let them blow in the mouth.

Take honey and alum.

Wipe out infant's mouth with its wet diaper. Do this three times a day.

Take chinaberries to make a necklace out of them, then wear it around your neck.

Toothache

For this purpose nothing is better than a split fig, roasted, and laid on the gum.

Split an onion, roast it, and bind it on the wrist while still hot over the pulse on the opposite side from the tooth.

Put vanilla flavoring on a cotton swab and put on tooth.

Soak a piece of cotton in some whiskey and put it on tooth.

Soak a piece of cotton in laudanum and put on tooth.

To prevent toothache, trim fingernails only on Fridays.

Put snuff on the toothache.

Put camphor on tooth.

Put lice or a mouse head on tooth.

Have a man or a woman to kiss you.

Tuberculosis

Bury the victim face down when he dies to protect others.

Warts

Tie a horsehair around it.

Let someone take a bean leaf and rub the wart with it. Then let the person hide the bean leaf without you watching where they hide it.

Get an old bone, rub on wart, and throw the bone over left shoulder.

Hide a dirty dishrag under steps.

Get a greasy rag from somebody else's house, and rub the wart real good. Then go and bury the rag.

Rub the wart with a stolen dishrag, and then hide the dishrag in a tree stump.

Open the wart with a needle by sticking it three times. Then hide the needle where you will never find it.

Bathe the wart with water from a hollow stump without thinking of a fox.

Rub with a bean; throw bean away.

Rub with salt pork; bury the meat.

Tie knots in string for how many warts you have, and put string where someone will find it. That person will then get the warts.

Some people can rub it and say something to themselves, and warts go away.

Put water and cornstarch on wart.

Put iodine on the wart.

Get a lady to rub bear grease on it, and let her bury the grease and not tell anyone where. Have faith the wart will go away.

Put castor oil on wart.

Rub your wart with a rooster's comb. Then bury the comb.

Find a bone, look at it real good to make sure you know how it was laying. Pick it up and rub the piece of one that was on the ground on the wart. Put it back down the same way and place it was laying. But don't tell anybody.

Whooping Cough

Get a mare and milk her, and give it to the person.

Take a mixture of turpentine, sugar, and honey.

Take cod-liver oil.

Catch a toad frog, tie a string to both of his hind legs, and hang him over the door you always walk in and out of. When it dries up, your cough will be gone.

Sip red clover and elderberries.

Drink a little coal oil and sugar mustard.

Put a cloth in a little turpentine, then put it in your mouth.

Eat honey.

Worms

Swallow chewing-tobacco juice.

Mix three drops of coal oil, a half teaspoon of sugar, and a big dose of castor oil. Take for three days.

Sip sugar and turpentine.

Go to the cow pen and get one cup of milk. Don't strain it; drink it.

Put three or four drops of turpentine on sugar and eat for nine nights. Skip nine nights, then repeat the treatment.

Use coppers and some pine resin. Make some pills out of that and take one every night for nine nights.

Eat a yellow duck steeped in vinegar.

Take the seeds from Jerusalem oak weeds. Make a syrup candy and put the seeds in it. Eat the candy.

Yellow Jaundice

Eat sweet food and candies.

Eat turkey-dung bitters warmed from wood bark.

Faith Healing

Linnie DuBose, seventy-seven, is a faith healer who lives in Pineland, Texas. She has had a busy life of service to others, including work as a midwife. She has a deep and abiding faith in the Lord, and gives all credit to Him for whatever she has been able to do to help people. This aid has always been freely given, for she believes that not all possess her gifts. Two other healers, Ollie Prince and Sybil Whiddon, who offered additional information, share similar attitudes.

In the following interview with *Loblolly* Mrs. DuBose tells of her ability to "draw fire" out of a person. The belief is that after a person has been burned, the fire continues to flame within, and unless drawn out, makes recovery slower and more painful. When she speaks of stopping bleeding, she means bleeding not of natural causes. Thrash (or *thrush*) is a childhood disease, with symptoms of blisters around and inside the mouth. This can spread to the mother in the case of breast-feeding. If not cured, the child could eventually die.

—Loblolly

Q.—We understand you can heal by faith, and wonder how you got that power.
A.—I got it from the Lord.
Q.—Are Bible verses used?
A.—For stopping bleeding it is, but I can't remember where. I think it's the sixteenth chapter of Ezekiel.
Q.—Do you remember where you got the ability to do that? Did someone tell you or did you just find out?

A. – Found out through the Lord. I found others done it, too. I don't think I ask for unreasonable things of the Lord. I don't think that's right. I broke my arm, broke my ribs, sprained my foot, and I have a crooked spine to go with it. Straining through a lifetime of working has done it, and I put that all on myself. The Lord did not do it. He can only help me deal with it. He put these herbs and medicines here and give us knowledge and understanding how to use them, you know. Well, he didn't give everyone the same power. Some know more than others.

Q. – How would you stop bleeding?

A. – By the verse of the Bible. You don't have to touch them. You just talk to the Lord and it's all right. It stops the bleeding quick, I understand. But I never did this myself.

Q. – What about thrash?

A. – Why, you could have an old piece of bacon, and use it to make Christ's cross on the bottom of an old smutty skillet. It could be any kind of meat you could get good and smutty from the skillet. Then, use it to rub the baby's mouth real good and then give the meat to a black dog and forget about it. It's cured, just like that. Of course, it takes time to heal up, but then it will not break out again. But it's got to have time to heal. You know his mouth gets smutty and his lips, too, because it's supposed to, but you don't go wash it off. You let it wear off.

Another thing is if you hold a baby up in the sunlight and get its mouth open. Let the sun shine down its little mouth before he's three days old, and he won't never have thrash.

Another thing you can do if you have a little baby with thrash and it caused your breast to be infected or something like that, it could be rubbed and it will go down. It will do that, I seen it tried. Another way you can cure that, and I think it will cure the thrash, too, is that some takes a baby down into the woods and get some kind of leaf and rub its mouth. I don't know the details about that.

A man or a woman can take and smother [crush] three of these things they call mold. The mold runs under the ground, you know, and makes them little runners. You can take and smother three of them, and you can blow it in the baby's mouth and cure the thrash. Or you can rub the mother's breast and it will go down if it is risen.

Q. – Have you treated anybody for snakebite?

A. – Well, I was told how by somebody, I forgot who, but it will work on the wasp bites. I shouldn't tell for fear of losing the power. But I don't ever use it anymore. But if it's the Lord's will, I guess I could. You rub your hand on the bite and say: "Julia, Julia, are you dead?/Go way down south and come no more/And this we ask in the Father, and of/The Son and of the Holy Ghost/Amen and amen." Just like that! But you got to have the faith there.

Q. – Do you have a cure for bruises?

A. – Naw, not exactly, but if you got bruised and it swells up real bad, just go out and pick you some buds off some tender sassafras bud. And beat them up and put you some ice water on them, make you a poultice out of them. Put it on the bruise; it'll draw every bit of that swelling out. Best you can do for swelling.

Q. – Did you use sassafras tea, too?

A. – That's right. It's good blood medicine. It keeps your blood thinned up to where you can stand the heat during the summer. It tastes good, too. I've got some cured roots there in the kitchen; you can buy them in the store now. You can tell a sassafras tree by the smell.

Q. – Do you know about getting rid of warts, too?

A. – Yeah, it's done kinda like a snakebite. You have one on your hand and you just say: "Wart, wart, go away,/Go away down south and come no more." You forget about it, and next thing you know, you look there and it's gone.

Q. – How do you draw fire?

A. – Blow on it and talk to it. Like you was burnt on your hand anywhere, don't make no difference where, you can blow on it. Just do it as hard as you can, and talk just as many words as you can as long as that breath lasts. Get another long breath, and blow again till you get it all recited. And do that till it quits burning. It'll quit. Say: "Come out, fire, come in frost/Follow thy Lord, thy Son,/and thy Holy Ghost/Amen." You may have to get breath between words and syllables like that, but blow just as hard as you can with your breath on that place. And it'll work – does for me. The directions to that is not to tell nobody who is related to you. You can cure your kin just as long as you don't tell them. I learned to do this from an old lady named Fanny Bell Wright. She's dead now.

One of the neighbor children got burnt pretty bad and they sent for me and my maw. She could take the fire out, too, and we both worked on that child half a day. We cured it, too.

When I lived at Buna [Texas], there was a child who had walked through a bed of hot coals barefooted. He had hopped through on one foot. He just burnt it real bad and hadn't wore a shoe for a week. His mother heard about me, that I could do that, and she brought that little boy to me. I worked on him an hour or two that night. And she went on back home, and she said next day he put on a shoe and never had more trouble with it.

Q. – Do you have any other cures?

A. – I know another thing that might be of help to anybody, and anybody can fix it. And that is with this poultice outfit when you hurting and can't get no relief or nothing. One time a man got a hook caught in his side while working in the woods. It tore the stripping loose between his ribs and his intestines, and air got in there. Well, the doctor doctored him two weeks and he couldn't hardly bear to be turned over and he couldn't turn himself. He thought at first he had pneumonia, but he didn't. They wanted to send him to Lufkin. But before that happened, a doctor's wife who was living close to me wanted to fix a poultice and put on him. So she took a box of dry mustard, two boxes of flour, a half cup of syrup, and a half cup of vinegar. She stirred that all up together and got it hot. She put it on him and it eased him. That will remove pain of pneumonia and stuff when everything else fails. Keep it warm; you may have to take it off every once in a while. If not, it'll blister. And wash him, put some oil on him, warm the poultice and put it back. Get him easy—but it'll work.

Q.—Can you tell us about the chicken pox?
A.—Well, you just make sure you got your chickens penned up. Next morning take whoever is sick out there, and let the chickens fly over them. They say it will work, cure them. I never did try that.

But I've tried this other. Kill an old black hen and scald her. Pick her like you was gonna eat her. But anyway, you save that water. Usually it's children that has the pox. But anyway, you save that water and give them a bath in it. Give the kid a bath, and it will cure the chicken pox.

Oh, yes, I've also used a cure for the itch. My kids all had it. I just got some sulfur and grease, and rubbed it on them. Some tell to have them wear their clothes for nine days, then burn the clothes. They think it will cure the itch. I done my kids that way and it didn't work. Someone told me if I'd put the kids in running water the first three mornings in May before sunup, it would cure it. That's what I done and they got all right. Just like I tell you, you've got to have faith in anything before it'll work.

Boil hives are what kids have when they are little. Well, when everything else fails, give them all kinds of tea. Make it out of all kinds of stuff nearly for the hives. When all that fails, take a razor blade and between the baby's shoulder blades make Christ's cross—just enough for it to bleed a little, not deep. Give that child that blood. Get it up with a spoon or something another, and give it to that child. And that'll cure the boil hives. We call it scarifying them.

Mrs. Ollie Prince

Oh, yeah, there's a verse in the Bible that you can repeat over three times. I can show it to you boys, but not girls, or I'd lose my power to heal. My boys had been cut a-many time and I stopped it. One time, when J. W. was about ten or eleven years old, he cut his toe off—cut it completely off and it was just a-bleeding. He was running up to the house. His sister was just a-hollering, "Mother, get the Bible! Mother, get the Bible!" And I got the Bible, read that verse over, and it stopped. One time down here at the Trades Day, Mr. Youngblood had a horse down there that was just a-bleeding and J. W. come and got me and said, "Mother, go down to that horse and stop it from bleeding." I did, and the bleeding stopped. It's done by faith and that verse from the Bible.

Sybil Whiddon

This old man, Mr. Eaton, he had been our friend for a long time, and everybody that would get burned would go to him to get the fire talked out.

When my oldest child was about three or four years old, he was climbing up on the mantle and fell in the fireplace, in the bed of ashes, you know, the coals. And I took him to the man. Well, he cured him. Now, if nobody believes in it there's nothing to it. But if anybody believes in prayer, they ought to believe in this. People laughed at me sometimes, but I won't tell anybody about it unless I trust the person real good. 'Cause if they don't believe in it, and they don't seem worthy of my trust, I won't tell them. This old man, he told me of his gift 'cause he trusted me and didn't think he would live much longer. He said he wanted to leave the knowledge with me, so he told me. And then, if anybody that wants to know how to talk the fire out, well, they could come to me, and if I thought they were worthy, I would tell them. I could only tell one man, and if I told any more, the power would be taken away from me. My mother could stop blood, but she told too many people how, so her power passed away from her. It's just a matter of prayer and your belief in God.

One time my little granddaughter got burned on her little hand on the top of a heater. She lived in Deadwood, and her mother brought her down to my house when I lived in Joaquin, and she just screamed all the way down there. After I talked the fire out, they headed back home, and by the time they got to the river bridge she was asleep.

Another time, I just didn't know to put my trust in the incident. Robert Sears married my daughter Brenda. She carried him some coffee one morning when he was in bed, and he spilt it on his side. He said, "Go call Mama and talk the fire out." I told Brenda I'd never tried it on the phone, but I'd try. And just from her calling me, it didn't even blister. And then one of my neighbors, the arm was badly burned, black, and she came over and I talked the fire out. The next morning it wasn't even sore. Just lots of people I've helped.

I don't tell what I say when I'm talking the fire out. I just say it to myself so I won't lose the power. And I blow on the fire while talking.

My mother could stop blood till she told too many people. Anybody you know or an animal—she could fix it. She didn't actually have to see them. I have a brother-in-law; he can stop blood. I had a big rising on my leg one time, and I was picking at it. It came out spouting—it scared me to death. My husband was in the field so the kids ran to their grandmother's to get my brother-in-law. And it stopped all of a sudden. That's what did it, whatever he said. I can't do that myself but I know others can. My mother found she had lost her power when she tried to help a baby. She couldn't do any good and the doctors couldn't. The baby died. She gave up on it then. She didn't even cure horses anymore as she had been able to before.

All this is by God helping, and believing in His power. I have been thankful for the gift and being able to help others.

Coming to Texas: Two Settlement Tales

"If only you'd shown up with the tape recorder twenty years ago! . . . Old Mrs. Monroe could have told you wonderful stories about the subject, but now she's gone." That melancholy refrain is heard a lot at *Loblolly*. Oral history as a process for recording the grass-roots traditions of East Texas can work only with the living memory. The wonderful stories the dead could have told us remain forever beyond our ken.

In the case of the following accounts, however, circumstances contrived to record the oral testimonies of two pioneer ladies born around 1850. The account of Mrs. De Steiguer was recorded in a 1940 interview by George Kright; she was ninety-one years old. Susan Patton's story was written by her daughter, Lester Patton Miller, and was a result of notes taken down over the years during conversations with her mother. Together, the stories offer a fascinating glimpse into the settlement period of East Texas and of life on the home front during the Civil War. Each of these settlement tales begins with the account of an epic journey to Texas, and ends happily— with a marriage.

—*Loblolly*

Mrs. De Steiguer

I was born near Selma, Alabama, in 1848. When six years old, with my father, Alan Bryan, mother, brothers and sisters, I moved from Alabama to Panola County, Texas.

My father had already purchased 4,444 acres of East Texas land which was part of the wilderness at the time of purchase. He came with his own wagon train, fifty Negro slaves, a hired overseer, and a considerable herd of cattle.

We crossed the Mississippi River at Romney, a little village about halfway between Vicksburg and Natchez, Mississippi. The river, to my childish mind, looked as big as an ocean, and I expected any minute for it to swallow me up. It took some time to cross the river, as the ferryboat had to make several trips to haul all the people, cattle, and wagons across.

At night we camped in the open and cooked our supper by campfires. Some of the older boys and men always stood guard with guns through the night as a protection against horse and cattle thieves and wild animals.

Finally, after seven weeks on the road, we arrived on my father's land in Panola County. The entire tract was wild and primitive. We made a camp; everybody went to work building houses. The foreman and some of the Negroes started clearing land to plant the crops next spring. Despite the fact that we could get neither lumber nor nails, we soon had a comfortable log house to live in. The logs, hewn in the woods, were hauled by oxen to the building site. In place of nails to fasten the logs together, we used wooden pins, boring holes in the logs with an auger for the pins to fit into. The nearest lumber was at Shreveport, one hundred miles away, too far to haul lumber with oxen.

We operated several spinning wheels and two looms. I have spun both cotton and wool, and wove cloth many days in our early Texas home. We made cloth for all wearing apparel, wove our own blankets and bedcovers. Good weaving was considered an art, and the womenfolk took a special pride in weaving beautiful cloth.

Father was in poor health when [the] War Between the States started. He was a loyal Southerner but had little hope that the South could win. He believed the odds against the South were too overwhelming. I recall, when two of my brothers joined the Confederate Army, we kissed and waved them good-bye. An older sister admonished: "Don't you come back here shot in the back."

For four years during the war we had neither sugar nor coffee. We used cane syrup for sweetening and for coffee substituted parched wheat, parched corn, or thin strips of hard-baked sweet potato, ground first. The only coffee I saw during the four years of war were a few grains hidden away that we found by accident.

My father died in 1862. We continued to live on the farm, which Mother managed as best she could.

Some of the things I did during those days would be considered unusual now but quite common then. For instance, I not only spun and wove, but sometimes helped out with syrup making in the fall, and I've even taken home-grown and home-cured tobacco and rolled it into cigars for the men. It was several months after Lincoln's Emancipation Proclamation before we knew the Negro slaves were free. Mother called up all the slaves and told them that they were free, could either stay on the place or leave. If they stayed, they could farm as tenants and get one half of the crops they produced. The Negroes were not overjoyed to be told they were free. Some of them cried, and most of them remained with us.

War Between the States had deprived the neighborhood of doctors. There was one woman, a doctor's widow, who had nursed and studied medicine. She was always called in to attend the sick. People for miles around would send for this good woman to come down to their aid when illness struck down someone in their family.

During the war many articles, including food and medicine, could not be had at any price. I recall the only flour we had was home-grown wheat, ground on a gristmill which turned out bran, seconds, shorts, and flour, all in the same sack. If we wanted to bake a cake for a special occasion, we sifted this flour through homespun cloth and sweetened the cake with homemade cane syrup.

Our family would have fared badly durin the War Between the States had it not been for the faithful Negro men and women who remained with us throughout the war. They farmed the land, raised hogs, chickens, fed and looked after the livestock. Also, they would fight at the drop of a hat in defense of we womenfolk.

Dr. De Steiguer and I were married at my home in Panola County in 1868. I wore a homespun dress. We lighted the home with tallow candles, and the cake was made from home-grown and home-ground wheat.

We began housekeeping with nothing except faith, hope, and love. It was a hard struggle for several years because the war had taken most of our property and practically all of our money. People in those days didn't think the government or anyone else owed them a living. It was root, hog, or die. But people helped one another without being asked to do so. They shared their food and clothing with the needy.

My children, and even some of my great-grandchildren, seem to think I am old. But I don't feel old and I don't expect to ever get old. I never worry about anything: "The Lord is my shepherd. I shall not want."

Susan Patton

The year 1857 saw many wagon trains and settlers moving into Texas. One train of some eight wagons was coming down through the bottoms of Louisiana in early spring. They were headed for the crossing known in later years as the Gaines Crossing, as many of the ox-wagon trains favored the place without steep banks.

Rain and mud had plagued the wagons all day. The oxen were tired, the horse riders besmattered with mud and dirt, and all were ready to make camp for the night. Soon fires were going, stock was watered and fed and cared for. Then the men had time to look about.

The Louisiana side of the Sabine River was low, swampy, with big and small trees of all kinds. The river was on a big rise, the water over the banks, and the fast current swirling tree trunks and refuse along the middle of the stream. It was wide, and there was no sign of the small rope ferry that usually operated in this place.

The men consulted and agreed that the river must run down some, then they must locate and cut down palmetto trees, and, tying them alongside the wheels, use them to float the wagons over. So far, on their way from Little Rock, Arkansas, they were ferried across the widest rivers and had been lucky with the smaller streams.

These people were mostly related families. The Pickard name was on three wagons. Childers, Windhams, and Franks were along, and cousins from other related groups rode horses alongside. Two of the husbands had gone ahead on horseback to Texas to prepare for their families and knew people already settled in Sabine County, in Shelby County, and what was to become San Augustine County.

One of these husbands was John Pickard, who had consigned the care of his family to the relatives and the young cousins to make the trip. Pickard had gone to Rusk, Texas, and bought property, but would meet the train at the Sabine crossing and join his wife for the rest of the journey. His wife, Rachael Ann Pickard—with her five children and all their possessions, two faithful oxen, a horse, and cow and calf to look after—rode high on the wagon seat holding her baby boy, age one year, while standing behind her much of the time were Susan, five years, and Amelia, seven years. Henry, proud of his eleven years, rode the horse, while Wash (short for Washington) managed the oxen with his mother's help. One eighteen-year-old Childers cousin came along to drive and help out when the going got rough.

For two days, the party waited and rested and the river began to run down, although the current in the middle still ran strong. Mr. Pickard had not arrived, and Rachael Ann became nervous. She thought of the baby and the small children, and the calf which rode in the back of the wagon, the cow leading behind so she could see it and not bawl. How would they manage to get the cow to swim?

The men made careful plans for their wagons and stock. They could not afford losing anything. Everything they had was in the wagons, and their women and children could not swim.

The wagons were loaded as lightly as possible. Yet they were full, some bringing bedding, clothing, seeds, and a few implements, some a box of chickens, or a duck or two, and in one were a dog and pet cat—the cat in a slate box, the dog tied up. The women all sat high on those spring seats for comfort in riding, but all feared the water.

Several young fellows were riding horseback alongside. They had come from Texas to assist the train, and two of the young Pickard cousins had helped to cross the Sabine before, when they had to float the wagons.

They planned to attach the logs alongside the wagons after running them into the water. Ropes would be attached to the wagon pole in front, and two horseback riders would swim in front of the oxen to guide and pull across.

Two other riders would swim alongside the oxen to help the driver and also carry long poles to push under the heavy yokes if they dragged the oxen's heads under or if an oxen faltered. Other riders led livestock or watched for logs or debris in the water to get it out of the way.

Mrs. Pickard grew more nervous, hoping her husband would get there in time to help, but he did not come. She made the long journey to Texas without him by her side; now she had to face up to this last and worst part alone. Each man was assigned his work and place. It was decided the young Childers cousin would be the driver for Rachael's wagon, for he was a good oxen driver. Wash would exchange places with him, and, riding his big, fine horse, would lead their cow behind the wagon so she could keep an eye on her calf while swimming.

Rachael Ann took her place up on the spring seat, holding her baby, Charley, in her lap, and placed her girls, Amelia and small Susan, behind her, standing and holding onto the seat on either side of her. She warned them not to cry out or make any disturbance. "Don't make any sound," she told them. "If you get scared, just look up at me and do as I do."

One by one, two other wagons were driven into the water and outfitted with the palmetto trees attached alongside. Then, with the two riders pulling on the wagon pole out front, swimming their horses, and the two side riders with their poles at the oxen's heads, with much "hallo"-ing and yelling and wielding the sustaining poles under the heavy yokes, they inched across the fast current and made the other side. As the wagons were helped up the incline over there, Susan looked up at her mother and saw that her eyes were tightly closed. She had not looked one time at the scene, nor moved a muscle!

When it was time for them, Cousin Childers came and climbed onto the spring seat by his cousin Rachael. She said to her girls, "Remember, now, what I said," and she tightened her arms around her baby boy.

John Childers "hee"-ed and "haw"-ed to the oxen, handling the reins expertly down to the water, and there the same palmetto trees had been brought back across the river and now put on their wagon. The two horseback riders got the ropes on the wagon pole up in front, swimming their horses ahead, pulling and guiding. The two other horseback riders with the poles were alongside, ready for helping with those heavy yokes in the current.

They started, and the two little girls fixed their eyes up at their mother's profile, rather than to look at the muddy, dangerous, deep-looking water. About the middle, as they reached the current, the wagon lurched from the swirling, and one of the oxen almost went under, his head low in the wave, until one of the men hurriedly lifted it with his pole and the oxen swam on.

Completely frightened, the little girls still looked at their mother, when they saw she was still not making a sound, but big, silent tears were rolling down her cheeks unchecked, her mouth was clenched, and her hand was over Charley's mouth, too. So they clenched their mouths to make no sound, but big, silent tears rolled down their cheeks, too. In this way, they finally reached the other side, but they never remembered going onto the bank or what happened next.

The palmetto trees went back and forth until all the wagons got over. There were none lost, but the men, oxen, horses, and all stock were completely worn out. The other women in the other wagons confessed to crying, and some loudly in their distress. They had not been prepared for this situation.

Mr. Pickard arrived next morning from Rusk, Texas, after a long, hard horseback ride, encountering swollen creeks and dangerous crossings to delay him. There was no barbed wire down in the lowlands or creeks, but there were snakes to consider, and few roads and no bridges.

This group was to settle in Sabine County, Shelby County, and the Pickards over at Rusk, Texas.

Three years later, the Pickard children were orphans. John Pickard died from pneumonia about a year after their arrival in Texas. Rachael Pickard followed him to the grave from grief and overwork. The children were separated and lived with other families. Later, Henry, who was eleven at the time of the river crossing, was able to bring them together again. Susan, Lester Patton Miller's mother, later married George Patton, and reared six children. In her later years she recounted memories of life in East Texas after the Civil War, and her daughter retold them.

The early settlers were attracted to Texas because of the fertile soil. There were some Indians still, but they were leaving the eastern sections. There were opportunities to obtain land cheaply, and most of the affluent settlers brought slaves with them at first. Around Jefferson, Texas, were people of means who used the waterway for transportation and importing goods for leisure use. Rusk, between the Angelina and Neches rivers, began as a thriving area because the red soil encouraged fruit and vegetables, and there was plenty of water.

While thinking of clear skies, rivers of clear running water, and agricultural soil, the settlers forgot to consider climate. East Texas gets bitterly cold when the northeast wind comes in with rain. And people and animals were thankful for the windbreaks of the forests and the lean-tos easily constructed of brush poles.

The settlers' log houses were bitterly cold, and the wood houses that quickly replaced them were noted for cold floors. The housewife began making rag carpets to cover them. They gathered all the old linsey-woolsey skirts and worn men's heavy trousers, old blankets, and any gay pieces of wool cloth. These they split and cut in narrow widths, then sewed them together and began rolling into balls of at least eight inches. They gathered these balls into a large sack for months and began hunting about the country for someone who had a carpet machine to weave the rag carpet. So many balls produced so many lengths, usually thirty-six inches wide or forty inches wide, and as long as the housewife wanted for her room. Multicolored, this carpet was woven so that the crosswise lines were the warp.

When she got her rug home, the housewife had to prepare the parlor floor for it. First, all the furniture was removed. Then, she scoured the floor, having spread fine, white sand over it along with a few shavings of lye soap. Then she rinsed well, and the floor was smooth and clean. (The ladies used to pass along to each other where they found the best beds of fine, smooth sand for scrubbing.) Finally, they scattered fresh, clean hay over the floor to make a pad. If they could get some Louisiana moss, they used the moss as a pad.

Starting at one end of the room, they laid the carpet in strips on the floor and began tacking it down, stretching it with hay rake prongs to hold the fullness taut. As they went, the housewife sewed the lengths of carpet together at the side seams with heavy carpet thread, whipping it securely. They continued with the tacking and the rake prongs to hold it smooth. It took a lot of work and back bending to put down a rag carpet in rooms fourteen feet, as they usually made them in that day. But how proud of them they were.

The housewife swept this carpet with a broom, if she was lucky enough to own one. She dampened pieces of newspaper and threw them around to absorb the dust on the surface. Often, they had to make their brooms from broom weeds, tying them with willow thongs and calling them a brush.

Wet, muddy boots were not welcome on these carpets; hence the men often removed their boots at the porch and slipped on cloth gaiters of dark woolen flannel in order to come in by the fire and warm themselves. On the porches were to be seen the "boot stops" of wood blocks with a V cut wide enough to fit and hold a boot.

The furniture of the best room included a bed, made up with a high feather mattress under the woven spread. The ladies pieced their handmade quilts in their spare time—and there was never enough. When clothes were worn out, the ladies took the best parts of men's and boys' pants and cut squares, sewed these heavily with cotton, and tacked them together here and there with cord. These britches quilts were mighty comfortable during a blizzard.

In the best room the pillows were stuffed with down from domestic ducks, or even the fine down from Dominicker hens. And some ladies even made little capes for the small children and filled the quilted yokes with the softest down to provide warmth.

The mattresses were often filled with the moss, which had been combed out, or even with shucks from the cornfields. The treasured feather beds were turned every day to ensure a high rounded look. Square pillow shams or extra covers were removed at night from the pillows and laid in place each day. These were often elaborately ruffled and embroidered to enhance the tall wooden headboards then in vogue. Such headboards kept out the cold air behind the bed of the lucky owner.

The ladies often helped each other sew their new dresses and wraps, and these all-day meetings promoted the "friendship quilts." They would exchange a few of the leftover scraps for some of their own and begin to lay them on a foundation, higgledy-piggledy, and then sew them down and embroider around them elaborate stitches with embroidery thread called sansilk in pretty colors. These embroidery stitches all had names, handed down through the years. Many of the stitches had come direct from England, by way of Tennessee settlers or from the Kentucky mountains. Often the ladies embroidered the name of the donor, and the year, or date of a wedding piece, or drew a design or a fan.

Quilts were then, and are now, conversation pieces, as each piece of cloth has its history and association. Also, each lady prided herself on the precision and imaginative use of color in placing her stitches.

My mother called her quilt, begun at Rusk before 1877, a "memory quilt." In it were pieces of cloth from her girlhood friends, also pieces of their wedding dresses, as well as her own. There were pieces of fine broadcloth used in men's coats and pieces of the velvet used to make "therevers" on those coats. Her own wedding piece was a green moiré silk, very heavy, and there was also a piece of her "enfaire dress" of golden brown ribbed silk. She kept on with this quilt, making dainty, precise stitches, each with a name. I remember one was "hen and chickens," but when I tried to learn to do it I found it extremely difficult to do well.

After the Civil War, clothes were hard to come by for Mother and her sister, for they were orphans. But when the sewing machine was brought into Rusk by a salesman, traveling in a wagon, everybody wanted to learn how to use it.

This salesman gave demonstrations and used charts for patterns and could accommodate the size of any lady. The charts were heavy white paper noted by inches as to size, and my mother's stayed in her trunk for safety. Her machine was a Seamstress and had the wheel with the rubber band and the foot rest for the feet. The top was removable and sat on top when not in use. We still have this machine, bought about 1875, and it will still sew. The original parts are still with it: the ruffler and the tucker, shirrer, hemmer, and gatherer.

In caring for their clothes the girls learned to use the "sadirons" the slaves had used, although they both complained at having to heat them outside on open fires—which was necessary in summertime—which only caused more ironing. It was too hot then to use the fireplace for ironing.

They enjoyed taking their wash down to the nearby spring on a nice, sunny day, both for the outing and because the spring water was soft and clear. They would build a small fire and place three rocks there and fill a small tin tub to boil the soiled clothes. They took along their "battling stick" and their lye soap and literally battered the soapy water through the soiled garments spread out on a large, flat rock. Then they rinsed them and hung them on nearby bushes to dry. While the clothes were drying, the two girls would hunt black hens and blackberries, then wade in a little trickling stream, enjoying the cold water flowing over the white sandy bottom.

They acquired a "fluting iron" to make their cotton ruffles stand up, and they knew how to make starch from mixing a ball of flour in water, then washing it over and over and over, and boiling it. It could stiffen men's collars perfectly. I never could quite do it so well, and Mother was glad to begin using Faultless starch. I was too, because in the boxes were cute little booklets of pictures and stories and puzzles.

Making lye soap was necessary in those days. All the freshly killed hog skin was saved and boiled down for fat. Old lard or used fats were saved in syrup buckets. Age did not matter, but it was strained.

The washpot was filled with water, a fire built, and the fat put in with the proper amount of lye. We boiled and stirred for hours. At the end of the day the mixture was covered and allowed to cool. The soap rose to the top of the pot and could be cut in squares, by layers, and stored in a dry place for future use. It had a pale, yellow color, or could be a creamy color, depending on the cooking and amounts of fat and lye used.

The ladies were jealous of their ability to turn out prize soap, and justly so. In later years, many beauty hints speak of the fact that beautiful hair and healthy scalp react well to the constant use of lye soap and spring water for shampoos.

The two sisters had long hair and spent much time dressing it. Mother had black curly hair, but she spoke of making spit curls of sugar water, as that was the style. Also, she braided her hair at night and wore little nightcaps tied under the chin. Both girls crocheted snoods to wear while riding horseback, which they loved to do. They had sidesaddles. The seat of Mother's was a flowered brocatelle velvet, and the pommel was black leather. Mother was a graceful rider in her riding skirt and wasn't afraid of any horse.

Canning and preserving were necessary. Also, trips were made for berrying or picking peaches or wild plums and persimmons, and haws, both black and red. These were all for making jam and jellies for the winter use.

The new courthouse must have been built in Rusk before 1878. Both the Pickard girls enjoyed the all-night dances held there. These were real balls, well planned and chaperoned, with very good music.

At this time they were all together as a family near Alto, and enjoyed the groups formed to ride the nine miles over to Rusk to these big affairs. The arrangements then were for a young gentleman to send a written invitation to his lady friend to accompany him for this dance. He would lead a riding horse to her home, and she furnished her own saddle. Two by two, the six or eight couples would gather with a married couple for chaperones, and they left for the dance, the young ladies carrying their dresses and their dancing shoes in a pillowcase. They would change when they arrived at the dressing room of the new courthouse. They had the grand march, polkas, schottische, two-step, waltz, and heel and toe. They often arrived home at dawn, having danced nearly all night.

Their church was Methodist, with much sacred harp singing, and both girls took part in the singing. Mother sang second tenor, which must have been alto in today's music. In those days she sang many songs, having a good voice, and both of the young ladies attended, together with their brother Charley. The singing school was held in the schoolhouse out from Alto, Texas. They each paid the teacher fifty cents and used their own books. The school ran school hours for two weeks, with much fun and frolic during the recess periods.

Still living near Alto, Susan planned her wedding to George Patton. He was located at Waxahachie, being a land buyer or agent for people back in Kentucky. There were Kentucky friends in Rusk, and he met Susan there. They each had a horse to make a team and planned a covered-wagon honeymoon, moving with all Susan's household goods and taking her sister along over the country to live at Waxahachie.

Sewing the aforesaid wedding dress of heavy green moiré and planning a wedding at home, the young bride was entertained at Rusk at an "enfaire" dinner. She wore the golden brown ribbed silk. Sister Amelia made herself a burgundy-colored silk, with a wool short coat of the same color.

Mr. Patton presented Susan a small bow-top travel trunk for her things to be packed. It had a little compartment up on the bow top to put her hats. Amelia also had one and that was packed to go.

The family owned a huge bow-top trunk, which held all goods. The Windham Bible belonging to Rachael Pickard was there. In it was kept the cashmere shawl Susan prized so highly which her brother, Henry, brought back from New Orleans, together with the gold earbobs, for which she had her ears pierced. This trunk became the family packing trunk. It went along with Susan on the occasion of the "enfaire" dinner at Judge Boyd's home in Rusk, and after Susan's wedding, all her friends told the couple good-bye and they got ready for leaving Rusk.

Courtship, Wedding, Shivaree

The *Loblolly* staff found that courtship and marriage were subjects that most all of their friends and neighbors had experience with and opinions about. Clearly, courtship was very different in those days when young people were more closely observed by friends and family. Nevertheless, despite the closeness of family surveillance and the obstacles of poor roads and slow transportation, love usually found a way. *Loblolly* also learned of the "shivaree," that boisterous harassment of bride and groom beside which the modern version seems pale! Read on and learn about courtship, wedding, and shivaree a half century ago.

—*Loblolly*

Courtship

Yes, it was love at first sight when I saw my husband. I was standing on the back porch with the blues, and Daddy was unloading pine. Vernon came up with his daddy, and I said, "Howdy." Then I ran in the house, closed the door, and stood behind the window, watching him. When they left, I went outside and asked Daddy who he was. "He's one of those Collins boys." I asked if he was single, and my daddy said that his name was Vernon Collins, and he was single. After that, I didn't put on for several months. Then one Sunday evening, he came over and asked me to go to a singing. I was thrilled for the opportunity. We would go to the cane patch, cut a stalk of cane, peel it, and chew it. Sometimes we would all get together and make pictures.

Daddy moved to what is called Sugar Farm Hill, which is near Cave Springs. Vernon had a Model-T Ford. Sugar Farm Hill was sandy and steep. It was so steep that the car wouldn't make it going forward, so he had to turn around and back up to the hill.

We went together for three years and three months.

Dating and courting then was only done by allowing a family member to ride along with them to church or to a party. The boy and a girl were never left alone at any time until after they were married. Some couples would pass notes in church or by a friend that they were sure wouldn't tell, because if you were caught, you weren't allowed to even see each other for weeks at a time.

On Sunday afternoon, a boy could be with his girlfriend from one until five, but no sooner and no later. When five came around, the boy had to go no matter what time he had got there. If the girl had a sister with a boyfriend over for the afternoon, both couples were allowed to sit in the parlor away from the family, but if there was only one couple, they had no privacy. They had to stay in the other part of the house with the rest of the family and were never left alone for one minute. There was no low talking, and no secrets were told. If two couples were in the parlor together, and one couple was caught kissing or touching one another, the other couple went and told right then and there! They weren't allowed to be around either of them again. The boy had to go home then, and the girl was restricted and given extra work to do around the house or in the garden. That couple wasn't allowed to see or be with each other again, unless they were at church, and then they weren't allowed to sit together.

The couples then really had it bad. If the boy was to help his date up on the wagon or steps, he was really considered lucky by other girls and boys.

In those days, we had a certain time we had to be in from a date. When my daddy looked at me and said for me to be in at a certain time, I knew to be in. And things that were interesting to us, just simple things, are just foolish to the majority of young people now. We had "play-parties," and people would have singings in their homes. The first time my husband ever went with me, I went to a singing at Mr. Johnny Newman's house.

Used to be everyone had ribbon-cane patches. In the fall of the year, we would get permission from the owner of this cane patch, and just ten couples would go to the cane patch. Things that young people take as a matter of course weren't thought of then.

Now, when we went to the parties, we would play games such as the Irish Trot or Mulberry Bush in kind of like square dancing. First everybody would sing: "All hands up in the Irish Trot/Irish Trot, Irish Trot/All hands up in the Irish Trot/As we go marching on!" Then you and your partner would break off in pairs and dance like you were square dancing.

The Mulberry Bush was whenever everyone would form a line, while one person would stand outside of the line, and the others would make a figure eight around him. Right at the last, everyone sang and coupled out.

Then you would swing your partner and promenade.

On Sunday afternoon, from fifty to seventy couples would gather at my house for a fellowship. We would have a picnic and make pictures. A lot of times, our boyfriends would just come to the house. We would play a game of forty-two with dominoes and make popcorn balls and eat them.

Wedding

Marriage was not a big celebration then as it is now. There were few engagement rings or wedding bands given, and engagements and weddings were not announced in the newspapers. Showers were always given after the wedding, but the gifts that were given were not luxurious—they were necessities. Most girls had hope chests, and many of the necessary items were found there. Girls also had dowries. This was important to the boy and his family.

There were few church weddings. Weddings were usually held in the girl's home. After the wedding, there was a large feast given by the bride's parents. At the feasts, the beverage the people drank was usually lemonade served from a churn.

Some couples, however, ran off to get married. They usually went to the justice of the peace to be married. There was an unusual custom where, if the floors were hardwood planks, the couple had to stand with the planks instead of across them. Some couples married hurriedly, not even taking time to get out of the car.

Lots of families got together and planned their children's marriages to keep wealth and land ownership in the family.

Most weddings were in the months of June, July, and August. The date was between the first and the tenth. The best time was between ten o'clock A.M. and eight o'clock P.M.

Most wedding dresses were white or light blue that were high waisted with high collars. Good-luck jewelry was usually a watch, ring, necklace, and/or rabbit's foot. The wedding ring was a small gold band. Some had very small diamonds in them. The bride carried mostly field flowers and orange blossoms.

The preacher's pay was two dollars and fifty cents.

Old shoes were thrown after the bride by her father. This was a sign of the transfer of authority from her father to her new husband.

There weren't any wedding pictures. Most of the time, the family was all that came to the wedding. The dress was long, and they wore ruffles under them. If a mother had a wedding dress, she would save it and pass it down to the daughter. Then, when her daughter got married, it would be passed down to her. In the wedding party it was just the bridesmaid, the best man, and the bride and the groom.

Back in those days, we didn't have wedding showers and big weddings.

The preacher would sometimes come to the house. Most of the time, the couple would go to the preacher's house.

We got married in 1926. I never shall forget my ring. It was white gold with orange blossoms and wedding bells carved on it. My wedding band got too small because I just weighed 103 when I got married. I had a blue georgette dress. It's a real thin material, and I got my cousin to make it. She fussed the whole time she was sewing, "What do you want with a dress like this?" I didn't tell her it was my wedding dress, and when she found out it was my wedding dress, she said, "I would have made a mess of it." I still have this wedding dress in a chest. The last time I looked at it, I said to myself, "Was I ever that small?" I had to be. I had a blue hat and white slippers, and my brother carried us to get married on the nineteenth of June.

The traditional wedding calls for lots of things handed down from ancestor to ancestor, such as a white wedding dress that stands for purity and a penny in your shoe for luck. Of course, the groom was not supposed to see the bride before the marriage, or it's bad luck. If it rains on the wedding day, that was also bad luck.

The wedding ring is traditionally worn on the third finger of the left hand, which had a vein going to the heart.

You might say we flaunted all tradition. I received my engagement ring one evening in early October, and then we went to the West Texas Fair. I was just as happy with our marriage. I wore a blue crepe street dress. Odell wore the loudest striped western shirt he could find, including the colors red and purple, with gray western pants and boots made of green alligator leather with big white eagles over the instep. We probably shocked the preacher. We were both new in town and we didn't know a preacher. Some friends set it all up for us. We were married by a Methodist preacher in the parsonage, which we haven't seen since. I realized later my mother and father were married by a Methodist preacher, and neither of them were Methodist either. I guess they had some good friends, too.

I ordered my wedding dress, but it did not come in. Since it didn't come in, I had to wear another new dress. I wore artificial flowers.

We were married in a house. We went to my husband's parents' house for our honeymoon. We gathered cotton and picked peas on our honeymoon.

We offered to pay the preacher, but he would not take any money. We gave him a sack of pecans during the fall.

Not long after my mother's health broke, my husband was called to preach. There was some interesting things that take place with couples getting married. Our old home was down in the corner of this yard. I lived thirty-two years in one house. I don't know all the couples he married. During the Depression, he nightwatched Gary. Of course he had to have a deputy card, and he carried a pistol and blackjack. One night on the railroad, by a flashlight, he married a couple. When he started marrying couples he told me, "I'll give you the money they give me." He married one couple that gave him thirty-seven cents. Another time, an elderly couple came to our house to get married. And the man had on patched overalls. She had a hat that must have come out of the Ark! Another couple, the girl groaned so hard the whole time she was getting married, I got tickled. An old couple came to the house at two A.M. to get married.

Usually the bride wore a homemade corsage made out of flowers that grew in the yard. Usually it was a cape jasmine.
The mothers usually cried because they hated to give their children up. Sometimes the bride and the groom also cried.
We very seldom had what they call receptions.
If the couple were to go in a buggy, guys would take parts of it and hang them up in trees. If they went in a car, they would set the wheels on watermelon rinds so it would just sit and spin. Sometimes they would jack up the back of the car, and the wheels would just sit there and turn.

Shivaree

Pranks were pulled then as they are now. The wagon that the couple had planned to leave in was decorated with rags tied all over it. Also, the cans were strung all around. Many times the guys would kidnap the groom and keep him overnight in an outhouse, while the girls did the bride the same way. Things were done to spook the horses, and a lot of times they would tie the horse's feet together so they couldn't walk. Sometimes heavy chains around the hoofs were used to keep them from going anywhere. Many times on up the road a ways, the couple would find where the ropes had been tied from one side of the road to the other to where the horses could not get by.
Some couples were "shivareed." They were awakened in the middle of the night by people marching around the house playing music, singing, or ringing cowbells. Stove wood was thrown on top of the house to make the couples with tin roofs to wonder what was a-going on. The guy would also be tied to a board in his underwear and run all over the countryside with other guys carrying the board upon their shoulders. At times during the night, about every thirty minutes to an hour, the couple was disturbed by different ones taking turns knocking on the windows and doors over the house.

There weren't any pranks pulled on us, but I know of some that have been pulled before. I remember one time some boys stole the groom and threw him in a pond. This was in January, and you can imagine how cold it was. He caught pneumonia and almost died. And one time the groom had his car full of gas, and some boys siphoned gas out of it. He got about ten miles out of town and ran out of gas. Some couples had buggies instead of cars. People would decorate the buggies by putting tin cans, cowbells, and anything else they could find behind the buggy. Sometimes people would serenade couples by getting together, bringing pots and pans. They would be banging them together, and sometimes they would shoot shotguns.

We did have shivarees. When we were married some of the men came to the house and started ringing bells and making a lot of noise. Then they started throwing rocks at the window. When the groom went to the window and opened it, they grabbed him, blindfolded him, and tied him up to carry him about three to four miles down the road. They set him down beside the road, gagged him, and left.

We wouldn't play any pranks on the couple before the wedding. We'd wait and serenade them after they got home from their honeymoon. The couple never did know when we were coming. I've seen as many as sixty-five at one serenading. It was mostly the older people doing it. To serenade someone, we would all get together one night when we would be least expected. Then we'd tie cans and cowbells together. Then someone would give the signal, and the bells would start ringing, the cans would start rattling, and the windows would start a-raising. A bunch of the men would get the groom and put him on a pole and ride around in the pasture. Then some others would blindfold the bride and spin her around and make her walk in the yard all by herself. Boy, was she scared!

Ever been to a shivaree after a country wedding? Now, I know that there were some that were not so welcome, but not in our community. We just didn't consider a couple really married until they had a proper shivaree.

No matter how hard the couple tried, or pretended to try, the folks all knew where they would be after the wedding. Just about ten at night, the newlyweds would hear the awfulest noises all around the house. There would be bells, whistles, horns, and all manner of noisemaking. Then it would get quiet as a church. Then the singing started. People don't sing like they used to! For about forty-five minutes, the house would ring with the good old songs; then there would be a knocking at the door. The groom would come to the door and find his front porch crowded with people demanding to be fed. He would, as a matter of good social form, protest that he didn't have enough food for so many. The crowd would push inside, but not with empty hands. They brought all manner of good things to eat. Most of the houses were too small for the crowd, so they would bring in two or three buckboard wagons and park them in the yard. Tablecloths appeared like magic, and the food was spread. For a couple of hours, the crowd would eat, tell jokes, and have a grand time. Then, almost as if there were a signal, they would all wish the couple a long and happy life and leave. Most of the guests left gifts for the new family. Then they all went home. We never had any rough shivarees. They were all fun.

Death Lore

The customs and folklore of death seem to hold a fascination for all of us. And if this is true today, it was certainly true in the past of East Texas.

Loblolly wanted to find out about death beliefs and customs in former days and to record factual information about how arrangements were made and affairs carried out in that more self-sufficient time. Families themselves did what had to be done with the body, while a neighbor made the coffin in preparation for the trip to the graveyard. As the *Loblolly* staff talked to people about the burial arrangements, they learned more and more of the folklore surrounding death. Omens and portents of impending death were known by many, and there were precautions to be taken to avoid another death in a family.

This is not a cheerful report on the story of death, but it is an interesting one.

—Loblolly

Sandra Youngblood

In less modern times, people were not as concerned with death as we are now. If one died fifty to one hundred years ago, he was simply left at home, not rushed to a hospital. Good neighbors came in, helped bathe and clean the body, and dressed him in his Sunday best.

In those days before funeral homes, they tried to bury the person before dark if possible. If not possible before dark, and they were held over to the next day, the odor would start. Generally, while neighbors were tending to the body, other friends or relatives would build a coffin. A few people could afford to have an extra box built out of pine to place the coffin in.

Some people were simply buried without a preacher or sermon, which seems sad, but most had a preached sermon. Many people compared life with the seasons of the year.

There are many beliefs of death—probably more than you could write in a book. An aunt told me of a relative dying when she was younger, and the cats started meowing very loud and long without stopping. She also said she had heard when small that cats would eat a dead person, but she doubted that.

People used to say if they dreamed of a wedding there would be a death shortly. Have you ever had your ears to ring? Some say these are death bells and that someone died. A farmer may say if a rooster crows three times before dawn, someone is going to die.

Of course, the gamblers or gypsies believe that if you are dealt the ace of spades, it means death. But that's probably only superstition, but many people think they have premonitions of death, and sometimes it comes true. It makes you wonder, doesn't it?

Robin Hooper

Zach William Hooper was a coffin maker. He was also my father. When someone died, the family notified him. He would build the coffin. I can remember having to hold a lantern all night on many occasions while he finished a coffin for someone to be buried the next day. He could make real nice coffins, or just plain ones. It just depended on how much time he had to build it.

I can remember the children saying that a bad person's coffin was built out of chinquapin wood. This was said because this type of wood pops when it's burned.

As for the direction of the graves, the feet are east of the head. The face is looking into the east so it looks into the rising sun.

There is a man in the Timpson cemetery that is buried crossways with the other people. He went crossways with the rest of the people all his life, so they buried him that way.

Floy H. Latham

My father, James L. Heaton, better known as Jim Heaton, was a carpenter and farmer. By 1890, at age twenty, my father was already known as a good carpenter, and people began coming to him to make coffins for their dead. In those times, funeral homes and ready-made coffins were unknown in these parts.

The material used in making a coffin and the vault was a good grade of pine lumber, one by twelve inches, known as boxing plank. After the wooden coffin was made, the inside was padded with cotton and lined with soft, white, silky material. The tacks, color of the material, were placed in an orderly pattern. Inside was tacked a winding sheet of the same material to cover the deceased. A small pillow was placed at the head. Around the top edge and hanging inside was white lace, and over this on the top edge was one-inch satin ribbon. The inside of the lid was covered with the same material.

The outside of the coffin was covered with the best grade of white or gray or black sateen. White was used for babies and young people, while gray and black was used for older ones.

The decorations or ornaments were beautiful. They looked like highly polished silver. There were pretty handles on the sides. Around the edge of the lid was lace and ribbon, and on top a lot of ribbon. The ribbon was tacked with metal screws on the lid, and on the upper center was placed a large, beautiful rectangular plate with an inscription such as "Our Darling," "Our Love," etcetera.

When a request was made for a coffin to be built, the measurements of the deceased was brought so the coffin was made to fit. The measurement was usually taken on a piece of cane fishing pole. Material was brought, and men came to help. Mr. Jesse McGee was an excellent helper, and Uncle Dave Heaton was good. Most of the men knew nothing about coffin building and were more or less in the way.

My mother cooked lunch for the men. She made the winding sheet, scalloped and notched it. When I was old enough to use scissors, I helped. Sometimes, neighbor women came in to help with the sheet.

One day, when the men had gone to the house for lunch, two of my brothers, John and Ebb, and a Negro boy, John Alex Williams, who lived on our place, decided to take a look at the coffin. They thought it looked rather small. Since John Alex was about the size of the deceased, John and Ebb decided to put the Negro boy in the coffin to see if it was the right size. John Alex had other ideas, and of all the kicking, fighting, squirming, he put it out! You can guess that the boy was not used for size. It would have been much easier to have put a wild Brahma yearling in the coffin.

My brother Doyce who was about three years of age, went to town with Mama one day. Back in Hull's store was a long-bearded elderly man who had palsy badly. Doyce was afraid of this man and hid behind Mama's skirt. Every time he peeped around, the man, shaking badly, was looking straight at him. The man was fond of children and wanted to be friendly, but he was scaring the kid half to death. About three weeks later, one cold day with snow on the ground, a man in a top buggy stopped at our place. Being curious, Doyce went with my dad to the door, and lo and behold, there was that bearded man! The child thought he had come for him. Down the hall and out the back door the boy scooted. Really, this was not the man who was seen at town. This bearded man had come for my father to make a coffin for a baby. It being so cold, the coffin was made in the house. After it was finished, they noticed that Doyce was missing and began a search. He was found in the hen house half frozen.

There were times when people would be waiting for a coffin to be made before my father had finished the one on which he was working. I have seen him work on them all day and all night. He made them for people far and near. He made hundreds of them.

While he was in town one day, a friend asked him to make a coffin for a relative. He said, "All right. Get someone to help me. We'll make it at the lumberyard." Soon another carpenter was there to help. The man had hardly come up when he asked, "Jim, what are we getting for this?" My dad replied, "I've been making coffins for forty years, and I haven't been paid for one yet, so I'm not expecting to be paid for this one." In a moment, my dad looked around. The man was gone. My dad remarked, "Well, I wonder who he expects to make his coffin." In a few years that was answered; the man died, and my dad built his coffin.

Since embalming was unknown, a coffin had to be made as soon as possible. Regardless of what my father was doing, if he was requested to make a coffin, he began immediately.

One time he was building Mr. Tilman Hall a new house, and he received a request for a coffin. Since the tools were at this house, the coffin was built right there. Just a little finishing work remained to be done when my dad went home for a little sleep. Taylor Hall, the oldest son, had been stopping by as he came home from work to see how the new house was coming along. It just happened that he was really late coming home that night, but he stopped by as usual. There was that coffin. Boy, oh boy! Was he seeing things?

Old-time funerals at home, at the church, and at the graveyard were quite similar to those of today. The main difference was no funeral homes, no embalming, and no hothouse flowers. The corpse was carried to the church in a two-horse or two-mule wagon by close friends of the family. Sometimes, a buggy was used if the deceased was a baby. The procession was a long line of wagons, buggies, surreys, horseback riders, etcetera. Homegrown flowers, if any were in season, were used. Friends dug and covered the grave. The older people of this vicinity will remember Mr. Will Laird as being the one who put the finishing touch to the grave. He made it look very nice, indeed.

Mrs. Mildred Beheler

I remember that people had a belief that cats would eat the body of a dead person. Well, my grandmother had a lot of cats. When she died, they didn't find her for two or three days. The cats had not touched her, although they had been in the house all the time. Another thing that is strange about her death is that she had a Civil War sword hung over the head of her bed. It had hung there for years and never made any attempt to fall off the wall. When they found her, she was clear across the room from her bed where the sword had fallen on her pillow.

Ellen Starkey

One time I was walking down the path from a friend's house, and a white horse appeared in front of me on the trail. The next night my husband died, and I figured this was an omen of his death.

Teresa Ritter

When a shooting star starts, it is a sign of death.

When a person is on a dying bed and calls a loved one's name that is already dead, they are fixing to die.

When a person is on the deathbed, and their life flashes in front of them, they are going to die.

Mable Clark

I was riding in a wagon down an old road, and a fireball rolled across in front of me, not over twenty feet away. Then it rolled off in the woods. Three times this happened. Right then my father died in the living room at home. We didn't have much of a mourning period, because it was right in crop time, and the crop had to be harvested.

Mrs. Billie Robinson

A sign of death is if you dream of a wedding; you will hear of a death. And after someone in the family dies, the clock will stop. Another sign of a death is if you hear three knocks on the door; you will hear of a death in the family.

The coffins were made out of different kinds of wood, such as pine, cedar, etcetera. They were different shapes. They would go pick flowers and put them in a vase with water at the grave. There was nowhere to buy them.

The body laid in rest at their home, usually in the living room or parlor. Then people would come and stay up all night with them.

The mourning period was from one to two years. The wife wore black or dark clothing to the funeral. Men carried the body to a wagon and took it to the graveyard. The wagon went first, and the others came in line after it.

Tom Havard

During the 1920's, Tom Antley and Holden Havard built coffins in Gary in the back of a store in their spare time. Mr. Havard had a tailor shop. He used steam from the steam cloth press to shape the boards for the coffins.

Mr. Havard's wife helped in coffin making by putting in the lining, such as silk, lace, old quilts, etcetera. They usually used pine and sweet gum, or whatever they could get for the coffins. They built the lid for the coffins flat in the shape of the coffin. They put the lid on with four screws.

Herman Venson

When I was young, I can remember that it rained three days in a row. On the third day, when the rain had stopped, Pa and I went outside. We looked up at the sky to see if it might rain again that night. Well, when we looked up at the sky, we saw three doves. My pa's face turned sort of black, which it always did when he got mad or was afraid of something. He looked at me and kind of mumbled something about something terrible going to happen tonight. I didn't quite understand what he was talking about right then.

When we went inside, my mother saw how he was looking. She asked, kind of weaklike, "What in the good Lord's name is wrong?" Pa just looked at her and said kind of weakly that something terrible and black was going to happen tonight. Ma asked him why he thought so. He said that for one thing, it had rained for three days in a row. When he had gone outside to see if there was any chance of it raining again the coming night, he had seen three doves flying around. Ma and Pa just looked at each other for a while; then we heard the tolling of the church bells. We sat there listening and counting the bells. The bell had rung thirty-two times when we heard a knock at the door. Pa jumped up and ran over to the door to answer it. There was a man at the door who was about out of breath. He looked at Pa and told him that something bad happened. Pa told him to come in. The man sat down, looked over at Pa, and told him kind of slowly that Pa's brother had died.

Pa sat there a little while. Then he got up and went to the door. When he got to the door, he turned around and told Ma that he was going on over to his brother's house to help get his brother ready. He wanted Ma and me to wait until morning to come and bring some food with us. When we got there the next morning, they had cleaned out the parlor. My uncle was on one side of the room, and there were chairs placed all around the room. My uncle must have known that Death was coming after him, because the week before, he had gone down to the general store and bought him a casket for five dollars.

I was trying to find me a mirror to comb my hair in, but couldn't find one. I asked Pa where one was. He said that they had been taken down and put up. I asked him why, and he said that if you saw your reflection in the mirror after someone in your family had died, you would be the next one to die.

I went back in the parlor to see my uncle, and he had pennies over his eyelids. Pa said that was to keep his eyes from opening. That evening, they buried him with his feet facing the east. They took him to the cemetery in a wagon that was draped in black. We mourned his death for two weeks.

Bobby Reider

When a person died, the neighbors bathed the corpse, shaved and cut its hair. They then dressed the corpse in the best clothes they had. The corpse then was laid out on a cooling board until just before the funeral. Then they were placed in the coffin. The coffin usually wasn't finished until just before the funeral. The funeral service was held either in the church or at the graveside.

If a person died with their eyes open, they wouldn't stay closed. So usually quarters were placed on the eyelids to hold them closed. Also, a rag was tied around their head to hold the mouth closed.

Sometimes when a person was dying, they were in such pain that it took several people to hold them on the bed. People sat up in shifts of hours.

A cat was not allowed in the house at any time that the corpse was in the house. The belief was that a cat would eat the corpse's eyeballs out.

The coffin was made of soft pine or cedar, depending on what was available. Sometimes they would hand-dress rough lumber with a plane. Jim Heaton and Frank Walton made most of the coffins in this community. The coffin was lined usually with a black material on the outside. The inside was padded with cotton, then also lined with what color cloth the family had. A bow of ribbon was put on the coffin. People would bring flowers from their yards.

The coffin was loaded in a wagon, then a sheet was placed over the coffin with a quilt placed over the sheet. Two men usually rode in the wagon seat, and usually someone sat in a chair beside the coffin. The people would ride to the cemetery in wagons and horseback. Four men lowered the coffin into the grave with ropes. Just before the corpse was lowered in the grave, the lid was nailed on the coffin.

Mrs. Faye Humber

For many, many years, people have believed that if an owl perched on or sat on top of your house at night and hooted or screeched, there would be a death in the family within twenty-four hours. Still others believed if you swivel a cane-bottom chair or rocker around, tilted to the side, there would be a death or critical illness within twelve hours. We always got rid of a hen that crowed, because this also meant death within the immediate family.

Another belief which one can notice will almost always be true is when there is one death in the community, there will be three close or within a week. This is true most always. So many people say they have dreams or premonitions of deaths. Many come to pass exactly as they dream.

We must all agree, though, certainly, that there's a higher power that controls our lives, if we but seek His guidance and will in each of our lives.

Country Epitaphs

*I am not afraid to meet my God,
Friends, how is it with you?*

Texas pioneers sleep in thousands of country cemeteries across the state. We see the cemetery signs pointing up side roads as we drive the main highways—signs to Six Mile and Snap, Red Rock, Long Branch, and High Grove. In many cases, the signs invoke the names of rural communities that themselves have passed away.

If we take the trouble to seek them out, these country cemeteries often seem to tell us more about the living than the dead—about their attitudes toward God, family, community, and the inevitable end of life. In the days before the "mow-over" gravestone, both mourners and mourned often availed themselves of a last word in epitaphs whose tones range from pathos, piety, and warning to celebration and rough humor.

An English writer named George Puttenham has well described their purpose in *The Arte of English Poesie* (1589): "An epitaph is but a kind of epigram applied to the report of the dead person's estate and degree, or of his other good and bad parts, to his commendation or reproach; and is an inscription such as a man may commodiously write or engrace upon a tombe in a few verses, pithie, quick and sententious, for the passer-by to peruse and judge upon without any long tariance."

"Pithie, quick and sententious" messages from the living and the dead, here are epitaphs from a score of country cemeteries, including Gary, Six Mile, Snap, Shady Grove, Long Branch, Boynten, Blair, Woodlawn, Mt.

The Loblolly Book

Bethel, Clayton, Greenwood, Tennessee, Mt. Olive, Macedonia, Corinth, Concord, Old Red Rock, High Grove, Alexander, and Cedar Creek.
—*Loblolly*

Country epitaphs take many forms and express a variety of emotions, but perhaps most common are those that are essentially tributes to the dead.

A life like theirs has left a record sweet
For memory to dwell upon.

Grace was on all her steps,
Heaven in her every gesture, divinity and love.

Her children rise up and call her blessed.

He did what he could.

Life's duty done, as sinks the day,
Light from its load, the Spirit flies,
While Heaven and Earth combine to say,
How blest the righteous when he dies.

Warm summer sun, shine kindly here,
Warm southern wind, blow softly here,
Green sod above, lie light, lie light,
Good night dear heart, good night, good night.

Others combine tribute to the deceased with clearly implied consolations for the survivors.

Asleep in Jesus.

God's finger touched him—and he slept.

He giveth his beloved sleep.
                Psalm 127:2

Mother and Son.
He took them from a world of care
An everlasting bliss to share

*Asleep in Jesus' blessed sleep,
From which none ever wake to weep.*

At rest with Papa.

*Farewell, Faith, Hope and Charity.
He said to me, "Mother, God will keep his promise."*

*Thou art gone, but 'twere wrong to deplore thee,
When God was thy ransom, thy guardian and guide.
He gave thee, and took thee, and soon will restore thee,
Where death has no sting, since the Savior has died.*

*The pains of death are past,
Labor and sorrow cease,
And life's long warfare closed at last,
His soul is found in peace.*

*She sleeps in the valley so deep,
But her soul has taken its flight.
Lo, her form is but dust 'neath our feet
While she is an angel of light.*

*God in his wisdom has recalled
The boon his love has given,
And though their bodies moulder here,
There souls are safe in Heaven.*

A special kind of tribute epitaph is that directed at those patriots who fell in war.

*He stands in the unbroken line of
Patriots who have dared to die that
Freedom might live.*

In Tender Living Memory of Uncle Cap

*The grave of a southern hero,
Who fought for love and right;
He was as brave a soldier
As ever dared to fight.*

*He led the Leon Hunters,
That noble, gallant band,
Who sallied forth to battle
For home and fair southland.*

Country Epitaphs

He followed Hood and Longstreet
Through sunny Tennessee,
To Appomattox Courthouse.
Yes, he was there with Lee.

He was just a captain in the ranks;
History scarcely tells his story.
He stacked his arms on Jordan's banks
And went to Heaven for glory.

Rest in Pattaya Beach, Thailand,
Grandson.

Sometimes the living speak directly to the dead in country epitaphs, vowing to meet them again "on that other shore."

Death is the close of life's alarms,
The watch-light on its shores;
The clasping in immortal arms
Of loved ones gone before.
"Yes, we'll meet beyond the river."

On that bright, immortal shore
We shall meet to part no more.

Farewell dear mother
Sweet thy rest
Weary with years and
Worn with pain.
Farewell till in some happy place
We shall behold thy face again.

My love goes with you and my
Soul awaits to join you.

And sometimes, especially on the oldest gravestones, the dead speak to the living in tones consoling and cautionary.

Weep not for me.

I am not afraid to meet my God.
Friends, how is it with you?

Blessed are they that are persecuted
For theirs is the Kingdom of Heaven.
Though worms destroy this body,
Yet in my flesh shall I see God.

Go home dear friends, dry up your tears,
For here I be till Christ appears.
As I am now so you must be,
Prepare for death and follow me.

Occasionally the pains of loss overwhelm the living, and the epitaphs give vent to emotions of grief and bereavement. For example, at the grave of a fifteen-year-old bride who died in childbirth in the 1860's, we read:

In love she lived,
In peace she died.
Her life was craved,
But God denied.

Other sorrowful epitaphs read:

Rest, mother, rest in quiet sleep
While friends in sorrow oer thee weep.

Mama, your babies will miss you.
                    Papa

A precious one from us has gone,
A voice we loved is stilled,
A place is vacant in our home
Which never can be filled.

Then as now, perhaps the greatest challenge to the survivors' sense of the fitness of things was the death of children. The country graveyards often set aside a special area for children's graves—a sad reminder of the high rate of infant mortality that prevailed in the nineteenth century. But in most of the children's epitaphs, the families of the dead seem reconciled to this loss of innocents, taking refuge in their deep religious faith.

Fold him Father in thine arms
And let him henceforth be a messenger of love
Between our human hearts and Thee.

Sleep on in thy beauty,
Thy sweet angel child,
By sorrow unblightened,
By sin undefiled.

A little flower of love
That blossomed but to die,
Transplanted now above
To bloom with God on high.

Farewell, dear Sammy.

Little Tottie
Beautiful, lovely, she was but given
A fair bud on earth to blossom in Heaven.

*Sleep on dear child and take thy rest,
In Jesus' arms forever blest.*

*The soul of a child is the loveliest flower
That blooms in the garden of God.*

He is not dead, but sleepeth.

Hant Stories

You may wonder what people did for entertainment when there were no televisions, radios, movies, and not too many magazines. Well, the black man developed the art of storytelling, especially ghost stories. The highlight of the evening was to sit around the fire while roasting potatoes and peanuts in the hot ashes and to hear about the ghosts that haunted old houses and guarded buried treasures.

—Black Gold

Born in 1875, just ten years after the Civil War ended, the grandfather of one *Black Gold* staff member could spin the most hair-raising, nerve-tingling stories about "hants" that you ever heard. Among his favorites was the following, retold by his granddaughter.

On Saturday nights someone would almost always give a hoedown at their house. This was a square dance and general party where the old and the young would get together to dance, drink, and have fun. People would come from miles around to be a part of the festivities. The young people especially liked these get-togethers, for much sparking would be done. Some would come on horseback, some in buggies, and some would walk.

This particular hoedown, Granddaddy, who did not have a horse, decided he would walk instead of riding with someone else. Since he had never been to this part of the countryside, he was not too sure of the exact place the dance was being held. As Granddaddy rounded a bend in the road, he heard the sound of music and laughter coming from a house just up the road a piece. When he got closer to the house he could tell a dance was in full swing. The fiddlers were playing and someone was doing a good job of calling the set. Granddad picked up speed to reach the house and join in the fun. This was before he met Grandmama, and he was looking forward to getting in a little sparking as well as a lot of dancing. But just as he stepped up on the porch, the light in the house went out, the music and laughter stopped, and not a single sound could be heard anywhere!

Thinking that his friends were playing a joke on him, he opened the door and went inside. He called out, but no one answered. After several calls, he decided to see what was going on and spoil their trick. Granddad brought out a match to light the kerosene lamps. He struck the match and, whoosh, someone blew it out! Granddad tried again. And this time, whoosh! Out went the match! He was getting a little tired of their joke, so he turned and walked out. Just as he reached the edge of the yard, the strangest thing happened. The lights came back on, the music started again, and the dancing commenced.

Well, Granddaddy could not resist the urge to go back. He was convinced that it was some of the boys playing a joke on him. He tried again. When he stepped up on the porch, the same thing happened as before. All sound of life stopped. He went inside, tried to light a match, and, whoosh, out it went. By now Granddaddy was good and mad about the whole thing and decided that he did not want to join them if they were going to continue to play tricks on him. This time, when he reached the edge of the yard, a buggy came by and stopped. The driver, a man that Granddad knew, asked if he was going to the dance. Granddaddy inquired, "Where is the dance tonight?" His friend replied, "Oh, it's being held about two miles further down the road." With this Granddad gladly hopped in the buggy and got away from the "hanted house."

Another story Granddaddy loved to tell us took place when he was a small boy about seven or eight years old.

As the story goes, my granddad and several other boys and girls, including my granddad's sister, were playing hide-'n-seek late one afternoon. Long about dusk, they were on their last game before having to go inside. Granddaddy's sister, who was about ten years old, ran to hide in the chimney corner. The girl became so scared of something that she began running around and around the house screaming, "Mama, Mama, woman, woman! Mama, Mama, woman, woman!" By this time, the adults inside the house came out to see what was wrong. All the children were so scared they could hardly move, and of course, they did not know what was wrong with her. Near hysterics, the girl was finally rescued by their mother and told the following story. She had gone to hide in the chimney corner, as she had been doing earlier. But this time, when she tried to get in the chimney corner, she found it already occupied by a little old lady. The old woman had on a long dress, an apron, and a bonnet, and had just stood there smiling at her. She was no one the girl had ever seen before in her life. So never again did the kids run to hide in the chimney corner — especially Granddad's sister.

According to the storytellers, all ghosts were not so harmless. If the hant happened to belong to a grouchy, mean, or evil person, then their spirit might try to hurt you. There was only one way to stop a hant, and that was by not letting the hant know that you were afraid. It was believed that if you would just stand there and not run, it would go away. But it seems that almost no one had the nerve not to run! As an example of a malevolent hant, my mother used to tell us about a visitation of the spirit of her dead father. According to Mother, he was a very mean and hateful man in his lifetime.

On the night after his funeral, the family was sitting by the fireplace talking. Well, the fire burned low and needed to be replenished. For convenience, firewood was stacked outside a sliding-board window which was built right beside the fireplace. Mother's brother, who was about fifteen or sixteen years old, opened the window to get some firewood for the fire. As he tried to draw the wood through the opening of the window, it seems that something caught hold of the other end of the log and began to pull, scratch, and claw on the wood. After several attempts to get the wood inside, my mother's brother gave up and quickly shut the window. Then the scratching and clawing grew so fierce that it frightened them almost out of their wits! Much too afraid to try to spend the night in the house, the three of them — my mother, her brother, and their mother — slipped out the back door and headed across the field to the neighbor's house. Soon the ghost discovered they were escaping and took up a hot pursuit. They could hear him running and panting, trying to catch them. Fear had put wings on their feet, and they were running for life. Finally, they came to a little old creek and jumped across to the other side and safety. According to my mother, this is the only thing that saved them from the horrible clutches of the hant. When it reached the stream of water, it stopped. They could hear it shrieking and panting. Hants could not cross a running stream of water.

The next day they came back and moved their belongings to another house and was never again bothered by Grandpa's spirit.

The old folks told many bloodcurdling tales about hants and other things with supernatural powers. As the previous story illustrates, they believed that hants could not cross running streams of water. Thus, if a person being chased by a ghost would cross a stream of water, they would be saved.

It was also believed that persons hid great sums of money in the ground under old stumps and underneath houses, in pots and buckets. After that person's death, their spirit would come back to guard the treasure and haunt the hiding place. If someone was lucky enough to be led to the treasure, there were certain rules which had to be followed in order to get the treasure out of its hiding place. First, the ghost would appear in various shapes in order to frighten the person away from the site. Instead of becoming frightened and being chased away when these weird things would appear, the question "What in the name of the Lord do you want?" was to be asked. Secondly, while digging for the treasure, regardless of what kind of ghost appeared, the rule was to say nothing but this one question. As the stories go, extraordinary things would appear, and tales were told of huge treasures being unearthed, only to sink out of sight when a digger became so overcome with joy or fear that he forgot and said something. Needless to say, the tests were always too hard to pass and no one ever got to keep the buried treasure.

One of my dad's favorite stories about hidden treasure was the following:

It seems that a white landowner had a tenant house that was haunted by a ghost who was guarding a buried treasure. Because of this, he couldn't get anybody to stay there and farm the land for him. So he offered a big reward for anyone who could stay there all night and do away with the hant once and for all.

Many tried and failed, but there was this one man who felt he could do it. He got some supplies together and moved into the house. He built a fire in the fireplace, put his coffeepot on the fire, made him a bed on the floor, and took out his Bible and lay down to read.

After a little while, the first hant appeared in the form of a long black snake. The man looked up and then continued to read, ignoring the snake. It disappeared.

Later, another hant appeared—this time a big black bull with red eyes. The bull came in pawing and snorting. Again the man ignored the ghost, and it went away.

By now it was getting to be about two o'clock in the morning. The man had grown tired and sleepy and had dozed off to sleep when he heard the door open and close. In came this man with no head who walked up to the fire and put his hands to warm them. As he did this, he turned to the man and said, "It's kinda cold tonight, ain't it?" This time the man was scared half to death. He reached and got his Bible and ran out the door. He ran for several miles until he was too tired to run anymore, then stopped and sat down on an old tree log and let out a long sigh. At this, he heard the hant say, "Whew, that was some race, wasn't it?" The man jumped up and said, "Hell, you ain't had no race yet!"

A lot of unexplainable things were considered as being supernatural. For instance, warm air spots were regarded as hants or the spirits of someone who had died quite recently.

There were reports of strange lights, clanking chains, and dogs and horses—even snakes—appearing out of nowhere and disappearing the same way. Big black bulls with red eyes, men with no heads, black cats, and big white birds were all figures used to illustrate ghostly shapes and hants. It was commonly thought that if a hant called someone by name, that person would die very soon.

Ed Bell: Truths and Windy Tales

Ed Bell was born in 1905 and spent his early life on the headwaters of the Frio River in Real County. His family settled on several hundred acres near Seawillow in Caldwell County in the early 1900's. Mr. Bell and his wife, Alma, live at the foot of Iron Mountain, where they raise cattle and tend their large fruit orchard and garden.

> —*The Plum Creek Press*
> With Thad Sitton

Truths

My daddy was a kind of a broncobuster when he was a young man. He had to be with that horse ranch. And Mama was the doctor. How could you afford a doctor in those days? A doctor would charge about five dollars just to come out and see us. Once Papa was riding a mean horse—he wasn't really a bad bucker; he was just mean—and he reared up and went over backwards on my father. My father'd usually jump out of the saddle quick enough, but that time he didn't manage it, and the saddle hit across his leg, the thigh bone, and broke the bone. There it was, sixteen miles from a doctor. No telephone. The nearest neighbor lived eight miles across the mountains, but that was two or three hours away.

So Mama got him and got some sticks all ready and set the bone herself. Put the splints on his leg, bound him down there, and made him as comfortable as she could. By that time, it was too late to go get the doctor. The next morning she hooked the team up to the surrey and made the trip down there pretty fast. She let that team out and they would run. The doctor told her that he wasn't going out that fast, and he had to take his

Ed Bell talking non-stop

rig. So, anyway, they got back, seem to me like it was around noontime or later. Well, he got out there and checked my daddy over. He took the splints loose a little bit and felt of them, put them back in place and said, "Mrs. Bell, you've done everything that I could do. There's nothing in the world I could do more than you have. Now, I'm going to give you a little bit of advice how to take care of him. You see that he stays still for two or three more days till that bone begins to knit." So she did. She watched over him like a hawk there and took care of him. At the end of three or four days, she'd let him go out on the porch.

Well, by that time we was out of provisions. No groceries to eat at all. Done fixed the last of everything. I think we lived one day on flour gravy. So Papa said, "Mama" (he always called her Mama) "Mama, I'm going out on that porch, and I'm going to kill a buck." That's a he-deer, you know. He took his .38 Winchester out there with him. Well, the approximate distance that a .38 will hold up is hardly two hundred yards, and they're not a bit accurate after two hundred yards. So my father set out there a little while. First thing you know, you hear "bang!" There wasn't no other shot. We all ran out on the porch with Mama, the ones that could—Susie and I was old enough to get out there. Arnolia was a baby; she was too small to even wiggle off the bed. So we got out there, and Papa said, "Mama, he was on the other end of that open glade over yonder on the side of the mountain. It's a little too far. I was a-getting kinda hungry; I shot him and knocked him down. He got up and come across this little creek over here and went into that blind canyon."

So Mama took Susie and I and went on down to that blind canyon, and just as she walked into it, she set us up on a little ledge about even with her head. She took the butcher knife and started towards that deer, and him just standing there. I could see froth and blood coming out of his nose. He looked wicked to me. I just knew he was going to kill Mama; she couldn't fight that deer. But she had the two dogs, and they was well trained. They were traveling on each side of her kinda half-crouched, watching that deer. Well, that deer throwed up his head, shook his horns, and here he come pounding right towards Mama. She says, "Git 'm!" And those two dogs hit him! They got that deer by the side of the head, and he just turn a flip. As he went by Mama, she reached out with that butcher knife and ripped his throat. Hoofs just a-flying, dogs and deer everywhere. She cut that deer's throat just as he hit the ground.

Then she grabbed him and went to skinning him out. She'd skin out a quarter at a time, and then she'd take Susie and I and go over to the house. I believe it was three or four hundred yards anyhow. She'd hang it up over there, then she'd take us two kids, go skin out another quarter. She brought in that whole deer that way before she stopped to cook something to eat. We hadn't had anything to eat in about two days but a little gravy and bread. We had plenty of flour. In those days you bought flour by the hundred pounds, or by the hog's head.

Mama says I can't remember it, but I remember every bit of it just as though it was yesterday. I remember lots of things that happened up at the ranch. I remember I was six years old when we moved away.

I was born on the head of the Frio River in 1905. The big springs of the Frio is in my daddy's ranch. Thirty-three hundred acres in there and those beautiful, beautiful springs. Papa traded the ranch up there for about a hundred-and-some-odd acres down there on Plum Creek river bottom near a little place called Seawillow. It was just before the beginning of the First World War, and we moved out to Seawillow by train from Sabinal. It's a distance of 145 miles, and it took thirteen days to make the trip. My father had taken the top off of an old surrey and built a big chicken coop on it. And he had two wagons, so he loaded one of the wagons with plow tools and implements and hardware and heavy stuff. The other wagon wasn't loaded very heavy, had mostly room in there to sleep. We had to have room to sleep, you know, if it was misting rain or anything. Both wagons were covered over with big wagon sheets.

We had a herd of cows, two or three small calves, and a bunch of chickens. Well, my father hooked up a four-up team to his wagon because it was heavy. And these cows, us boys drove them, and we had one saddle horse. We'd take turn about riding this saddle horse. We'd just plod along and let the old horse graze. Thirteen miles a day, approximate, because my father knew every water hole on the entire trip, and we'd make it to a water hole. If we got there at four o'clock, we'd camp. If we got there at six o'clock, we'd camp. We just made it to a water hole. In those days, just lay down and drink the water out of the river. It was perfectly all right.

He kept that place on Plum Creek for, well, it was during the war, and we was nearly starving to death because you couldn't hardly get any flour, and I don't remember what all was scarce. So Papa traded the place on Plum Creek for an old half-section piece of sand hills. It wasn't very good land, but they had about forty-five head of fat hogs, and the whole place was fenced hogproof. The first thing we did after they consummated the deal was to move a load of stuff over here. My father and I brought a load apiece, and we butchered a big hog.

We got this butchered hog back over to Seawillow, and my mother baked one of those big old hams. And she just cut a big slab of it off to keep there with them and sent all the rest of it with us on the next trip over. Well, my father thought I was a good driver, so he had me drive a wagon and he drove a wagon. We both of us had a drinking-water jug in the wagon, always in those times, you know, because it might be two or three hours between water holes, maybe ten! Well, we got over here and unloaded and started back, and Papa says, "Well, it's about noontime. Let's eat." I still didn't know what that ham would taste like. I got one bite of it in my mouth, and I went crazy. I could see red, blue, yellow, everything in the world. I began to just guzzle it, and Papa says, "Here, Buddy, slow down, slow down! I know you're hungry for meat, but, hey, take it easy!" Well, I slowed down a little bit.

Finally, Papa told me after about the third slice, "Son, that's pork. I'm afraid it's going to make you sick." Well, I didn't care much whether it made me sick or not, you know how a boy is. We got in the wagon and started on back toward Seawillow, and we hadn't gone but about a mile till my stomach began just to wind up. It come around about three times, and then it began to tighten. It come on down, and pretty soon I thought I was going to die. I just couldn't imagine what was going to happen. I couldn't vomit; I couldn't do nothing. And the sweat was popping out all over me. I was a sick human. Papa was on down there ahead, and it was pretty hard to whip the old team up and make them trot because they was used to walking. I knew I couldn't get any help from Papa. Well, I looked down at that water jug and reached down and took a drink of it, and everything was all right immediately. And I found out now when I eat too much fresh pork, take a drink of water and everything just straightens out, all right.

Us kids knew where everything to eat was in the country. My father never would have enough, you know, for ten kids, really. But we knew where good fine grapes were. And we knew where the persimmons grew over at the Old Britton Field, knew where the big mulberry trees were that made the finest mulberries. We knew which kinds of grass we could dig up that had nuts on the bottom—we could eat it. We knew where the wild onions grew and the wild lettuce—it just leafs, it don't make a head at all. We just might nearly lived off the land. It's absolutely unbelievable that people could learn to live off the land so much.

But there's nut grass out here that makes little nodules on the bottom. And these old bull nettles that sting so bad, that's the best coconut in the world. Oh, those seed are out of this world for eating! You've got a little trouble getting them, but you learn how not to get stung much by them. We made medicine out of what we call ice weeds: those weeds that grow up about four or five foot high. And when it comes a freeze, the stalk will bust open at the bottom and shoot icicles all around there. That's the reason we call them ice weeds. The roots of that are good medicine, awfully good. My mother was always fixing her own kind of medicine out here. She gave us several different kinds. She also showed us how to make chewing gum. We had great times out here in these hills when we was kids.

I made a bale of cotton one year. I think I got a hundred dollars for it. Man, I was real rich. And I'd been riding a burro. Us kids rode burros to school. Why, I'd ride a burro all the way to Luling! So one day Papa says, "Buddy, you've been wanting a horse and saddle, we might as well go to Luling and get you one." Right in there close to Frank's feed store used to be a great big corral. Horse traders would come in there and put in their horses and trade them and sell them. Well, anyway, we got down to Luling that day, and I said, "Papa, there's the horse I want! There's the horse I want! Isn't he pretty, fat, and round?" And Papa went over and felt of him and said, "Buddy, you don't want that horse." I said, "Why not, Papa?" He said, "He's been fattened on soda, and he's been fistuloed." Papa said, "This horse here, if you don't feed him soda all his life, he will just waste away and die. He's been fattened on soda, and so you've got to keep him on soda." Well, I'd never heard much about how they soda-fat a horse 'cause Papa wouldn't do it. He refused to. If a horse had to die, now, he just had to die. He didn't keep him alive on soda.

Well, he looked over on the side, and he said, "Buddy, here's the horse you need." Well, it was an old, gaunt white horse. He was regal, all right. He looked like he had a lot of Arabian stock in him. He sure could have been a beauty, but he was all rawboned, back stuck up in the way, you know, and his great big old knees on his front legs. I asked, wasn't his knees fistuloed. But Papa says, "No, Son, they don't fistula on their knees." He says, "That's a cow pony past ordinary. They've roped a lot of big bulls on this horse and jerked him to his knees. That's what's made his knees big." He said, "You can ride this horse all day, and he'll stand up to it. That horse over there, you'd kill him the first day you got on him."

I didn't like the idea a darn bit because, lookee here, there was that prettiest horse in the lot, and he wasn't any good, and this old rawboned horse was. I gave thirty-five dollars for the horse; now, that was a top price. Then we went down there, and Walker Brothers, I believe, was the one that had saddles then. Well, Papa let me pick the saddle pretty well. He told me two grades of saddles was about all that was real good. So I picked out one of them, and Papa says, "Well, that one's gonna cost you a little more because it's got a lot of handwork on it, but it's as good a saddle as the other one."

Forty-five dollars! Forty-five dollars for a saddle! My golly, you'd ought to been able to buy one for ten dollars, the price of everything else.

I was right at sixteen when I got this horse. I was topping out as somewhat of a man, and I thought I was. I was feeling my oats! I don't know why; I couldn't go with the girls. The girls scared me. They didn't want to have much to do with me, and they'd kinda joke about me being awkward or something or other. But around the boys, now, I figured I was one of the men, one of the boys! I would go to Harwood on this old white horse, Old Gray, as I called him. Gray Eagle was his name. I'd ride Old Gray Eagle down there and fish in my pocket and bring out the cigar that I'd bought last trip to town. And just before I went out on Main Street, I'd unwrap that cigar and light it up, the old kitchen matches, you know. I'd hit Main Street, and I'd put my heels in this old horse's flank and jerk up on the reins, and he'd prance, single-foot, right down Main Street of Harwood. And the boys would say, "Look at Old Bell. Ain't he hot stuff on his pony." Oh, can you imagine! Back in those days that was the tops if a boy had a good saddle pony. It's just the same as if you have the finest, flashiest roadster ever built now.

I went to school down here at Rock Waterhole, and Hall School, until I got to the eighth grade. My daddy wanted me to go to Lockhart, and I wanted to go to Lockhart, so I went there. That's the year that those Page boys were ramping in football. Silly to think about staying out here and going to school. Time I could of rode a horse to Lockhart, why, school would be turning out. I went up to Lockhart, and I got a job working at the old Greasenbeck Hotel. There's not very many people know anything about that, because it burned down a year or two after I was there. But I didn't burn it. I believe I would have, if it hadn't been for that old lady, Miss Clara. The Old Lady Greasenbeck was a wonderful person, and Miss Clara was, too. But Miss Cordy was the schoolteacher type. Snap at you and growl. I couldn't stand that!

They give me a little room there. I think it was four by six. I think it'd been a closet. They put a cot in there, and I slept in that little old room, with not a light good enough to even read by, not a table to write on. I wrote on my knees if I did any writing.

I sawed all the wood, and they fired everything with wood. I mowed all the grass. When I caught up with that, I mowed the brother's grass over there, somewhere. On Fridays or Saturdays or Sundays, I forget which day, they had ice cream. They had a five-gallon ice cream outfit. I'd get out there, and I'd crank that old thing till I give plumb out. And Miss Cordy would come out and bawl me out every once in a while. I'd try to speed up a little bit, but my arms was falling off. You'd crank it for two and a half to three hours to make that ice cream; finally get the ice cream made, and she'd give me one little bitty dipper! That's all I could get. Miss Clara came by and she said, "Ed, is that all the ice cream you could get?" Because I couldn't eat in the dining room, now, with the paying guests, I'd eat in the kitchen. I said, "That's all Miss Cordy would give me." "Oh, Ed, what a shame, a growing boy can eat more than that." So, she grabbed that dipper and put four of them on my plate. Wait a minute, now! There was that Miss Cordy in there, and she was going to be back in just a minute, and she'd see all that ice cream, and I'd stole it! She wouldn't have it any other way. I just poured it down my throat. I liked to choked to death on that ice cream, trying to get rid of it before Miss Cordy would get back in there.

The same with meatballs. You know a young fellow like that, he's growing, he just sure does want to eat. I was trying to train for football, too. Miss Cordy'd give me one little meatball, and a little bitty helping of spaghetti. Well, the old lady come in, Mama Greasenbeck. Just as nice as she could be. She's always looking out for young folks, motherly type. She says, "Ed, is that all you're going to eat?" I says, "That's all Miss Cordy will let me have." "Well, that's silly, a growing boy, our guests eat two or three of them apiece." And she just put four of them over on my plate. Well, I liked to choked to death trying to eat that stuff up before Miss Cordy would get back in there, because I'd steal it, you know. I'd be stealing it!

I got in trouble with Miss Cordy and had to leave anyhow, after being so careful about not letting her catch me stealing ice cream or meatballs. One day I was out there, and "Ed! Oh, Ed! Come here!" I went around and hunted her up, and I said, "What do you want, Miss Cordy?" "I didn't call you!" I looked at her, and I know I was mad, but I just ducked my head and went back to raking leaves on the back side of the house. I was raking and raking and raking and raking. "Ed! Oh, Ed! Come here!" That's the way she always called me, just exactly. So, I went around there and asked her. And she said, "Are you going crazy or something? I did not call you!" I was fixing to sass her, but I knew better because I would have been run off right quick.

So, I went to raking leaves. I was raking faster because I was mad! I was getting after them leaves, come on around the corner, and all at once, "Ed! Oh, Ed! Come here!" I looked up there, and there was that darned parrot. She'd been calling me so much, the parrot got to mimicking her. He called me just like she did. But it didn't do him no good when he's right over me, because I saw him. I caught him in the act. So, I went ahead raking leaves and in a minute, "Ed! Oh, Ed! Come here!" I just kept on raking leaves, naturally. "Ed! Oh, Ed! Come here!" I just wished somebody would wring that darned parrot's neck. About that time, Miss Cordy grabbed me by the shoulder and spun me around and said, "Are you completely deaf, or you just don't want to hear me?" I said, "I've been going to you all morning when I heard you call." And I said, "I found out it was that darned parrot." And I said, "I can't go anymore because I never know whether it's you or the parrot, and I'm not going to go to a parrot calling." She says, "You're getting so snotty and absolutely miserable." Says, "I'll just have to let you go." So I had to quit.

Well, I was putting in four hours every evening and all day Saturday and all day Sunday working for her. Now, in those days, in those times, it was from daylight till dark. It wasn't even sunup to sundown; it was daylight till dark. I couldn't study my lessons. I had no time to study anything whatever. I made the first red mark I ever got on a report card in my life, except for deportment. I used to get red ones very often on deportment, but not on my studies. B, $B+$, A, and $A+$—that was all I was ever used to. Now, I get a red mark. It broke my heart, but what could I do? I can't study. The teacher at school kind of rectified it. She found out what I was doing, and she got me to stay in during recess and periods, and she'd help me. I got to getting a little bit better, but here I am now, without a place to stay.

I went to canvassing town, and I'd got acquainted with a man in a rooming house, right on the square, about over Bill's Dollar Store or pretty close to that. South side of the square in Lockhart. So I went over there and asked him, and he said, "Ed, I can't feed you." He says, "Really, I'm starving to death. I don't know where my next meal is coming from." But he says, "I'll let you have a nice room if you'll sweep up the rooming house." I said, "I'll sure gladly do that."

So I did. I had about four bits in my pockets. Man, that run out in a hurry, but on the weekend I didn't have to stay there; he let me go home. I went home and I told my daddy what was going on. He said, "Son, I don't have any money. I really don't know what money looks like, hardly. But Holland Page owes me a little money on a plow." He says, "I told him he didn't have to pay at that time, and I hate to ask anybody, but I'll go by and see if he can't pay some on that plow." Well, everybody was in hard shape then, you know. I guess even Holland Page was. Papa went to Holland Page and talked to him, and Holland let my daddy have five dollars, which, back in those days, about equaled two hundred now, I guess. Papa gave me the "two hundred dollars," and he went on back home. He didn't have any money. I don't know how they was living, but they were living pretty good.

I got this five dollars and went down to the store and immediately just socked in a bunch of that. I got a half gallon of Brer Rabbit syrup, and a loaf of bread, I believe, something to eat for bread, anyway. So, I went back out there, and immediately the school started hollering for writing paper, pencils, this and that, you know. Man, I'd look at that five dollars, and I'd go down to the store, and I'd sure hate to pay ten, fifteen, or twenty cents for something. But it just had to be done. It was sucking all that money away.

By the time the bread was gone, about two days, most of that five dollars was already gone. I still didn't have quite everything I needed. I promised the teachers I'd try to get them as soon as I could. I didn't tell them I didn't have any money; I didn't want to tell them that. I lived for five days on that half-gallon bucket of Brer Rabbit syrup. I'd turn it up to my mouth and drink a little of it. I got to where I'd gag and my stomach would turn over in knots every time I'd think about drinking any Brer Rabbit syrup. Papa came up there, and I told him about things. I said, "Papa, I think I'll go back home. I just can't make it this way any longer. I can't drink that Brer Rabbit syrup any more!"

Windy Tales

"True to a certain point, then it just couldn't help itself; it just busted loose."

The Mud Hole

This old boy was riding down the road, and he says, "Man, that's the awfulest-looking mud hole I ever saw in my life!" It was down there on that coast country. "I know that that mud's awful deep out there." Says, "Look, there's a new Stetson hat out there! I don't know how in the world I'll get to it, but I'm not gonna risk bogging this horse down." So he eased the horse over pretty close and got off of the horse and picked that hat up. And there's a man's head in it! The man looked up at him and said. "What're you doing, fellow, taking my hat away from me?" He said, "Excuse me, I had no idea that there was anybody under that hat." Man says, "Well, fellow, I got a damn good horse under me!"

The Tobacco Chewer

There was an old man over east of here named Lewis—the place is still called Lewis Ranch. That old man often told me all kinds of things that happened. I guess maybe it's happened to some other people. He had a friend that come to see 'm every once and a while, and the fellow just chawed Brown Mule tobacco all the time. Either that or Horseshoe if he couldn't get Brown Mule. So, he just spit whenever he got ready to spit—he spit!

Well, this Old Man Lewis hated to ask him in the house. His wife said, "If you ask him in, you got to get that spittoon out for him." So he got this spittoon. It's brass, and his wife had it polished up just as pretty as it could be. So he set it down there, kind of between Old Man Lewis and his company. So the old man was talking this big windy tale, and chompin' on that tobaccer. He started to spit, and he leant over, and there was that spittoon—pretty, clean spittoon! So he just spit on the other side, right on the floor.

Well, that woman had that floor just as pretty and clean as it could be. Course, now, it wasn't really pretty, an old rough floor like they have in the country, but it was clean. It was real clean. You could've eat off the floor, but you sure couldn't eat off it no more, 'cause that tobacco juice just splattered! Oh, she like to died right there. She run over there and got that spittoon and took it over and put it down on the other side where she'd had it first. Well, that old guy was busy talking and didn't pay much attention, and he got ready to spit—and there was that spittoon! So he turned around and he spit again the other way. She run over and got it and put it over there. So, he was busy telling these tales, and he happened to remember that that thing was in the way and not to spit, and he turned around there—he had already started to spit—and he saw that thing, and the spit run down his chin. And he wiped it off good as he can. And he said, "If you don't keep that dang thing out of the way, I'm gonna spit right in it!"

The Bee Tree

I was working down in the woods—I don't remember whether or not I was possum hunting, coon hunting, or just looking around. Anyway, right on the other side of Rock Waterhole Branch was a tree that was so stupendously big, that I had no idea of a tree like that in the country. I could see that tree fifty feet on each side of center, and I don't know how big it might have been. I never did really measure it to see how big it was. But it was a golly-to-whopper! I rared back looking up there trying to see how high it was, and about that time I noticed this black wave just coming out of a holler limb on it—great big old holler. I said, "That's bees! That's a bee tree! That's the biggest bee tree I ever heard of. There ain't no telling how much honey is in that tree."

So, I come back and told Papa about it. Course Papa said, "Son, you let your imagination run away with you all the time. I wish you'd quit talking tales like that because ain't nobody gonna believe you." I said, "Papa, the tree's there, do you mind if we go down and cut it?" "You and who?" he said. "Papa, I believe I can get Parm Williams and Alec Ford to go with me to cut it." "Well," he says, "if they're crazy enough to go down there to cut a tree that big, why, just go ahead." I said, "Papa, we'll be gone at least a week." He says, "Why, it's only just two or three miles down there, Son." I says, "Yeah, but it's gonna take a long time to cut that tree." He says, "You know, I guess that'll be all right. You can take old Buster and old Flaxie and the wagon and go down there."

So put on a bunch of camp stuff, our cooking utensils. Alec Ford and Parm Williams were just tickled to death to get to go out for a week's outing down on Rock Waterhole Branch. We loaded everything up, and we got all the barrels we could find, all the tubs, dishpans, buckets, just everything we could find—even took some fruit jars along. We was gonna put honey in all those things! Course, Papa and Mama both laughed at us for taking that much vessels to catch honey in.

Anyway, we got down there, and we had to cross Rock Waterhole Branch twice going down there or go about three miles out of the way. It made such big bends, you see. I said, "Let's just camp there, boys; we don't want to get too close to that thing. If it fell on the wagon, it'd bust it all to pieces." So we parked about two hundred yards away. Then we went over there and looked at the tree, and those two old boys were startled. They didn't know there's a tree like that over there. Well, I hadn't either. Nobody knew.

I said, "Let's eat dinner before we start chopping on that tree. That's gonna be a job." I said, "I figure it'll take us about five or six days." Parm laughed, says, "Why, three men chop that down in five or six days? Be well to do it in a month!" I says, "Well, whatever it takes, gonna be a job, so let's eat." So we went over and we cooked us up a bunch of stuff there. Mama had fixed it up for us so we could have something to eat on the first few days, then we'd have to do all of our own cooking.

Then we started chopping on that tree, and I was always one that liked to kind of pook off. I had the other boys working real good, and I'd try to find an excuse, you know, to throw off a little bit. These old boys, they was just chopping like that, and I says, "Say, Parm. I hear something ticking at this tree, seem like it's coming from the other side. I'm going over there and see what's going on." "Yeah," he says. "Anything in the world to get out of work. But go ahead, you found the tree. We'll keep on chopping."

So it took me well nigh an hour to walk around to the other side of that tree. And, you know, there's three boys around there chopping on the other side! They'd found it, too! There was their mark on the tree, just like mine! So it was legal. I says, "Boys, I guess we all have an interest in this tree." I told them we was chopping on the other side, and I agreed with them that we'd all just go ahead and chop it down and divide the honey. We didn't know what division would really mean on that.

Anyway, we went ahead and chopped on it, and sure enough, in six days we chopped it down, and it fell right across Rock Waterhole Branch. The branch was only about ten or fifteen feet deep and a hundred feet across there. It was dry, wasn't any water in it. The boys went to hollering about the time it fell, and I run over there to look. And there's another knothole right below where these bees went in, and it was about four inches across, and it was just a solid stream of honey coming out of that hole—just the prettiest stuff you ever did see! Then I think it was Parm hollered, "Hey, look, look, look!" And I looked over there, and a big old limb had broke off about the size of a flour barrel, and there's a roll of gray squirrels rolled out of that thing. For three days and nights, just come out of that thing solid! And I said, "That's the reason that limb kept bulging while we was chopping it down! Every time they took a deep breath at the same time, it made the limb swell up." Anyway, there was enough squirrels there to furnish everybody in the state of Texas. So we'd get two or three of them at a time until they run out. They all finally got away. And we was gathering up that honey all this time. We'd filled up all of the barrels and all of the tubs, all those dishpans and all the buckets—everything we had, even to those fruit jars. And the other party had done the same thing, only I believe they had more to put it in than we did. I accused them of being greedy. But, anyway, they got all their vessels full, and the squirrels had quit running out of the tree, and we wouldn't have any more to eat unless we went to work and boiled up some beans. We didn't hardly want to do that, so we decided to go on home. Well, now, mind you, while we was sleeping, that honey was running out of that tree, too, just same as it was in the daytime. We couldn't plug it up. So we started to go and when we got to the first crossing of Rock Waterhole Branch, it was level full! It was level full of honey! The branch was about ten foot deep at that place, so we knew we couldn't get that wagon across that branch with that much honey in there. I says, "Well, boys, it's gonna be a long way around." So we just took our time, drove plumb around that two-mile bend of Rock Waterhole Branch. We got back up to that other crossing, and sure enough, the honey had already got there. It was level full. Anyway, we got home with all that honey and like to never eat it all up. And for all I know, that creek's still running brim full.

The Incredible Hunt

My daddy had a muzzle-loading gun. It was one of them old two-barrel things. And he had a ramrod that'd been handed down from his great-grandfather, back in the days when diamonds weren't worth very much—course, they've always been valuable, but they wasn't nothing like the price they are now. Anyway, he had a handle in that ramrod that was built up with two rows of diamonds around each end of it for a hand grip. No telling how much that thing would've been worth, but it made an awful good handhold. And right on the top end of it was a sharp-looking spike. I don't know what they used it for, that was up to them. But anyway, you rammed the charge, the powder, and everything, down with the other end of this ramrod, and used that diamond-studded handhold to hold it by.

Well, I got after Papa to let me take that old twin barrel and go down to the river and hunt some geese. He said, "Buddy, there's not very often any geese or duck ever come to that river. I don't think you'll have much luck." I said, "Papa, I sure got lots of patience." He kind of grinned. He had been trying to teach me to have patience, you know, and trying to make me a superb hunter and a tracker and all that kind of stuff. He says, "Well, all right, Buddy. I hope you'll be all right. You better take a few sandwiches along to eat."

So that I did. I went down to the river, and the river kind of forked there, and there was an island right out in the middle — it wasn't much higher than the river, but it was a little bit, maybe. Made a good place to sit there and watch for geese or ducks or just anything that I could kill in the way of game. So I sat there for about five days, and I run out of sandwiches. I was getting tired of sitting there. Really tired of sitting there! The next day, the sixth day, I says, "You know, I can't stay here very much longer. I just can't do it!"

I'd been sitting there so long when I heard that honking noise, I thought I was dreaming at first. But I wasn't! I looked up the river and there came a thousand geese come swimming down that river. By golly! And I looked down the river, heard "quack, quack, quack," and there come a thousand ducks swimming up the river. I said, "Oh, my goodness. I can get the thousand geese, or I can get the thousand ducks. Ain't no way I know of to get all them things." Well, I was squirming around, you know. I had been sitting there still so long. And I looked across the river, and there was a buck deer over there, and I know that thing had forty-some-odd points. It was the biggest deer I'd ever seen in my life and just like a treetop on the top of his head!

I said, "Well, now, shall I take the thousand geese or the thousand ducks or that big old buck deer?" And I'd squirmed around a little bit, and all at once I heard something go "*bzz-z-z-z.*" I looked down right between my legs, and there was a big old diamondback rattlesnake that had crawled up there and coiled up where it was kind of warm, between my legs. Well, I knew he's getting ready to strike. About that time I heard "*grr-r-r-r,*" and I looked over my shoulder, and there was a grizzly bear coming up behind me! And that grizzly bear was mad about something. He wasn't a bit happy!

Well, I knew he was after me. And I said, "The thousand geese and the thousand ducks I can do without. I'm gonna die anyway. Either that rattlesnake is gonna get me or that grizzly bear will. I'm gonna get that deer; that's what I've wanted all my life." So I just pointed across that river. And, you know, every once and a while I'd packed down that charge down tighter in that old muzzle-loader. And every time you pack it, it gets a little more powerful! Man, you just keep on and it's liable to blow things up. Remember, I'd been tamping on that charge for six days. I just pointed that thing across the river and forgot to take that ramrod out of one barrel and pulled both triggers.

Well, that thing just blew up, blowed all to pieces, right there in my face! That ramrod went across the river and killed that big old buck; killed him dead, right there. The trigger guard had gone down and cut that rattlesnake's head off. The stock flew over my shoulder and knocked the grizzly bear in the head and killed him. One barrel went up the river and killed those thousand geese, and the other barrel went down the river and killed those thousand ducks.

Well, folks, it's a job to get out there and pick up that many ducks and geese! It sure does run into a lot of work. I had on my hip boots, but my goodness, I was about to give out! I waded out there, and the first thing I knew, I was in water over the top of those hip boots, and I was just dragging a big old bunch of those geese and throwing them up on the island. Then I'd have to pull the fish out of my boots. Every time I come out of the water, why, my boots was full of fish! So I gathered up all those ducks and all those geese and throwed them on that island. It was pretty well filled up with them by that time. Then I waded on across the river and looked at that old buck and admired him.

And I thought, "My golly, what killed that deer? Papa's ramrod! He wouldn't take nothing in the world for that ramrod. He'll skin me for sure. I don't know what to do. I'm afraid to go home now." Well, I looked on the far side of the buck and there was a big old tree just split open, laying out on the ground on each side. I looked and there was another one split over yonder. That was that ramrod doing that! 'Cause I had a powerful charge in that durn gun, I'd been packing them loads in pretty solid. So I just follered it. Finally, way out at the edge of the bottomland, I found that ramrod sticking into a big tree. And it had nine quail pinned on it!

Pure, Raw Bee Honey

People have long been fascinated by the process of bees gathering nectar and transforming it into honey. But this is only half the story. Around Albany, Texas, the other half concerns Mr. Alvin J. Schkade, a beekeeper since 1907. Born six miles north of Albany in 1893, Mr. Schkade still cares for close to one hundred beehives and processes on an average some five thousand pounds of pure, raw honey.

"Father [Earnest Schkade] gave me a few hives when I was eighteen; he had close to a hundred hives," says Mr. Schkade. His father began extracting honey in 1900. In the beginning he did not have much information on the process, and he asked the editor of a German newspaper in Giddings, Texas, for assistance. The editor then wrote to Germany and received instructions that he turned over to Schkade's father. Another son, Charlie, took a greater early interest in the bees. "I would take off when it came time to help Father with the bees, but here I am now the one raising them," recalled Mr. Schkade.

Honey is harvested in late May or early June from hives that are located all across Shackelford County. The hives are four or five boxes collectively called supers. Honeycombs made of wax are put in wooden frames and placed vertically in the supers. Outside the hives, plant life blooms, and the bees begin gathering their pollen and processing their honey, working from the center of the hive to the outside. Mr. Schkade says that during a good year, the bees in a single hive could gather ten pounds of honey a day. "Last year the early rains caused an abundance of wildflowers. We had four, five, and six honey boxes stacked, and we couldn't make the rounds to all the hives!"

The combs are removed from the supers and the frames—Schkade constructs his own comb frames—and the cover made by the bees is cut off with a hot knife. Then the combs are set in a honey extractor, which is similar to a centrifuge. The honey is spun out of the combs and placed in thirty- by thirty-inch steel tanks. Anything not pure is skimmed off the top by hand. Mr. Schkade emphasizes the two words "pure" and "raw." "Pure, raw honey means not damaged. Nothin' added and nothin' took out and nothin' filtered. That's what the word 'raw' means. We pour it and fill our tanks up and keep it an even temperature [80 degrees] so it will settle out; otherwise, it wouldn't be clear." The honey is then placed in either one-, two-, five-, ten-, or sixty-pound containers to sell. Normally, honey weighs about twelve pounds per gallon.

Mr. Schkade opens the caps on the cells with the electric knife.

No honey is wasted in the process. All the honey skimmed from the tanks is placed in troughs in the beeyard where the bees carry it back for food. After the honey is extracted from the combs, they are also placed in the yard for the bees, who take out all the leftover honey and chew the wax combs. Bees, according to Mr. Schkade, are very neat insects: "I've never seen any bees carry trash back in the hive."

Keeping bees and extracting honey is a combination of skill, knowledge, and luck. Even in good years, the honey crop can fail owing to lack of

Mr. A. J. Schkade with his bees.

moisture in the atmosphere. "The mesquites will be covered with blossoms, and when we go to check the hives, there will be no gain," Mr. Schkade says. However, too much moisture in either the ground or the atmosphere will prevent the catclaw from blooming and also hold honey production down.

When studying bee culture, one is surprised to learn that different blossoms produce different flavors and colors in the honey. In general, the lighter the blossom, the lighter and fancier the honey. According to Mr. Schkade, "People and books say that the mesquite and catclaw honey is tops." The books are *The ABC–XYZ of Bee Culture,* used by Texas A&M University, and *The American Bee Journal* and *Bee Culture.* The people

Mr. Schkade and his "ammunition," burlap set on fire and placed in a hand smoke which is used to "cam 'em down.

are Schkade's satisfied customers, who will vouch that his catclaw and mesquite honey is the best-tasting liquid ever slapped on a hot biscuit.

Many people are surprised to learn that the honeybee is not native to the United States or Texas. The early French settlers wrote of lacking beeswax, so it is believed that the Spanish, and later the Germans, introduced the insect to Texas. Mr. Schkade has two varieties of bees in his beeyard. "We have mostly three-banded bees and also some Caucasian bees," he told reporters from *Old Timer*. "The Caucasian type originated from the Alp Mountains near Russia. They are black with gray, hairy bands. They are the gentlest bee in the world: won't bother your neighbor. They are smart and won't carry too big a load. They fly faster than the Italian, and their range is nearly again as far from the hive. But on short range where you have a clover field or alfalfa field, Italian bees carry a heavier load and will put in more honey. But around here, we need a wide-range bee." He explained that his bees will range about three miles around the hives.

Bees that work in the hives, including the queen bee, live about two to four years. Worker bees only last for thirty to forty days. Their short life is due to the fact that their wings wear and become useless.

"A good hive of bees, hardy bees, will have as much as twelve pounds of bees in the hive. Some good years, we would have fifteen pounds of bees. There are thirty-five hundred to thirty-seven hundred bees to a pound." Mr. Schkade added with a laugh, "What if you had to pay taxes per head on 'em like cattle?"

Mr. Schkade stresses the importance of keeping quality queens in the

Mr. Schkade demonstrates the honey extractor

hives. "You got to have good queens. Sometimes a queen gets old and disabled. The old queen and a young queen will fight. The young queen generally whips the old queen because the old queen won't defend herself."

In 1950, his peak production year, Mr. Schkade owned 285 hives, but because of ill health, he was forced to sell all but 6 of his hives. He laughed when he recalled how a son told Mrs. Schkade to "sell every hive next time instead of saving a few." The son knew what was going to happen. From those 6 hives, Mr. Schkade again expanded to a total of over 100 producing hives. His honey has been sent all over the United States and is noted for its purity and freshness as well as its medicinal and "health food" qualities. Its purchasers think it the best anywhere and swear that there is no better food than a batch of homemade biscuits, some real butter, and a jar of Schkade honey.

—Jim Waller and Paul Stribling
Old Timer

Mules Remembered

Plowing a field with a mule is the most satisfying thing a man can do. And at the end of the day, looking over what you've done, you can feel a real sense of accomplishment, and that's a very rare thing.
— President Harry Truman
in *Plain Speaking*

    The mule has been with us a long time. Records indicate that they were being used at least three thousand years ago in Asia Minor. Mules are hybrids, the offspring of the male ass (jackass or jack) and a female horse (mare). Much less frequently a female ass (jenny ass or jennet) is mated with a male horse (stallion). This results in a hinny, an animal inferior to the mule. The mule is sterile but does exhibit hybrid vigor, combining the traits of strength and hardiness from both parent species.
    Mules were the most popular farm animal in East Texas and were used for a great variety of work from log hauling to being worked to a wagon. The mule population has dropped dramatically here since the 1930's. As you will see, it is about impossible to buy a working mule today. But in their day, they were a key factor in making East Texas a leading producer of cotton and food crops. These hardworking animals are missed today by those who spent much of their lives farming with mules.
— *Loblolly*

Raybon Ford

I was about nine years old when I started working mules. And I worked mules, I guess, for forty-five years. I logged with them, plowed with them. My daddy did, too.

Some mules are smarter than other mules, especially the mare mules. They're smarter than the horse mules. They're quicker to mind you, quicker to do what you want them to do. A horse mule is stubborn, but they are good mules.

Some of them live to the age of fifteen to eighteen years old. Some live longer than that, such as to twenty-five years. For the benefit of the mule, fifteen to eighteen years is all the good you get out of him. He'd get to where he wasn't able to do the work. That's the normal life for a mule.

I've owned some good ones, and I owned one or two bad ones. Mean mules had to be watched all the time. You had to make him do what you wanted him to do. And I owned some that would do what you wanted them to do without any trouble at all. With the mean ones you had to be cruel sometimes, but they learned.

To train them, you just start off working them, and you help them learn how you want them to work. One thing was to show them which side of the wagon you want them to work on. If you had a pair of mules working, you'd have one work on the left side and one on the right side. That's for working with a wagon, plowing, or logging double. Most of the time if you swap sides with them, you can't get anything out of them. They don't want to mind you; they don't behave right. They just like their normal side. What I mean is, if you break one on the right side of a pair when you were hauling logs, put him on the left side and he's not himself. He doesn't know what to do—he's lost. It's not on purpose; he just doesn't know how to work on that side. You break him then on the side you want him on. And you keep him there the rest of his life.

I'd rather have a mule than my tractor. I like them better, for you can plow better. Three years ago, I got my tractor and sold my mule. I go way back with mules. Me and my daddy logged with them for years. We loaded logs all over this country. Our mules learned to work well for us. As they worked in the woods, as I said, they learned to turn around, come right back to you. They learned the work and liked it.

I've had mules die from sickness. They have colic just like people do. They'll have sleeping sickness, and they'll die from that. But most of the trouble is overeating. Some eat more than others. Some will eat all night.

You hardly ever saw a mule in the woods kick from any kind of excitement, other than bumblebees or yellow jackets stinging him. He'll kick then, and I don't blame him. I've gotten four head of mules into yellow jackets in the river bottom. They were dragging a log, and I went off into a slough. And the log got into a drift, and that drift had a yellow-jacket nest in it. The log got hung, and the mules couldn't pull it. The yellow jackets were stinging them, and I had one gray mule that tried to lay down. I was

Early logging days

trying to get them loose so I could get them and me out of the nest. They were stinging me just as bad as they were stinging the mules. I couldn't leave the mules. I had to whip the gray one to keep it from laying down. If he'd laid down in their nest, they'd have stung him to death. I was finally able to get slack enough to undo them, and got us all away.

I've had mules get tenderfooted, mostly if you were hauling on the roads with them, or had a bruise caused from a bump. Some you'd have to put shoes on to keep their feet from getting tender. I never had many in my life that I had to shoot.

I was logging in the Brushy Bottom, south of 999, and I had that gray mule. He was nine years old and had come from West Texas. He had been around rattlesnakes. The men cutting logs in the bottom were watching for one because they had smelled him. That mule knew what one was. The other mules didn't know. The next morning we went down there to work. We watched all day because he smelled them, for he was snorting. My daddy and Tiny Smith killed six little ones about eighteen inches long. I went up on the side of the hill to get a log. I turned the mules around there and fastened the log, and a rattlesnake about three feet long came crawling at me and the mules. I stood there and let him crawl on, and the others came and killed it.

The best way that I ever found to train a mule is help him good and put him with a mule that already knew what to do. Me and my dad always put a new one with the smartest mule we had, and we let that mule help us to teach him what to do. If I went down the road and came to a bridge, the young mule might be afraid of it. That old mule would walk right on over it. The young one might try to push him off, but that old one would hold him to keep him on the bridge. Or he might meet a car and set back and be scared. But that old mule would walk on like nothing was happening. It would be a day or two and that mule would walk on across with the old one because he knew it wouldn't hurt him. That's the best way to train one. So you can see there's a whole lot of work in training a mule.

I wish I had a pair of mules right now. You can buy a pair in Louisiana. Some fellow sold a pair for $15,000 just the other day. In the past you usually paid $150 to $200. I gave $150 for that old gray mule I had. But work mules are gone, now.

They built this road right here to Gary, and they built it with mules. They started the road on the ground over the country. Then they put gravel on it. It stayed dirt for years. The man that built it camped on 999 out of East Gary. They had a water hole out there on that branch. He camped right there and built that road. They had a bunch of tents with people living in them who drove the mules. He built that road just like it is now. He had the mules doing work that bulldozers do now.

Mules aren't as good as horses to ride. About the best you can get out of a mule is a walk. If you trot, you get all shaken up. But they are wonderful animals. They're hardworking animals, that's really their life. That's what they're made for. I like to see them work and earn their feed. If you don't work him, he gets rowdy. You have to make him mind even if it takes a whipping. As long as you keep him in the harness six days a week, you got good work every time. If you give him a week rest, he'll try your patience. Most of them will try that anyway.

Mules will learn their name fast. If you call him, he'll pick up his ears and listen for it. They'll know their name, and they also would look for you when you called them. They are interesting animals and have been a big part of my life.

Jim Milford (age 95)

At Timpson they had lots full of mules. We've bought and sold down there all my life. A long time ago that was, but I don't know where they came from. We've owned lots of mules and some of them pretty bad, too. We kept them working all the time at farming, and some would break pretty good and some wouldn't.

I farmed all my life with mules. I've owned some good ones and some rough ones, too. I guess the way you handle them makes for a good mule. Some people could handle them better than others. My brother Flem was good, but sometimes he'd have to tie them up and give them a whipping.

I got ahold of a mule one time from one of the horse traders. He told me that it would work, but it wouldn't do much for me. So I traded for two young mules. The man I traded with wanted me to plow with mine first to show he'd work. He plowed then just as good as you ever seen. But after the trade the man couldn't do anything with my mule, either.

There was no particular breed of mule, you just took your chances. I remember mustang mules, though; they came from South Texas, I think, with a mix of the mustangs and a mule. A lot of times they had a "tough mouth." Well, a tough-mouth mule is hard to guide. When you pull on that line to go "haw," he doesn't want to go "haw." Sometimes you had to wrap the bits with wire to make them do what you wanted.

Sometimes we'd have to put "knee knockers" on a mule—something on their feet so they couldn't go so fast. You could take a little pole and tie it to their collar so the poles were in front of their knees. And if they went too fast, it would knock them across their knees. It would slow them down.

Sometimes you had to tie a mule's head up. A lot of mules want to keep their heads down to the knees and balk. But if you worked with them and had patience, they'd do what you want.

Marvin Wolfe

In training mules, especially where you raised them yourself, it is important to handle them while they are young. But don't pet them; you can pet a horse, but don't pet a mule. A pet mule is the meanest thing in the world. Their heels are their protection. They wouldn't bite you; they would kick you. When you start anything, don't let him outdo you. If he does it that time, he will do it again. The main thing in training them is to be firm. If he ever turns away with you, he will do it again, so don't let him get away with it because they don't ever forget as long as they're a mule. That is one thing a mule never forgets after he is grown.

Mules were all my daddy would use. He liked them. The reason people liked them is they would stand more heat and they could stand more endurance than a horse. General thing is, they ate less and cost less to keep them. Horses, the biggest percent of them, didn't want to work. They didn't like work. They would do what they call balk on you. You would have to give a lot of them a beating. But mules aren't that a-way. They were just stronger than horses to their size.

Of course, some men, when they get a tough-mouth mule, they would put haywire on their bits to hold them. They would mind you better. You could teach them in plowing. In this country, nearly everybody plowed single. They would teach them "gee" to the right and just not touch their lines, and "haw" to the left. They would mind you. They tend to be that way.

When you buy a mule, get one that is tight, made like a little barrel, and broad between the breast. You want a nice smooth-cut head on them. Some of them had a Roman nose. His nose tapered from about his eyes down. They always said a mule with a Roman nose was mean. They were, too. Papa raised one over at home that had a Roman nose; he was the meanest mule that ever lived. Get a mule that was broad across the forehead. They're more intelligent than straightheaded mules. One that's broad across the breast and long from his hip to his hock is strong. In other words, you don't want to have what they called too much light under one. His body is too high off the ground.

Yeah, boy, you can make a mule do work! When a horse wants to quit, well, you got a fight on your hands. There are a few good horses, but not like mules. Mules were put here to work. When they used to grade up roads, there wasn't any tractors or caterpillars, there wasn't any machinery to do it with, so they used mules. Maybe one contractor would have seventy-five to one hundred mules. They always picked big mules. To plow the dirt up, they used slips and those mules. They worked through the summer because that was their main month to work through. In the winter, it got all wet and muddy and they had to lot the mules, couldn't work them, couldn't work out there grading the roads. They would feed them oats in the summertime when it was as hot as the Devil. The mules would stay there when a horse couldn't take it. That's the reason they used mules.

They used to use them logging, too. They believed in mules. On an average it took less feed to keep a mule than it did a horse. They could just stand the heat better than a horse. That's the reason they used them. They will just take more hot weather—they won't get as hot as a horse will.

I have seen them log with mules that weighed about 800 pounds. They work pretty good, yes, but you had to feed them. The fellow logged over there where I lived, at the old place, he bought ear corn from Papa to feed his mules on. He lived in Garrison himself, but he had a fellow up there driving his team for him. They used four and six to the wagon, and he had four that weighed about 950 pounds apiece. He would go to feed the mules and would just pour a barrel of corn in their trough, shucks and all. It was good corn; he wouldn't buy anything but good corn.

They used to use steers to haul logs. Steers were slow; they never got into a hurry. In the early days people used steers, but after more sawmills came into the country and things began to pick up, they went to using mules. Some fellow started it and made a success with them. Then everybody went to hauling logs with mules. During the summertime, with all the pine tops cut down and green in the woods and wilting, it was hot in there. Ninety percent of them stuck to mules.

Rudolph Marshall

I worked mules up to about three years ago. I wasn't farming, I just had a pea patch or something like that. That's all the livelihood we had back when I was a boy growing up, up until I was grown and left home.

Well, we would raise these mules up to about two or three years old. Then we would break them and then plow them, and that's all we knew, and the only way we had to farm. That was the livelihood then, farming with mules or horses.

We had an old parrot-mouth mule we called Mat; that was her name. We used her a lot. We'd have new ground, you know, and we'd use what you called a Georgia stalk. And back then to lay the rows off with you used a cutting colter. I got one out in the barn now that Dad and Granddad used to use. I've used it since I was a boy. I used it some last year to plant sugarcane, to lay rows off with. And I remember this old parrot-mouth mule, old Mat. She never surged when she hit a stump; she was steady. You know, when you're plowing a mule, they're fractious. They hit stumps, and sit back, as we call it. Well, that makes their shoulder sore if they do it too much. And if they just ease against that collar when you're laying them rows off, it doesn't make their shoulder sore. You want to keep your mule's harness in good shape. And you want their collar, which goes around their neck that they pull with, you know, you want a good collar. Some people use a collar pad.

These rows we were talking about in a cane patch or corn patch — it's new ground, you know. First few years of farming we used this mule. She would mind you real good and she was awful gentle. She wasn't fractious, and that's the kind of mule it takes to plow in a new ground. One that would worry you to death is a young mule in plowing new ground. Of course, new ground is the best place to work a mule, because they'll soon learn.

Now a parrot-mouth mule is a mare, and her mouth is crooked and shaped sort of like a parrot's beak. That's the reason they called her the parrot-mouth mule. We had some mules that would like to buck with you, if you wanted to ride them. We never had any mules that we worked that we didn't ride. Of course, I am not going to tell you we didn't get thrown a lot of times, because we did. But we'd get back up on them and ride them. I guarantee you they were rode. We used to have three mules and two horses, and we would feed them all. We had a long feed trough and we would feed them all corn if we had corn, and if we didn't we would feed them oats. They had all they could eat, and they all stayed fat. We wanted them to be in good shape so they were able to work good.

I remember one time when I was a boy we used to have a dinner bell. My mother would ring that bell at eleven o'clock. We had a little mule, it was a mouse-colored mule, and she'd hear that dinner bell ring. If we were headed away from the house, that mule walks just real slow, but when you got to the end of the row and turned back to go towards the house, you better get ready to walk because that mule was gonna walk your legs off coming back! She knew that was dinnertime just as well as you did. She knew that dinner bell was quitting time.

Gus Davis

I retired in 1971 when I sold my store to my youngest son. Then I went to work. All I do now is work my garden. I've got about two acres that I tend, you see.

I swapped for this mule. The kids, all of them, use old Mandy, too. She's just a family mule. So all I do now is work my garden, fish, play dominoes. I went over to a neighbor's yesterday afternoon and we played fourteen or sixteen games and we quit even. Me and my partner got seven games and they got seven. We played all evening, nearly.

I've got a little of all of it in my garden. I'm growing watermelon, cantaloupe, peas, corn, butter beans, squash, pepper, Irish potatoes, sweet potatoes. I just got the last of my sweet potatoes laid by this morning. It's going to be a good garden this year.

This is the third crop I've made with Mandy. Mandy is old; I don't know exactly how old she is. She's bound to be around forty years old. She'd pass as a sixteen- or eighteen-year-old mule. From what I've been told about, who owned her before took care of her. I got her from Clifford Johnson.

Gus Davis and Mandy

Clifford maybe got her from Cub Starkey, who was a trader. He used to live across the road from Clifford. Jim Smith owned her before that, and had gotten her from Rudolph Marshall's daddy. She's been around a long time.

Mandy was trained right, broke in good, you know. And she's worked hard, but she's been properly fed and cared for. I feed her good, boy. As old as she is, she's still in good shape and can eat good to be an old mule. It's a wonder she'd have a tooth in her head, though. She can eat corn off the cob!

Mandy is big. I kinda have to reach to put the collar on her. I imagine she weighs 1,000 to 1,200 pounds. I've never had her weighed. Small ones can't work as well. That little mule I traded for Mandy weighed about 700 pounds. He wasn't very tall but he had a big body on him, had a huge neck. He couldn't do what Mandy does. With all the rain this spring, I did some of the hardest plowing in my life. The ground was full of water and it was harder than when I broke the ground, but she stayed right with it.

Mandy will be hard to replace. It will be hard to do. She's old but I'm no spring chicken myself.

Grandma's Moral Tales

Born and raised in Mexia, Texas, Max Haddick is a longtime friend of *Loblolly*. Among his many talents, he is a skilled storyteller of wit and wisdom.

—Loblolly

Now the stories I'm going to try to tell are not about Sam Houston, Lamar, or any of those early Texas heroes. Reason that I'm not going to tell any stories about them is because I don't know any stories about them. I'm sure there are lots of stories that could be of value, but I didn't meet any of those gentlemen personally so I can't vouch for any of their humorous sayings or humorous stories about them. Instead I'm going to tell some stories that my grandmother used in place of peach tree switching. She didn't believe in paddling, but being an only boy, I sometimes deserved a paddling. Instead of sending me out to the orchard to get her a nice peach tree switch, she would make me sit down and she would tell me a story that would illustrate the error of my ways. I'm not sure which would hurt worse—the switching or the telling of the story. But in any case, my grandma was a wonderful lady, and she managed to teach me a little bit about right and wrong. I try to live by the precepts that she has taught in her stories, and maybe somebody else would be interested in the stories she taught, so I'll tell them to you just as well as I can remember them.

Once, when I was about twelve years old, I thought I knew everything in the world. I was so positive and so set to my ways that my grandmother was concerned about me being the most stubborn person in the world.

Now this went on for some time, and she finally had just about enough of my stubbornness. So she sat me down to tell me a story about a farmer's wife who didn't know how to use any cuss words. She didn't use any profane, vulgar, obscene, or foul words of any type. Her only word that could be classified as an oath was "scissors," and she used it incessantly.

One morning the farmer got up and asked his wife, "Honey, is breakfast ready yet?" "Aw, scissors!" she snapped. "Go sit down and wait. I'll tell you when it's ready." After he waited for a while he came and said, "Honey, I'm awfully hungry. Could I get just a cup of coffee before breakfast?" She said, "Aw, scissors! You go sit down. I'll call you when it's ready."

Well, he went out and milked the cows, and slopped the hogs, and fed the chickens, and brought in wood. He used up about forty-five minutes, and he came in and breakfast was ready. He finally got his breakfast.

Then he went out in the pasture to run the cows out. And he went down, hitched up the horses, and plowed all morning. It was a hot day, and man, it was so hot, he was just sweating like everything. And he was tired, and he plowed until high noon. When he come in from plowing, he was hungry and thirsty and not in the best of humor. He said, "Honey, is dinner ready yet?" "Aw, scissors!" she come back. "I'll let you know when it's ready. You go sit down, and don't bother me." "Honey, could I have a glass of ice tea? I'm so thirsty I'm just about to die." "Aw, scissors! You don't get any ice tea. If you did, it would spoil your dinner. You go sit down and wait for me." And he went and sat down and waited, and he waited, and waited, and finally he just couldn't wait anymore. And he went back in and said, "Honey, I've just got to eat. Is dinner ready yet?" She said "Aw, scissors! Don't bother me anymore." He said, "Look, honey, I've heard that word for the last time. I'm full up to my Adam's apple with scissors, and I don't want you to ever use that word in my presence again. Now you understand me? Don't you ever use it again!" She said, "Aw, scissors! I'll say it anytime I want to. You can't tell me what to say. Scissors, scissors, scissors. I'll say 'scissors' every time I want to."

The farmer just had had too much. He thought about it for a minute. He said, "Honey, if you say 'scissors' just one more time, I'm going to drag you out of this house by the hair of your head. I'm going to drag you down to the pond, and I'm going to hold you under the water until you drown if you ever say 'scissors' again!" "Aw, scissors!" she screamed. "I'll say 'scissors' anytime I wish. Scissors, scissors, scissors! You're not going to do anything. I'll say 'scissors' all I want to!"

Well, that farmer had just about had it. True to his word, he grabbed her by the hair, dragged her kicking and screaming out of the house and down to the pond. And he shoved her under the water. At first she struggled violently, and bubbles came up, *"blub, blub, blub,"* and she just worked and tried to get away. But she couldn't get away, and he held her under that water. And finally she relaxed. And just when she totally relaxed, and it looked like she was gone, one of her hands came out of the water, and she held it up right in front of his face, and she made a snipping motion like she's using scissors!

Grandma said, "Now that's about the most stubborn thing that you could have in the world," and if I didn't want to be like that farmer's wife that said "scissors," I was going to have to cut out all my stubbornness. I don't know that it completely cured me, but at least when I was being stubborn about something from then on, I'd stop and think about that woman that said "scissors." My grandma knew how to tell me what was right and what was wrong.

When I graduated from high school, we had a local businessman as our graduation speaker. It was an awful hot day, and the city auditorium wasn't air-conditioned. We had on these old wool cap and gowns, and we were just about to melt. Sweat running down our back until it tickled, and we was about to pass out. And he talked and he talked and he talked. Lord, that man just never had a stopping place. I think he talked for about two hours, but it seemed to us about four or five hours. Anyway, when I got home from the graduation exercises, Grandma asked me what he had to say. She was sick that day and couldn't come see me graduate.

I said, "Grandma, I haven't got the slightest idea what that man had to say. He talked for hours, but I don't know what he had to say. He was just putting together a bunch of words, and we were so uncomfortable and hot and sweaty, we didn't pay any attention to what he had to say." She didn't like that. She thought I ought to pay attention when people were talking to me. And she said, "Well, I've got a little story about graduation that I want to tell you." So there was nothing I could do but sit down and listen to Grandma's story. So she started off.

She told me there was this professor of psychology in a university in South Africa. Every year, he made a practice of taking his psychology class out into the jungle to observe the behavior of monkeys. These students would work hard all day long, piling up this huge pile of firewood in a clearing in the jungle.

Just at dusk, they'd set fire to the wood and then hide in the underbrush around the clearing. When the fire got burning real good, the monkeys would come out and dance—dance all around the fire. They'd just have a wonderful time. But finally the wood burned away, the monkeys went back into the jungle, and all was quiet.

The professor took his class back to the classroom. "What did you observe?" the professor asked one student. "Well, I observed that young monkeys jump higher than old monkeys," the student replied. "That's correct," said the professor, "but that's not what you should have observed." Another student said, "Well, the boy monkeys showed off in front of the girl monkeys." "Well, that's right, too," the professor said, "but that's not what you should have observed." Another one said, "I noticed that the big fat monkeys couldn't jump near as high as those little skinny monkeys." He said, "That's right, but that's not what you should have observed." One by one, every one of the students made an observation, and every time, the professor would say, "That's right, but that's not what you should have observed." These students were getting just a little bit exasperated. One of them, a braver one of the bunch, said, "All right, Professor, what should we have observed?" The professor thought for a minute, and then said, "You should have observed that not a single monkey added a stick of wood to the fire."

Well, Grandma said that we were like monkeys. That all the time we was going to grade school and high school, we was dancing around the fire of civilization that was built by our parents and grandparents and all the people back to Adam and Eve. And we shouldn't be monkeys in this life. We had all this fun a-dancing, but now we had graduated from high school, it was time for us to go out and add some wood to the fire. I think about that real often in my work and think about how much Grandma meant to me and how much she taught to me about life.

There was another story that she told. It doesn't matter because of the messages. They're loud and clear for anybody who wants to hear it. We had an oil millionaire in our town who had oil wells and tank farms and all kinds of things to do with petroleum production. His name was J. K. Hughes. Anyway, one of the gaugers out on the tank farm made a bad mistake one time. You know, in those days they didn't have automatic gauges to tell when the tanks were getting full. Instead, they hired gaugers. And these men took dad lanterns or big flashlights, and they would climb up on top of these huge oil tanks out in the tank farm and take a cover off and shine a light down there to see how much oil there was in the tank. It was a deathly rule that nobody was ever to carry a kerosene lantern up on top of one of those oil tanks, because of the danger of fire. But this old boy left his flashlight one night, and he just didn't want to go back and get it. So he lighted up his kerosene lantern, went up on this tank, and opened the cover, and was looking in there when his foot slipped and he dropped that kerosene lantern. Man, it caught fire in an instant! There was fire all over the place, and he scrambled down off the tank and called for help, and they brought hundreds and hundreds of men—brought the fire departments from half a dozen towns. But that tank burned, and when it burst the burning oil went over and set fire to another one and another one and another one until they had about a dozen of those huge tanks of oil burning. And they burned all night. Big billows of black smoke just going all over the place. And all the men there worked as hard as they could to try to contain that fire, but couldn't put it out. They took big bulldozers and fresnoes and all kinds of earth-moving equipment, and they threw up a dam around those burning tanks and just dammed that oil off and let it burn. It took four days, and those men worked day and night for four days.

When it was all over with, the superintendent who was in charge of all the workers in the tank farm went into Mr. Hughes's office. Man, he was tired. His face was black with smoke, he hadn't eaten, he was mad, and he says, "I'm going to find that son of a gun who took that lantern up there, and I'm going to fire him. I'll run him off. I'll see he never gets back on one of our tank farms again." Mr. Hughes sat there for just a minute and says, "No, you can't fire that man." Says, "He's one of the most valuable men we've got here at the tank farm." The superintendent says, "I don't see how you can say that. He cost you a million dollars. We worked for three days and nights. He took a kerosene lantern up there and burned off all that oil. You lost it all. You tell me he's most valuable? I ought to fire him and run him off."

Mr. Hughes said, "No, sir. You can't fire that man. He's the most valuable man we got out there, because if you fire him you're going to have to hire another gauger to take his place. Now, a new gauger who never had had a bad mistake like that, he just might carry a kerosene lantern up on top of one of those oil tanks, but that man will never carry another lantern up on top of those oil tanks if he lives to be a thousand years old!"

You know, I've thought about that a lot. You know when a man makes a mistake sometimes, it makes him a better man, and that's what Grandma meant to tell me when she was telling that story.

Grandma taught me a lot of stories, but my grandpa taught me some, too. You know, that man was awfully smart. I didn't realize it until I was twenty-one, but he was a brilliant man.

One time, when I was about eight years old, they bought me a Steven's Little Scout .22 rifle. Naturally I had to go out hunting. Well, they didn't want me to go out hunting right then by myself, 'cause I just had gotten the rifle. So Grandpa went with me. We had a greyhound that was the fastest thing on four legs. That was the runningest dog you ever saw in your life. Boy, he was faster than the wind, but that greyhound had one bad fault: he ran by sight. He could chase anything he could see, but once he lost sight of it, that's bad. He couldn't scent-follow a trail at all. I think he didn't have any sense of smell at all. He just couldn't follow anything he couldn't see. But believe it or not, we had a little bulldog that wasn't near as fast, but that little bulldog had a good nose. I know bulldogs are not supposed to have a good nose, but this dog didn't know it. So he would follow a trail by scent.

Anyway, we jumped up a cottontail out there in the pasture, and that greyhound took off. And, man, it was hot! Oh, Lord, it was hot in August. It was just blazing sun, and that rabbit would run just as hard as he could, but that greyhound was gaining at every step. They zigzagged across the pasture, up and down, and finally that rabbit, just about wore out, cut through the canebrake down there, and that greyhound lost sight of him. That greyhound was so confused he didn't know straight up from straight down. And so he cast around a little bit, and Grandpa put the bulldog down on the trail and said, "Go get him, boy!" And that bulldog sniffed about three times and found that rabbit's scent, and off he went. He zigzagged through the canebrake and out the other side and down the creek, and we were running out there just as hard as we could go. He was following that rabbit every step he took. He zigged when the rabbit zigged, and he zagged when the rabbit zagged, but he followed him every step of the way. And that rabbit was so worn out that even that old, slow bulldog was gaining on him. Well, we tore out following, and we followed it down to the creek. We got down to the creek, and there was a tree right on the bank of the creek. The bank was sort of washed out, with water running under it, and that tree had almost fallen over. It was laying over about a 45-degree angle. And durned if that rabbit didn't run up to the third fork in that tree and was sitting there in the fork of that tree, just a-panting like everything. Boy, he's sitting there going "*th hu hu hu hu hu hu*." I ran up there with my Steven's Little Scouter, and I was about five feet from him! I couldn't have missed. But my grandpa reached over there and pushed that rifle down and said, "No, we're not going to kill that rabbit." And I said, "But, Grandpa, we got him right there. I can kill him; I know I can hit him." He said, "I know you can, but we ain't gonna kill that one." Says, "You know, we've been having lots of trouble with you lately, saying 'I can't.' You know, I'll tell you to do this, and you'll say, 'I don't know how. I can't.' And I'll tell you to do that, and you'll say, 'I don't know how. I can't.' " He said, "I want you to learn something from that rabbit." Says, "You know, even a rabbit can climb a tree if the dogs get too close. Anytime you're tempted to say that you can't do something, I want you to think about that rabbit and remember even a rabbit can climb a tree if the dogs get too close. Anytime you're tempted to say that you can't do something, I want you to think about that rabbit and remember even a rabbit can climb a tree if the dogs get too close."

Witching for Water (and Oil)

Call unto me, and I will answer thee, and shew thee great and mighty things, which thou knowest not.
Jeremiah 33:3

Many Texas farmers who may rely on modern technology for weed control and seed and fertilizer selection nevertheless revert to the mystic and ancient art of water witching in their search for underground water. Recently, this practice has been extended to the search for oil. The practice has many names and a long history. In England it is called dowsing; in the Latin countries, divining; and in Germany, wishing or striking. In modern-day West Texas, where it is very much a living folk tradition, it is termed witching.

In the seventeenth century, many people believed that divining was the work of the Devil, and the Church condemned the practice. In an effort to purify the divining practices, people tried everything from cutting the limb on St. John's Day to baptizing the rod and giving it a Christian name. Reports associating divining with witchcraft began to appear in the American press late in the eighteenth century. The association with witchcraft and the fact that the witch-hazel shrub was often used for divining rods gives a clue to the origin of the term water witching—a term that is probably the only truly American contribution to divining practices. Virtually all forms of water witching found in America, usually involving differences in the shape of the rod or the material used to make it, are of

European origin. Divining itself is very old. According to Emily and Per Ola D'Aulaire in the May 1976 *Reader's Digest,* archaeologists have found an eight thousand–year–old cave painting in the Atlas Mountains that seems to show a dowser, divining rod in hand, surrounded by a group of onlookers.

It's not just water that can be found by witching. People also search for buried treasure, pipelines, oil, and almost anything else that can be found underground. An article in the March 1978 *Science Digest* reports that in Vietnam, engineers in the 1st and 3rd Marine divisions successfully dowsed with bent coat hangers for Vietcong booby traps, mines, and tunnels.

Scientists in the Soviet Union are studying divining as a method for locating water, petroleum, and various ores; they call it the Biophysical Method (BPM). At a 1973 conference in Prague, Professor Aleksandr Bakirove of the USSR reported that "BPM lessens drilling costs and makes prospecting more efficient."

There are approximately twenty-five thousand practicing water witchers in the United States. Very few of these men and women try to make a full-time occupation of witching. Most of them only witch for their own needs or to help a neighbor. Hundreds of these diviners belong to the American Society of Dowsers. Every autumn, members arrive in Danville for the annual ASD convention, armed with their favorite divining rods.

How are these persons "recruited" to the craft? At age ninety-two, Texan Perry Cartwright is a master water witcher who has been witching for the last seventy-eight years. During his career, he estimates, he has witched more than seven hundred wells with his preferred divining rod, copper wire bent into a *Y.* As Cartwright pointed out to Bob Gates of *Texas Highways* magazine, green forked limbs are not always readily available in the Big Bend! Nevertheless, it was a forked limb that introduced Cartwright to the art when he was only fourteen.

"There was about a half-dozen people at my house, and there was no water well there. And one of these ladies could witch a little bit, so she took this peach limb and found a stream of water. Then three or four other people tried it. Well, they walked across the stream of water, and it wouldn't work for them. I was just a kid, and they said, 'Perry, why don't you take the limb and see if it will work for you?' I took it and walked across the stream of water, and it went right down on the water. Since then I have used it anywhere and everywhere with success. . . . You can use any kind of limb or wire that you want to. It's the talent that God gives you, and if He doesn't give you the talent, you can't do nothing."

Pete Kennedy, a protégé of Cartwright, agrees with him that it works for some people and not for others, and he offers a theory as to why: "I think it has somethin' to do with electricity in your body. Some people walk across and touch a light switch and they won't get shocked, but many people do. Now, you ask Mr. Cartwright, and he will probably say that it is the 'gift' of divining. You can get a different answer from anybody you

Witching for Water (and Oil)

Water witching Pete Kennedy

The Loblolly Book

Pete Kennedy

Pete Kennedy "counting the nods"

Pete Kennedy with tools of the trade

talk to. I think you create a certain wavelength, and you can pick up a wavelength from the water. If we ever get it proved scientifically, I think it would be good because water comes up in domes underground, and there is so much in witching that geologists don't even dream of."

The forked tree branch is usually thought of as the classic instrument for witching, but through the years many things have served as divining rods—everything from whalebone to pliers, even bare hands. Today, many dowsers prefer plastic, metal, or fiberglass divining rods. Carl Schkade of Albany, Texas, has been actively witching for oil since 1979. He has tried brass rods and copper rods, but now uses what he calls loaded rods. His loaded rods consist of two tubes, each shaped like an *L*. Each L rod is made by joining a long length and a short length of half-inch–diameter PVC pipe with an elbow. Then each L rod is filled with the substance being witched for—in Mr. Schkade's case, this is mostly crude oil. He holds each rod by the short part of the L so that the long part sticks out directly in front of him, parallel with the ground. He then walks over the land where he is looking for oil, and when the two rods cross each other, that is an indication that he is standing over an oil formation.

Schkade says that when he was a child, a man came out where there were some deep wells and could tell within two feet how deep the wells were. Schkade himself could never find depth by this method, but about two years ago, he found another method that works well for him. He notes, "I always can get within a hundred feet. That's my rule of thumb."

Considering the great depth of crude-oil formations, this is no small feat. Sometimes Schkade's estimates come out exactly right, and sometimes only within his 100-foot range. He says, "I went out here with somebody the other day, and I said, 'Don't tell me how deep the well is.' And that particular one I said was 500. It was 570 feet deep; I was still within my 100-foot range.

"I went out with another guy, and he had some wells. And I went to this particular one and said, 'Well, it shows it producing two barrels a day and it shows it's 600 feet.' And he said, 'That's exactly what it's doing!' I walked over there to another one three hundred feet away from it and I said, 'I don't know what's the matter, but this shows it's 500 and it ain't making but a barrel a day.' He says, 'That's right. That's a deeper well and this is a shallow one.' " Schkade notes that it is odd for two wells to be only three hundred feet apart and in two different production zones. Yet he was able to detect this with his divining rod.

On one occasion, Mr. Schkade estimated a well at 363 feet and oil was hit at 350. On another, his estimate was 410 and the well came in at 430. He notes, "I've only been working with it two years, and maybe two years from now I might have it perfected."

Mr. Schkade claims witching to be only about eighty-five percent accurate for finding oil. Sometimes a formation is detected and divining shows it should produce, "but when we get down there we get sandy shale formation. The formation was there, but it didn't have any oil in it." So, he says, if divining shows an oil well, there's no absolute guarantee you're going to get one. But if divining shows a dry hole, "I wouldn't drill it, and I wouldn't put a plug nickel in it."

Luther Helm, a retired Methodist minister now residing on a farm in Comanche County, witches only for water. For all the wells he has witched, he has used a peach or willow branch. He now has metal L rods, but has not used them to witch any wells. Mr. Helm was first introduced to water witching when just a boy. It was during a dry summer, and his family was having to haul water for their goats. "Papa had heard how people witched for water. He told me what to do, and I think he even tried it, too. We got out there with a forked peach tree limb and got to walking around. And, sure enough, we found a place that every time we walked across, it would pull that peach limb. So we dug down there, right where it pulled straight down, and we got water at about fifteen feet. It was plenty of water for the goats. Later on, we witched out for a well over on the other side of the place to draw water for the cattle. We did the same there and got water."

Mr. Helm tells of the time at Lakeview when he was trying to find a gas line to tie into for a new building. "We could see where it came into the old building, but we couldn't find where the pipe led off from there. So I just got out there in the cotton field and started digging. I dug two different ditches—I thought at first it came in directly from the north, then I decided it must have come in from the east. I went back over there and dug awhile. Then this fellow came along and said, 'Why don't you try witching for the metal line?' I said, 'I don't know how. I know a fellow can witch for water, but I didn't know you can witch for a line.'

"And he said, 'Yes, you can!' So he broke him a piece of barbed wire off the loose end of a fence there, untwisted it and broke the smooth part of that. He threw the barbed part back down and made a crook on one end of each of them and started walking across there. He got to where they pulled together and crossed, and he says, 'Well, if you dig right there you'll find your line.' So I dug right down and, sure enough, I found the line right where he said."

Helm believes that the stronger the pull on the divining rod, the more likely you are to find a generous supply of water. However, in one well he witched the pull was very strong, but there was not a great quantity of water. He thinks minerals may have had something to do with pulling the rod down. Sometimes the forked limb will pull extremely hard. "I've had it to pull so hard—gripping it so tight it couldn't turn—but it would twist the wood and break the bark loose. It just had so much pull."

Depth-finding works differently for different people. Mr. Schkade, who uses L rods, finds depth by pulling the rods apart and counting the number of times they swing across before stopping, and that is the number of feet to the first oil formation. Mr. Helm, who uses the forked branch, measures the distance from the point where the limb first begins to pull to the point where it pulls the strongest. This, he maintains, is the depth to the water. Perry Cartwright uses a piece of straight wire about a yard long and, as he says, counts the nods. As he describes the process, "You take this straight wire, grab the end in both hands, and you just set down on your knees. When it starts out, it moves sideways, then pretty soon it'll start dipping up and down. That's when you go to countin' the nods [of the wire]. Then, when it gets to the water, it'll start goin' sideways. But if you wait, it'll start to dipping again, and that is how far it is to the next water."

Mr. Schkade observed that if someone used his rods they would not work in exactly the same way as they did for him—they might not even work at all. "If they work for you, I don't have to tell you that they work. I can just hand them to you, let you walk across where there's oil underground, and you can feel for yourself." And, although someone might feel the rods react, he wouldn't know how to read their indications—wouldn't know how deep the formation was buried or how much oil it would probably produce. Schkade himself learned how to interpret rod movements by trying the technique on wells where the depth and production were already known.

Mr. Helm noted, "I think it's something that some people can and some can't. I know I've seen people take the switch and walk with it, and it wouldn't do a thing in the world for them, and I can take it and it'll pull right down." Schkade's wife can witch water with a willow switch, and he can't, but he can find the same spot with his loaded rods. He says, "I know it works, but why it works, I can't be sure."

There is no easy answer to why water witching works. Although himself a proponent of the "electricity theory," witcher Pete Kennedy of Alpine correctly observes that "you can get a different answer from anybody you talk to." Like Kennedy, Thomas Edison also thought that successful dowsing was related to electricity, and Albert Einstein believed the explanation was in electromagnetism. There has been some limited scientific research into divining, but it is difficult to control experiments in the field, and it is equally difficult to take witching to the laboratory. One scientific study, headed by American physicist Dr. Zaboj V. Harvalik, has found that "many dowsers are unconsciously sensitive to small disturbances in the earth's magnetic field." In tests, he had subjects walk across a low-intensity electromagnetic beam that could be turned on and off. Sensitive dowsers seemed to be able to pick up "dowsing signals" from it. Yet they failed to do so when certain parts of their bodies (the kidney area or the head) were shielded with heavy aluminum or copper foil. This suggests the existence of magnetic sensors in those parts of the body, Harvalik reports, "as well as a 'signal processor' in the brain which transmits the command for subliminal arm-muscle contractions that move the rod." Harvalik proposes that the divining rod and the way in which it is held make these small muscular movements noticeable as a movement of the rod.

One reason that water witching has its place in West Texas, says Pete Kennedy, is because "we don't have a water level where you could just drill and pick up water." In his article in *Texas Highways* (November 1980), Bob Gates wrote:

> Most water witchers think the water in West Texas is stream water and that some streams are less than a yard wide. The stream theory was advanced in 1960 when employees of the State Department of Highways and Public Transportation

drilled for water at a maintenance warehouse near Johnson City. Doyle Johns and his crew set the drilling rig over the stake that marked the location of the new well. They were interrupted by an elderly man who lived nearby. He greeted Doyle with the query, "What you doin', Sonny?"

Doyle replied that he was going to drill a well. The old man acknowledged the statement and then began to cut a forked limb from a nearby tree. After a few minutes of walking the area in the vicinity of the rig, he stopped about 10 feet from it and said, "Here's where you'll hit water, right here."

Doyle thanked the old-timer, but explained that he had to drill where his boss had indicated.

Four days later, Doyle's crew had drilled 900 feet—a dry hole. After much deliberation, they decided to drill 25 feet from the dry hole. Four days later, Doyle had another 900-foot dry hole. In desperation, he moved his rig to the spot the old-timer had witched. Two days later the drilling bit punched into sweet water at 460 feet.

Another instance supportive of the stream theory is told by Mr. Helm. "Now, over where I was born and raised, [there was a well that] was a dry well for several years. Then one day, the people living there heard a roar, and they went out and decided it was in that old well. They looked in there, and up about twenty feet from the bottom was water pouring in—just a big stream of it, just filled up in a little bit. They had barely missed the stream of water when they dug the well. Now, I think it had been witched for, but it was such a narrow channel there that they didn't get just exactly dead center on it, and they missed it just by a little bit. And when it broke in the well, then they had a good well."

The divining process can be sped up by witching from a moving vehicle. Carl Schkade tells that he can go down the highway at sixty miles per hour, and if he crosses over an oil formation his rods will pick it up. As Pete Kennedy observes, "We drive down a pasture road and pick streams out of a car. You may pass up some weak streams, but you will certainly pick up the big streams."

When I [Paul Quesenberry, the student who interviewed Mr. Schkade] first tried Mr. Schkade's rods, I had difficulty convincing myself that I was not moving the rods. Every time I passed over an imaginary line, the rods crossed. I backed up and tried again, but the same thing happened! When Mr. Helm demonstrated his method, I was given an opportunity to try the willow fork. The bark didn't exactly peel off in my hands, but as I walked over what could have been an underground stream, that willow branch made a 180-degree turn from pointing straight up to pointing straight down.

What I'm saying is that I *know* these devices moved in my hands, but

I still don't know what caused them to move. We still don't understand how a stick or wire can come to life in somebody's hands over a particular spot that frequently yields what is being sought, but this doesn't mean it is impossible.

"Call unto me, and I will answer thee, and shew thee great and mighty things, which thou knowest not," the Bible says. Certainly there are still many things in this world we "knowest not," and perhaps water witching is one of them. Pete Kennedy stands on his record of only four dry holes in over two hundred wells drilled from his witching. With that kind of record, dowsing deserves consideration from any of those in search of substances buried underground.

—Paul Quesenberry
Old Timer

Jack Pate: "I'd Rather Be a Cowboy than Anything"

Jack Pate was born December 29, 1903. It was only fitting that he took his first breath of life in the town of Fort Griffin, on the western cattle trail. Born in cattle country, Jack has been a cowboy all his life.

Jack was reared in Shackelford County, Texas, and was the son of a trail driver. His grandfather was also a stockman. He was part of a large family, having four sisters and five brothers. He "graduated" from school in the ninth grade, but contends that he is still going to school: "I went to that school of knocks most of my life."

Ranch work began as soon as Jack could ride a horse. He first worked alongside his father for some of the large ranches around his childhood home. Next he worked on the Bright Ranch, which is located north of Sierra Blanca, New Mexico.

In the early 1940's, Jack ran wagons, tending to cattle on two ranches in New Mexico that covered two hundred thousand acres of land. Jack worked as foreman on the Jones Ranch for twenty-five years, and he still considers this beautiful New Mexico ranch his home.

In 1927 Jack married Margaret MacMillian. She passed away in 1965, leaving him with their seven-year-old adopted daughter, Susie Marie. Eight years later, Jack married Etna Poer. Jack was sixty-nine years of age at the time.

Over the years, the Pates have reared many children besides Susie. These include three nephews and an orphan named Willie who later was killed in Vietnam.

At this time Jack and his wife are residing in Albany, Texas, the county seat of Shackelford County. He hasn't slowed a bit, and still works days on the surrounding ranches. In fact, on his seventieth birthday he began the tedious task of breaking a colt!

—Old Timer

I've been riding more or less all my life. I was just like all kids. I was always doing something I shouldn't-a done. I used to run off from school and things like that. The first day's work I ever drew wages for in my life, oh, I was probably nine. All I did was hold cuts [cattle that have been cut from the herd for some reason]. I got a dollar a day. I was in the money! I helped them five days, and that five dollars looked like five big bicycle wheels to me.

My parents never tried to keep me from being a cowboy. They wanted me to go through school, and I didn't do that, but it wasn't their fault—it was mine. I went to school out there on Diller Flat. I got through the ninth grade. There was nine of us kids. I'm the only outlaw in the outfit.

When I was about sixteen years old, I started working full time. I worked here when I was a kid when they were cleaning up the fever ticks in this country—about the time of World War I. Course, I wasn't but about fourteen years old, but the boys, most of them, went to the Army, and my dad, he helped everybody, and, course, I had an old horse or two, and I went and helped them, too. Course, I was in the way, I imagine. My dad was an old trail driver. My grandfather came to this country as a pioneer settler and of course they fought the Indians out of this country. I was working for thirty dollars a month. Just cowpunching fever.

I was busy all the time, but—well, I'd prowl them hills just like an old coyote. I had two or three ponies, and I was big enough to ride, and I knowed that country. I used to gather wild plums in plumtime and, oh, such stuff as that. I don't know why a rattlesnake didn't bite me. I've thought about it since, but I didn't think about it at the time.

I'd rather be a cowboy than anything. I'm not sorry. If I had it to do over, I'd probably do it again. I've worked for good people. I guess when I went to New Mexico was when I sure enough took over an outfit. I run a ranch at Magdalena, New Mexico, that belonged to Mr. Jones, and another one in Moore County, Texas. I had a home at both places and they was 302 miles apart and I run both of them.

Course they wasn't any trucks then; everything was on the train, and we shipped at Kent most of the time, and there was a lot of hoboes. That was back in the Depression time. Those people were out of jobs, couldn't find a job and just drifting over the country riding the T.P. One summer, I was in camp and at what we called the Deep Wells, right next to the railroad tracks, and we fed a good many hoboes there—boys that was hungry and between jobs, you know. Always, anybody come along hungry, we fed them. In a way, it's tradition with ranch people. It's been that way as long as I can remember. Those people never bothered us. Most of them was

Jack Pate—cowboy

just boys trying to get somewhere and wanted to go to work, and ever' once in a while, one of them boys would take a notion he wanted to work with us, and we'd get some pretty green hands.

I ran a wagon a lot in New Mexico. That outfit finally built up to where they had three ranches. They furnished me a chuck wagon and about eighty-six saddle horses, and I think we had about twelve head of mules.

I had a good cookie at the time. He was a good cook but he was a character. We'd get in around a town, and he was sure liable to get drunk on me. One time he got drunk and got back to the wagon, finally got back home, and we was camped and just had our bedrolls out on the porch about November or December; I smelled that coffeepot and I heard old Lilo moving things around in the kitchen and I said, "Lilo, what's the matter with you?"

He said, "You know what I've done?" He said, "Went and volunteered for the Army." But when he went up for his physical he couldn't pass it. We just had beef and beans and that Brer Rabbit syrup, you know, but he was a good bread cook. And everybody liked him. He always had time to do anything for you. He always took good care of his team and he didn't want anybody fooling with them. He worked for me about thirty years.

I like to be with a good bunch of cowboys. You take a good bunch of cowboys branding or gathering cattle—it's all fun. A lot of them are always pulling something on someone. There's not many dull minutes. But I'm a little funny about that picking on anybody. Anytime you see me picking on somebody, it's somebody I like. If it's some old boy I like, I might do anything to him; but if it's some old boy I don't know or somebody that might not take a joke right, I just leave them alone. We pulled nearly anything on one another. Pushed an old boy off in the cold water in a tank and he caught me then and rubbed my hair full of cockleburs. One old boy I used to stay in camp with, there wasn't anything I wouldn't do to him, but he was a big booger and I had to do everything I could to stay even. One winter, we was staying in camp and just had a little old shack with no roof on that we stayed in, and we had a hole dug in the ground outside where we done our cooking and fire building, and we had a horse that we wrangled our other horses on that was pretty mean to buck. We took turn about cooking breakfast, and the one that cooked breakfast always throwed some hot ashes under old Dusty to try to get the man wrangling horses bucked off. We didn't do that horse much good. That boy roped me one time and threw me down, and I let him think I'd forgot it for about a week or ten days. There was a little old gate that was torn down that we always come in to come to the house. One night, one of us would turn out the horses and the next time the other—we took turn about doing everything. So about the time he got to the gate, I stepped out there and threw a stewer full of water on him. He made a run at me and I'd tied me a baling wire up about chest high from one post to the other. . . . I stayed on the hill that night. But we had a lot of fun. We'd pen up a bunch of horses and flip heads or tails to see who rode first and one'd pick for the other.

We made most of our own fun all the time. We used to pitch horseshoes, play cards a little. Never did play poker much. We used to play poker for pecans a lot—we didn't have much money. I wound up with two big cake sacks full of pecans one time. We used to play baseball a lot, or get together and have a rodeo once in a while. We used our old horses that we rode. Take them over there and buck them at them shows and take them back home and go to working cattle on them.

In the wintertime, the snow would break down the fences on us a lot, and always those steers would scatter and go. You'd eat breakfast before daylight and you might eat dinner long after dark, too. We've laid out lotsa cold nights. I remember one night we laid out, and I heard the next day that it was twenty-nine below that morning. We had just stretched a tarp across from one tree to another to kinda break the wind off us.

It's easier like they do it now. I know there's been lots of times in my life that I never laid down on a bed that had springs on it—slept on the ground or on the floor, if I was in a house, but most of the time on the ground. I finally got me a little seven-by-seven tepee tent. I'd just roll my bed up in it for cold and for rain. I've rolled my bed up and got my slicker on and sit down over it like an old hen, too, to keep it from getting wet. I tell you, when a bed is wet in cold weather, it's pretty rough sleeping.

We always got up early. We used to get up four, five o'clock, especially if we was out with a wagon. If you didn't have somebody holding the horses—a night hawker—you'd have to go out and wrangle them. We didn't work from headquarters or nothing. When you was branding outside, it would take a lot of help. I've seen twenty or twenty-five boys with that wagon. You had to have help to hold the calves, and then you had to have flankers and men to drag them.

I guess I enjoy branding more than any because I always enjoyed roping. Catch them by both hind feet and drag them up to the branding fire and a set of flankers. One of them'll catch that rope and the other one'll catch hold of his tail and just jerk him over. One of them will sit down and hold a foreleg to keep him from getting up, and the other one will hold his heel so he can't kick. I tie them on. I like to tie. I don't want something getting away. If I'm roping outside, I tie all the time. A lot of time if I'm riding a horse that's not gentle that I think is liable to get in a jam in branding and dragging calves, I dally. But as long as I'm riding a gentle horse, I tie.

And if we were gathering cattle in the fall in rough country, it wasn't nothing to ride that horse forty, fifty miles. We had plenty of horses, took care of them, kept them shod, and they got hardened to it.

Some horses are stubborn and disagreeable, and it doesn't make any difference what you try to do with them, you can't get along with them. Once in a while you find people like that, too. I used to ride a gray horse a long time ago that I called Polka Dot that I just loved like a person, and I've had several since. I've worn out more horses than a lot of people have—ride them till they went to getting stiff where they was dangerous and old, and then turn them loose and set them free. Let them die at the ranch, you know. I didn't sell them.

That old horse I used to ride named Champagne, an old bald-faced horse, I think he was thirteen years old. He wasn't the gentlest horse you ever rode, but he went on and made one of the best horses I've ever seen. I could take him and I'd head or heel, either one, on him, rope calves on him, or take him to a cutting, and I tell you, it wasn't over till he got done. He was a real horse. And a deer hunter shot him right through and through one evening. That was about the hardest lick I ever had in my horse business. I've never went and roped or took any part in rodeos since, and that's been about fourteen years ago. He was a real horse. I couldn't hardly speak to a hunter for two years. He was right in his prime.

Those horses were something. Once I was out trying to get everything done I could because the forecast said a storm would hit about eleven that night. We worked and put a bunch of cows and baby calves in the barn. I was packing hay to some cattle in Franklin Canyon, about two miles from the house, to feed some yearlings. About the time I got there, that storm hit. You couldn'ta seen your hand. It would just pack that snow in the fork of my saddle, and you couldn'ta took a stick and packed it any tighter. That old horse just headed towards home and had to angle right into it. Sometimes, that old horse couldn't stand it, and he'd turn around with his head away from it, and there'd come a lull in that wind, and he'd turn around and start again. I knew I didn't know the way, but I knew he did. A boy down below me there who worked on a ranch down south of Santa Rosa, he was out on horseback, too, and he didn't make it in. He got off his horse and backed up against a tree to get out of it, and that's where they found him.

That storm we had seventy inches in twelve days, and we already had snow on the ground. Our cars was sitting at the end of the house, and it covered them up. A horse can't do anything when that snow gets up above the point of his shoulders. You've got to break a trail for him. And them cattle snowed in, you take these old blue spruce or pine and they'll get in there and tromp out a place and stay there. Well, that snow gets piled up around them, and you've got to find them and pack that hay in there to them. I've had them stay in them kind of places two or three weeks. I lost a good many little calves, but no cows. But them people down below me on the flats—we had hay stacked out in the meadows and in barns and everywhere, you know, but we hadn't had a bad winter since '64 or '65, and they'd got careless. And I'll tell you, them people lost a lot of cattle. They dropped feed out of them helicopters for the cows, but those antelope died in piles there on them flats.

That storm's when I lost all my good looks. The next morning, my old face was swelled up, the hide all come off, and I had to take a hot towel to get my eyes open. It wasn't funny.

Then there're always accidents to make things hard. I got hung to an old gray horse one time and I thought he was going to kill me. He fell with me and the saddle horn caught on the inside of my leggings—broke that string and pulled my boot right up to the saddle horn. He finally pulled my leggings loose. Why he didn't kill me, I don't know. He kicked knots on me and then kicked them off, but he never did kick me in the head. I got into the hospital on Thanksgiving night and stayed there until the second of February and went on crutches about eight months. He was a gentle horse but he got scared. That was the first horse that ever made me afraid of a horse. It was a lesson to me. Later, I got in another jam that was another lesson to me. I had a horse fall with me, and when he quit rolling, I had a leg caught plumb up under him and he had both hind legs straightened out wedged down in the fork of a mesquite and he couldn't even touch the ground with his front feet. He couldn't get up, and I couldn't get out from under him. Them broomweeds was just as high as they are right now, and I stayed there until Talmage Palmer found me. And I thought about all the mean things I'd done until old Palmer found me, too. Never broke a bone in me. But that was a lesson to me. I never have stayed by myself and broke horses since. Never stay by yourself and ride them kind of horses.

Another job that was to do sometimes was hunting bears that were killing stock. A bear will whip all the dogs in the country. You take an old bear with cubs: she'll go up a tree and take them cubs up a tree and she'll come down and you can't get enough dogs around her to whip her. Bear is a lot more dangerous than a mountain lion. Course, a bear is gonna get away from you if he can. I'm not much of a killer, but if a bear gets to killing calves or killing goats. . . . One time, we had a little bunch of goats at the ranch, and an old bear come through there and killed thirteen just for fun, you know. I took a couple dogs and put him up a tree and I killed him, but I never killed anything I didn't have to for some reason.

I had some good dogs and I used to also go hunt wild cattle for people. They was Catahoula and Border Collie—good dogs. I found one bull that was so big, I couldn't handle him. I later got him, but we killed him loading him. He had took up in what we called Ortega Springs, and you couldn't get a vehicle in there to haul him out with, and he was too big to neck to something. That old bull, I imagine, was six, seven years old. He was a Hereford bull, a sharp-horned bull, probably weigh fourteen hundred pounds. I let them dogs chew on him till I seen that he wasn't going to come out, and I just called them off. And this Mexican boy, we decided we'd get that bull. We found a cow in heat and took eight other cows and calves over there with us. About five or six miles across there, and we spent all day coaxing him back to the corrals and getting them in. Well, we got that bull in on the scales, and we had a good set of scales, made out of two-by-sixes and two-by-eights. And that bull seen them gates was locked on him, and he just hooked the whole end out of them scales and out of there he went.

Well, we went in and changed horses, and we went to work on him again and finally got him back in. We opened the gates, and there was cedar posts there at that gate set in cement. When he went through there, I caught him and just jerked my slack and pitched my rope over it. That bull hooked ever' board off that fence; everything that joined that post, he cleaned it up. I got that old bull wrapped up around it and finally got enough wraps on it where I could tie over to the other post. And I went and called Jiggs Potter, and he sent a boy up there the next day with a power wagon and a winch on it and a stock tank on it made of pipe—something he couldn't tear up. So we got the chain hooked around that old bull's horns—course, his old head was sore by then and I was letting the slack off that rope and old Juan was trying to pull it up in there. And he got his nose in there, and that old bull jumped just as high as he could and come down and broke his neck. Every cowboy in that country had tried to get that bull. You know, he could kill a horse. He was a sharp-horned bull, and you had to watch what you was doing.

I like early of a morning. I guess it's my favorite time of day. It's always cool and the air is clear and everything and it smells so good of a morning early in the high country. Spring of the year is the best. It's not hot, it's not cold, and that's branding time. It is the climax of what you've been working for. The spring of the year is when you're trying to save your calves, and then when they're up big enough to brand, you're checking what you've done and know what you've done.

Yeah, these old doves holler and these old redbirds holler, and I like to hear these old dogs bark—tree a lion or run them wild cattle, either one. It'll grow on you. I like to hear a cow bawl. I don't like to hear them bawl when they're hungry, but I like to hear an old cow bawl up her calf of an evening. I like to smell the pines. In the spring of the year, you get in those high pines—I think it's a smell anybody would like. That's living close to nature when you're punching cows.

I think sundown of an evening is a pretty time of day, too; and the mountains, I guess, is the prettiest sight I ever seen. You get up above ten thousand feet and you can look back across and the sun's going down—especially if you're about fifteen miles from home trying to get in. You'll see some pretty sights thataway. It'll make you like to be a cowboy.

The reason there's not a lot of good cowboys like there used to be is so many more things that boys can make more money at. Instead of following cowpunching for a trade, they follow something else. I never did have much money. You never seen many cowboys with much money. I'd like to have a hip pocket full. Money's not everything, but it's a good thing to have. I guess a man could live without any, but it would sure be unhandy. If a man has principle and his friends and money to go with it, he's a real successful man, I'd say. But most important is just be honest, try to help people, and do what's right. I think cowboys is as good a class of people as any. They might not have as much money as some, but money don't mean everything. It's just whatever you're happy doing. I'll tell you one thing. Most cowboys—if they've got a dollar and you need it, you can sure get four bits of it.

Would I recommend it? Well, really, I don't guess I would, but I wouldn't change my own life. Do what you're happy doing. It's poor pay and hard work, but I think living outside and eating cow meat and gravy keeps you young!

From Skiprope Rhymes to Sacred Harp

The *Loblolly* staff has often been impressed with the major role music played, and still plays, in the lives of the people of East Texas. Because of this, it decided to devote an entire issue to a review of the area's traditional music and musicians.

Dr. F. E. Abernethy, who teaches at Stephen F. Austin State University and is secretary-editor of the Texas Folklore Society and an active member of the East Texas String Ensemble, told *Loblolly* much about the folklore and history of East Texas, and added to the story by singing and playing his guitar. *Loblolly* also received help from others from as far afield as Nashville and New York. The areas of local musical tradition that were looked at most closely were folk music and country-and-western music. *Loblolly* discovered that for many persons, past and present, music seemed to be as great a necessity for human life as eating and breathing!

Folk music is that body of verse and melodies that is in folk performance at a given time and place, and whose authors or origins are little known or forgotten. The songs themselves have survived, although changed (and constantly changing) with time and place. The versions of folk music popular in East Texas are often very different from the versions of the same songs brought over from the British Isles or carried west across the Mississippi. East Texas folk music usually came by two routes: either west along the southern Gulf states, or by a more northerly path through Arkansas.

These pioneers were of an adventurous nature and looking for something better, and their music usually reflected this optimistic spirit. One such song was once popular at "play-parties" and was called "Shoot the Buffalo." Its message was intended to persuade the young ladies to join the men on the road to Texas:

> Rise you up, my partner dear,
> And present to me your hand,
> 'Cause I know you want to marry
> And I'd like to be the man,
> Where I know you want to go.
> And we'll rally round the canebrake
> And shoot the buffalo.

Some offsetting advice was offered in another play-party song, which demonstrates the characteristic dry humor that often accompanied the optimism. "Texas Boys" said:

> Come all you young ladies and listen to my noise,
> And don't you go to marrying these Texas boys,
> 'Cause if you do, your life's gonna be
> Johnny cake and venison and sassafras tea,
> Johnny cake and venison and sassafras tea.

Like the music itself, early musical instruments were folk-made and traditional. Fiddles were constructed of gourds or even cornstalks, while banjos and guitars were made of whatever was at hand. Crude though they were, these instruments were put to good and competent use.

The individual's experience of folk music often began with what were called children's songs—rhythmic rhymes and chants associated with such childhood games as skipping rope and bouncing ball. Many of these rhymes, chants, and songs (for example, "Froggy Went A-Courtin'," from sixteenth-century England) were very old, having been passed down for hundreds of years across the generations of childhood.

Another type of musical tradition was the love song. These songs often carried a moral theme as a core meaning—for example, "Barbara Allen" (dying for love) or "Careless Love" (guilty love punished). Obviously, country music owes a great debt to these love songs of an earlier time.

Where it was allowed, dance music was popular with East Texas pioneer communities. Much of this music can also be traced back to the British Isles. Often it was danced to the sounds of crude fiddles made from gourds or cigar boxes. Such music was "out" in some communities because of the folk belief that fiddle players received their skills as a gift from the Devil. But in areas where they were allowed to play, the fiddlers were men of prestige whose services were much in demand. They sometimes added to their value by also doing the calling at community dances. A popular old fiddle tune was "Sally Goodin," whose call goes in part as follows:

> I ain't dead,
> And I ain't wooden,
> And I'm in love
> With my sweet Sally Goodin

> I love pie,
> I love puddin',
> And I'm crazy about a gal
> That they call Sally Goodin.

In the communities where dancing was not allowed, play-parties were popular as a musical alternative. At most play-parties, the only allowable music was vocal and the dancers were redefined by the community as "players" or "marchers." These were truly community affairs, for it was "come one, come all" whenever a play-party took place in a local home. The action, which took the forms of ring games and reels, was considered a game and not a dance. Some popular tunes for play-parties included "Hog Drovers," "Old Joe Clark," and "Weevile Wheat." In play-party games, hand swings were allowed but not waist swings. Boys and girls had to abide by play-party rules, but such parties offered them one of their few chances to socialize in public. Persons who did not march or play found play-parties a good occasion to meet and talk with friends and neighbors and to monitor the doings of the young.

Another type of music popular in East Texas was sacred harp singing. This strange and beautiful religious music often featured Christian verses set to traditional tunes and spread to East Texas from its origins in the nineteenth-century South. Sacred harp is increasingly rare but may still be heard at certain churches where people sing in the old ways.

Country-and-western music is in many ways a direct extension of the folk music of the rural South. While the music is mainly Anglo in origin, its instruments reveal multicultural roots. Because of the general cultural conservatism of the South, the forms of folk music discussed above lasted longer there than elsewhere in America. With the communications revolution of the 1920's, these folk traditions were transformed into "hillbilly music" and extended to a mass audience by way of radio and phonograph. In the early days, this revised music was called "hillbilly." Later, following World War II, the term fell into disuse and was replaced by "country and western" or just "country." This boom in popularity has caused a loss in authenticity and simplicity from earlier times, but this is still a music belonging to the people.

So the music of East Texas survives as a continuation of rural traditions. It is the music of a people who have seen their world change greatly, often with violence and disruption. But its themes are still the folk themes of family, patriotism, and morality. The original optimism is still there.

—*Loblolly*

Skip-Rope Rhymes

Skip-rope games and the rhymes that go with them have been a lasting type of playground activity for younger children. There are a wide variety of games and hundreds of rhymes that are chanted or sung in the course of play. Here is a sampling.

Once in My Life

Once in my life,
Twice in my life,
A boy asked me,
To be his wife,
He asked me once,
He asked me twice,
But I told him he wasn't very nice.
I told him so many times,
I would never hear wedding bell chimes,
Then one day he called me dear,
So how many chimes did I hear?
One, two, three, four, five, six, seven, eight, nine, . . .

Theresa Smith

The Little Turtle

There was a little turtle,
He lived in a box,
He swam in a puddle,
He climbed on rocks.
He snapped at the mosquito,
He snapped at the flea,
He snapped at the minnow,
He snapped at me.
He caught the mosquito,
He caught the flea,
He caught the minnow,
But he didn't catch me.

Kelly Jones

By the Night Before

By the night
By the night
By the night before
Twenty-four robbers came knocking at my door
As I ran out
They ran in
Ask 'em what they wanted
And this is what they said:

Spanish dancer turn around,
Spanish dancer touch the ground,
Spanish dancer do the splits,
Spanish dancer run out quick!

Beverly Lyons

Cinderella

Cinderella went to town
To buy some mustard,
On the way her girdle busted,
How many people got disgusted?
One, two, three, four, five, six, seven, eight, nine, . . .

Kelly Jones

Alligator Purse

Mother, Mother, I feel ill,
Call the doctor over the hill.
In came the doctor,
In came the nurse,
In came the lady
With an alligator purse.
Out went the doctor,
Out went the nurse,
Out went the lady
With the alligator purse.
Doctor, Doctor, shall I die?
No sir, no sir, close your eyes
And count to ten.
One, two, three, four, five, six, seven, eight, nine, ten . . .

Beverly Lyons

Nineteenth-Century Weepers

These songs were sung to William Moore, ninety-one-year-old resident of Timpson, Texas, by his parents when he was a small boy. Mr. Moore was born in Kansas, but his family moved to Oklahoma while he was an infant. The family moved on to Texas by wagon shortly thereafter.

The two songs that Mr. Moore sang for his visitors from *Loblolly* are known as nineteenth-century weepers. These are melodramas put to song which tell heartrending tales of family tragedies and of cruelty to children. Even though these are "made-up" songs of long ago, they still can deeply involve the emotions; the remembrances and sentiments from the past brought tears to William Moore's eyes as he sang.

Orphan Girl

"No home, no home," cried an orphan girl
At the doors of a rich man's home,
Trembling stood on the polished hall
And leaned on the marble wall.

Her clothes were thin and her feet was bare
And snow had clad her head.
"Oh, give me a home," she feebly cried.
"A home and a bit of bread."

"I'm free," she said and she sang to the floor
And strove to cover her feet.
"Please give me a home," she humbly begged.
"Yes, a home and something to eat."

The rich man sleeps on his velvet couch
Dreaming of his silver and gold
While the poor little girl on a bed of snow
Murmurs, "So cold, so cold."

Now the rich man sleeps on his velvet couch
Dreaming of his silver and gold
And proudfully frowned and scornfully said,
"No, no bread for the poor."

The morning dawned and the snow fell fast,
She still lay at the rich man's door.
But her soul had fled to a world above
Where there's room and bread for the poor.

And I rode on in the midnight charm
Call out if you knew well
Now the poor little girl had a home in heaven
While the rich man squirmed down yonder.

Drunkard's Dream

I dreamt I staggered home last night,
So oft I've done before.
I missed my wife; where could she be?
A stranger at my door.

She's dead, poor thing, I heard them say,
She lived a wretched life.

For grief and want have broken her heart
For being a drunkard's wife.

Her little children standing round
And to the father said,
"Oh, father dear, go wake up Ma,
The people said she's dead."

"Oh, she's now dead," I faintly cried,
And rushed to where she lay.
And there he kissed her on the cheek—
It was as cold as clay.

"Oh, Mary, speak to me once more,
I'll never cause you pain.
I'll never grieve your loving heart,
I'll never get drunk again."

The night was passing very slow,
I thought I'd lost my bride
But woke and found my darling wife
Was kneeling by my side.

The Dying Cowboy

Several years ago, Leon Choate of Carthage discovered a letter in an old farmhouse in Panola County. The letter was written in 1888 from William F. Mayo to a Miss Mary E. McCarthy. Mr. Choate had done some research on the people involved and shared what he had found with the *Loblolly* staff.

The letter contained an early version of the folk song "The Dying Cowboy." This famous cowboy song is also known as "Oh, Bury Me Not on the Lone Prairie." Like many Texas folk songs, it was something else before it came to this part of the country. Frank Dobie in *Ballads and Songs of the Frontier Folk* noted that the song was first published in 1850 as "The Ocean Burial."

Whatever her response to Mayo's letter, Miss Mary E. McCarthy was later to marry James Cooper. Where William Mayo learned the song or why he sent it to a girl in 1888 is unknown, but here is his version as it was in the letter, including his original spelling.

August 12, 1888

The Dieing Cowboy

O Burry me not on the Lone Prairie this words come
   low but moarnfuly

Tame the frallie lies of a youth who lay
On his dying couch at close of day

He wasted and pined til are his brow
Death gloomy shades are garthering now
He thought of home and the loved ones thare
So the cowboys gathered to see him die

In silence we listened to his well known words
To the free wild winds and songs of birds
He thought of home and cottage house
And sceanes he loved in childhood hours

I have always wished to be buried when I die
In the old church yard on the green hillside
And by my father O let my grave be
O bury me not on the lone prarie

It maters not so I've ben told
Whare the body is lay when the heart grows cold
But grant o' grant if boome to me
And bury me not on the lone prarie

O bury me not on the lone prarie
Whare the wild coyotes will howl ore me
In the narrow grave jest six by three
O bury me not on the lone prarie

O bury me not on and his words failed thare
But we heeded not to his dying prayer
In a narrow grave just six by three
We buried hom thare on the lone prarie

Whare dew drops fall and buterflies rest
And wild rose homes on the prarie crest
What the wild coyotes and winds pass free
We buryed him thare on the lone prarie

wrote by W. F. Mayo
for Miss Mary E. McCarthy

Play-Parties

Teen-agers were the usual participants in play-parties, and they marched to the rings, squares, and reels of the play-party songs. Three basic instruments were sometimes allowed. These were the violin, accordion, and French harp.

According to Monroe Brannon, ninety-year-old resident of Gary and a long-standing friend and informer of *Loblolly,* "I was a teen-ager from

From Skip-Rope Rhymes to Sacred Harp

W. F. Mayo's letter

1899 to 1906 and these plays were very popular for my generation: (1) Thimble, Thimble, Who's Got the Thimble?; (2) Drop the Handkerchief; (3) Snap; (4) Go In and Out the Window; (5) Skip to My Lou, My Darling; (6) Fancy Four; (7) River Bend; (8) Ocean Wave; and (9) Irish Trot (my favorite!)." Mr. Brannon, who attended many play-parties in his younger days, was very eager to talk about them.

Monroe Brannon

We would usually announce the play Monday or Tuesday, in order for the word to get around the community, because we had no telephones. We'd ask some family to give us a play-party and they would agree that we could have one on Friday night. On Friday evening, the people of the house would clear their largest room of all the furniture, which usually consisted of a bed, a few chairs, a Singer sewing machine, and a lamp table. Then they would go out to the woodpile, where there were stove wood blocks about fourteen inches high, and bring in these blocks, setting them at intervals of about five feet around the wall of the room. Then they would get one- by twelve-inch pressed-pine planks and put them on those blocks of wood for the ladies to sit all around the wall. That would give us the whole big room to put on our play. Of course, that was just seating places for the girls. Us boys would be on the front and back galleries, in the hallway, and sometimes in the yard. When we'd get ready for a play that required a partner, a boy would come in and ask a girl if she'd be his partner. If she said no, figuring that her main beau might come along and pick her up later as his partner, all the girls in the room heard her refusal, and it was impossible for him to get a partner, because they would say, "No, I don't want to be second choice." He would have to go out on the gallery, in the hall, or yard to get him a partner. Then we would all play Irish Trot and other games, such as River Bend and Ocean Wave. All the people came by torchlight about eight o'clock on Friday night from various directions. Someone would go ahead, and the crowd would gather in from all directions and even from trailways. They would save some of those splinters until the party was over so they would have a torch to go home by.

The way the girls dressed for the parties was what was so beautiful. They all had various-colored calico dresses that their mothers had made on Singer sewing machines. The dress usually opened in the back down to the waist and then was solid all the way down to her ankles. The top body usually wore a whalebone corset, and the neck of that dress came up under the chin, and the sleeve came out to the hand. No exposures. They had their hair in two plaits that hung way down their back, and on the end of that, they would have a little bow of red ribbon.

They normally wore one of three colors—red, pink, or blue—and the girl would select which color she wanted, and all that she wore would be that color or would match it. She would wear those little pieces of ribbon on the end of her hair and a bow at the back of her neck and then a larger bow pinned at the top of her head. She was pretty! And, of course, around her waist she brought two-inch ribbon around and tied it in a bowknot and that gave her shape. She would pin that together to keep it from coming undone and the end of that sash would hang down about twelve inches. Some girls were trimmed in red, some in pink, and some in blue. The girls' shoes were coarse and high, lacing up about six inches in the front.

The boys had homemade hickory-striped shirts and hand-me-down suits bought at a store, not tailor-made. Some of the boys that were really dressed up had these white bosom-pleated shirts that had several pleats for the front to make it stiff and thick. It was starched real well. It even had a flap at the lower end of the shirt that would button to his top pants button to keep it from flaring up in his face. There were little holes in the front of the shirt, and if he'd bought some little shiny trinket from a peddler, he would put it behind those holes. The shirt opened in the back, and he had a standing collar about four inches high. It buttoned in the back and came around to the front where there was a button that would separate, and he would put the stem through that, and the collar was on. Then he wore what you call a tie but was then called a cravat. It had a string that came around the collar and had a large knot tied at the top of the collar. He took a large piece of whalebone and a piece of string and tightened it around his neck.

We all wore very coarse shoes. There was no such thing as patent-leather shoes. Those shoes really tore up a floor. You could hear that party a heap farther than you could hear the music.

We usually had a French harp, maybe two, an accordion, and a violin. We would sing those songs and the instruments would play them and it was really fun.

[*Loblolly:* Other persons remember play-parties where musical instruments were strictly forbidden. Grace Burns told *Loblolly,* "We made our own music by singing. We were not allowed any other kind of music, like musical instruments or record players, as that seems to bring out evil. You see, if one is kept busy thinking about the words in a song, they would not have as much time to think on evil things."]

We had play-parties as often as our neighbors would grant us one. We would try to have one every Friday night, at least every other Friday night. There were few people that would give us play-parties. Over in the Mount Bethel community, Uncle Myles Dudley would let us play over there. Here in the Gary community, Uncle Bud Hall would give us a party now and then.

If this party was on Friday night, you could stay until midnight before the old man broke it up. But if it happened to be on Saturday night, the party had to break up at eleven o'clock because you were supposed to get some rest for church on Sunday morning.

After the party, if the boy had nerve enough to ask his girl for a date next Sunday evening, that was all fixed before they got home. Little Brother walked ahead, on the way home, carrying the torch while the couples walked down various lanes and trails to deliver the girls home. Little Brother would wait out at the road until the last one had delivered his girl and then he walked back down the road and the boys would join in with him in going home. Of course, we took the shortest path home. For example, we often walked in pigs' trails. But we young folks would have liked the longest way home because when you're courting, "the longest way home is the sweetest way through."

At a play-party of that kind, there were always a few wallflowers. Some girls that weren't pretty or too fat wouldn't get to play much because the boys back then, and probably still so today, would pick the best-looking girls to dance with. But I always had sympathy for them. I'd select me a girl that I would notice had not had a partner so she would have a good time, too. We had great fun.

Here are the words for two of Mr. Brannon's favorite plays.

Irish Trot

Choose your partner for the Irish Trot
Choose your partner for the Irish Trot

Choose your partner for the Irish Trot
Way down below.

All join hands for the Irish Trot
All join hands for the Irish Trot
All join hands for the Irish Trot
Way down below.

All march around in the Irish Trot
All march around in the Irish Trot
All march around in the Irish Trot
Way down below.

Rights and lefts in the Irish Trot
Rights and lefts in the Irish Trot
Rights and lefts in the Irish Trot
Way down below.

Swing your partner in the Irish Trot
Swing your partner in the Irish Trot
Swing your partner in the Irish Trot
Way down below.

All promenade in the Irish Trot
All promenade in the Irish Trot
All promenade in the Irish Trot
Way down below.

Go hog wild in the Irish Trot
Go hog wild in the Irish Trot
Go hog wild in the Irish Trot
Way down below.

Skip to My Lou

In somebody's big white house,
In somebody's garden,
I'll step out and get somebody's darling.

Chorus:
Skip, skip, skip to my Lou,
Skip, skip, skip to my Lou,
Skip, skip, skip to my Lou,
Skip to my Lou, my darling.

Ma make butter in Pa's old shoe,
Ma make butter in Pa's old shoe,
Ma make butter in Pa's old shoe,
Skip to my Lou, my darling.

Repeat Chorus.

Rat in the wood box big as a mule (repeat 3 times)
Skip to my Lou, my darling.

Repeat Chorus.

Can't get a young man, an old man will do (repeat 3 times)
Skip to my Lou, my darling.

Repeat Chorus.

Sacred Harp

On Easter Sunday several years ago, Kay Griffith and *Loblolly* adviser Lincoln King attended an all-day sacred harp singing held at the Mt. Ararat Primitive Baptist Church six miles east of Henderson, Texas. There were over one hundred people in the church. Both men and women song leaders were using the old sacred harp songbook, and the young as well as the old took part in leading. Each time, the leader would give the key, then all would join in. Different denominations from all over Texas had come.

There was a great amount of enthusiasm and Christian spirit present that Easter Sunday. Someone said, "I can remember singing that song over seventy years ago." The songs included "Wonderous Love," "Wayfaring Stranger," and many others.

Mr. F. David Waldrop of Tyler, Texas, has been singing sacred harp songs all his eighty-three years and believes that there has been very little change, except that modern singers do not sing the notes as much as did the earlier singers. He told us that the *Sacred Harp* is a songbook odd in shape, with an odd name, and, as some think, with odd-sounding songs sung by odd people. The book contains largely a collection of very old tunes used a long time ago, origins often unknown. Most of the songs were brought from England by Puritan and Huguenot pioneers. Some tunes had words not very suitable for the Puritans' minds, so they put in new words.

The following is from a letter that Mr. Waldrop sent to *Loblolly*.

F. David Waldrop

In the late 18th century the Southern frontiers took old tunes people knew and put to holy words. This grew from mass music to camp meetings and singing school. Many of the songs are tunes used centuries ago in road houses. When the pioneers came over they already knew these tunes, so they applied more appropriate words. Now found in mostly Primitive Baptist churches, most are original Great Britain folk melodies. For example, "Wonderous Love" is a tune of "Captain Kid." Words of old Harp songs were of sad people who were fatalistic and knew of sufferings.

The tunes in early days had not been written. Singing was by *note,* and I find many singers who are very popular and can't read music. When the

The Loblolly Book

F.D. Waldrop leads *Sacred Harp* singing

old tunes were put to music, only four notes [shapes] were used: *fa, sol, la,* and *me.* Notes were always sung first and followed by the words, a practice still used by many today. Hence, this type of singing was referred to as "fa-sol-la" singing. In the western part of Panola County, Texas, where I was raised, we did not know any tunes for church except what was in Sacred Harp. This was true for much of the south in the county. For use in our churches we had a very small hymn book called "Ever Green" with about one hundred hymns printed in it. An interesting thing probably never observed is that in these old hymn books at the top of each hymn you can find characters like: "CM," "SM," "LM," and sometimes figures like 7-8-9, etc. In our older Sacred Harp books you can find the same characters. Now this little hymn book is small enough to carry in your pocket and has the same characters as the big book, which has music. Many hymns will have the same "CM," "LM," etc. in either book. That is the meter inclination. So any hymn listed "CM" will sing with any tune listed with the same meter in the Sacred Harp. It is the same with all other characters. So "Amazing Grace" (CM) will sing with any tune listed as

Sacred Harp Singers

CM. Old leaders in revivals could sing all day on the same tune and never use the same words. This type of singing was referred to by Shakespeare in his dramas. Other references related to Sacred Harp Singing includes: *South Carolina,* by Oxford University Press, N.Y., 1949, and *History of Sacred Harp* by George P. Fullen. David Crockett also loved and sang these old tunes, and in fact was known to be an excellent singer.

The first known Sacred Harp published as such was in 1844 by B. F. White in Philadelphia. This book with several revisions is still used in various parts of Texas, Alabama, Georgia, Tennessee, etc. The following are some of the annual days and places where Sacred Harp Singers meet each year: Easter (location determined by invitation); 3rd Sunday in May (Beckville, Presbyterian); 4th Sunday in May (Lufkin, Old Union Church);

3rd Sunday in June (Pine Hill, Zion Hill Church); 4th Sunday in July (Pine Grove, near Pine Hill).

The customary way of singing has changed very little in my memory. These tunes were taught to us by our parents largely, but we also had singing schools in our communities. The Sacred Harp Singing has inspired love and friendship very close amongst the singers. Most of us are very consistent church people.

The Sacred Harp Singings are open to all and all are welcome to come regardless of denomination.

Here are the partial texts from several sacred harp songs.

Hinder Me Not

In all my Lord's appointed ways my journey I'll pursue,
"Hinder me not," yet much loved saints, for I must go
   with you
Tho' floods and flames, If Jesus lead, I'll follow where
   he goes;
"Hinder me not" shall be my cry, tho' earth and hell oppose.
Hallelujah
And let this feeble body fail, and let it faint and die;
My soul shall quit this mornful vale, and soar to worlds
   on high,
And I'll sing hallelujah, and you'll sing hallelujah,
And we'll sing hallelujah, when we arrive at home.

The Royal Band

Hosanna to Jesus, my soul's filled with praises,
Come, O dear brethren, and help me to sing;
No music so charming, no look is so warming,
It gives life and comfort, and gladness within.
Hosanna is ringing, O how I love singing
There's nothing so sweet as the sound of his name;
The angels in glory repeat the sad story
Of love which in Jesus is made known to man.

Loblolly sought more information about sacred harp from Dennis Jones, a master on sacred harp history and singing. *Loblolly* found him at a nursing home in Tyler, Texas, where he lives purely as a matter of convenience, because he is still a man on the go.

Dennis Jones

Lots of those old songs were brought over here by our forefathers when they came to America. They did not have the notes then, so they would sing by memory. Later, they put down the round note system, then they went to the shaped notes. The first *Sacred Harp* used only four notes in their scales. It is identically the same as the seven shapes as far as the numerals are concerned.

In our older states, Alabama, Mississippi, South Carolina, and Tennessee, they sing that old music. Quite a few of those people came from the early history of America and brought their music with them. I had an uncle who was a professional singer. He came from Georgia. He didn't know much about the science of music, but he could give you the key note. He had it down by ear like a lot of people play on instruments. He was a real good singer.

That old music was dearly loved. Back in the early days of America, most people were sincere and religious. I think the old book has some of the most religious songs in it that can be found. A lot of the songs were taken from Bible scriptures. Psalm 137 will tell you about the children of Israel in Babylonian captivity. When those people were down by the Babylon rivers, the natives of the country came around singing their songs. Making fun, the natives said, "Let's hear one of your songs." The Israelites said, "How could we sing one of our songs in a strange land?" Songs like that have deep meaning to people who love the Bible.

The Old East Texas Sacred Harp Singing Convention was organized before the Civil War. It was stopped during the war. In 1868, the convention was renewed. They met at a church about six miles east of Henderson.

We used to meet at those conventions for three days. People never got tired of singing day after day. They came from almost every county around. I don't know how the women did it, but they would get up and fix something for us to eat every day. They never complained about it, because they loved those singings. There was always a wonderful spirit in which it was carried on.

We do have many people in sacred harp who do not know a sharp from a flat, but they can still sing. I've seen lots of old men come and sit throughout the convention. They didn't sing, but you could see tears streaming down their eyes. They loved the music. I think the secret of the music lasting so long is because it was founded on true religious principles.

A good while ago, when I could get around better, when they would call a page number out, I could go ahead and give them the key before I found the page because I knew it almost by heart. I would miss sometimes, though. We never did use an instrument. I understand they do use an instrument now in Alabama and some of the older states.

Hall Rousseau added some of his remembrances of the sacred harp. A great regret for him is that he can't still make all the singings.

Hall Rousseau

First, I'd like to say that according to my grandparents, the sacred harp music was brought to this country from Europe by the Pilgrim fathers, way back yonder, and it's with us still.

We had very few songbooks in my early days. I remember over at our church at Zion Hill, we had what you call Little Hymnal Books. And they had memorized the truth of these songs. The song leader would get up and announce the song and he would read one verse and they would all sing. No one had a book but him. He'd read another verse, and they would sing again. Well, later on, about the time I became ten or twelve years old, this was done away with and everybody had songbooks. I remember a songbook known as the *Gospel Gleaner*. Well, it seemed, as best I can remember, that there was competition between the *Sacred Harp* and the *Gospel Gleaner* which didn't live very long. The *Sacred Harp* was our church hymnal at Zion Hill until about 1943. When they loaded the old Model T's up to go to church, why, the old *Sacred Harp* always went along. But from around 1943, we got the church books, which gave more of the poetry and so forth. A number of old songs that are in this *Sacred Harp* (for instance, "Sweet By and By," and songs like that) was in there and kinda carried over the *Sacred Harp* to the present.

The sacred harp music, the best I remember when it got into full swing, was originated in Dothan, Alabama. Fella by the name of White was the publisher of it. When I began to try to sing a little and attend song services and so forth, his picture was always on the front flyleaf of the songbook. The *Sacred Harp* has changed some. They've taken a few songs out, but not many. Instead of changing and getting a new book, they have gone ahead and just put annexes over in the back. I can remember when I first started noticing that there were almost three hundred song pages. Now in the *Sacred Harp* book there are close to five hundred. These have been added from year to year, down through this time of history. Some of them I like and some I don't, but that's for them and not for me to judge.

I remember my father plowing all day long and looking to me as if he was tired all out. But after supper, he'd get in a rocking chair on the front porch and rock at least one of the children asleep. He'd sing sacred harp music until they went to sleep, and sometimes it looked like he was going to sing himself to sleep. My granddaddy and grandmother were great sacred harp believers, and they'd even travel from DeBerry to Smith County on the other side of Troup.

My granddaddy would often sit out on the front porch in the evening. Then you'd hear him singing sacred harp songs.

I had two uncles that were great fox hunters. One of them was single, and he lived there with Grandpa and Granny part of the time. The other one lived about two hundred yards from them, and they had a pack of hounds. Well, you'd hear Grandpa start humming. The next thing you knew, them dogs would get out there in front of him in the yard in about a half-moon circle and start howling! It was the most wonderful thing you ever saw, them old hounds there. After Grandpa would sing five or six songs, he'd, you might say, come alive, and see them old dogs out there howling. Off the porch he'd go, get him some rocks and sticks, and chase them off. Well, he'd get back up there, nod, and watch for a while. Finally, he'd start singing again. You'd see an old dog reach his head out, and directly he'd come out. Another would come out, and the next thing you know, they were all howling and Grandpa was singing. It was an unforgettable scene.

Once you get sacred harp music in your system, you'll never in the world get away from it. You'll always appreciate it. In fact, I think sometimes that almost all of these songs was strictly inspired by the Holy Spirit.

Fifty Country Proverbs

Patch grief with proverbs.
— Anonymous

Whether short and sweet or short and sour, proverbs are characterized by brevity. Nevertheless these single sentences are memorable, for they embrace the wit and wisdom of Texas folk.

The social conditions under which a people live, their observations of situations, and the manner of their thinking are all reflected in their proverbs. It is understandable, therefore, that proverbs were once used in the education of the young as a handing down of the wisdom of the old. Here is a selection of fifty "country proverbs" from the Texas grass roots.
— *Loblolly*

A dry well teaches the worth of water.

A hit dog always hollers.

Any woman who doesn't know true value can throw out more with a teaspoon than a hardworking man can bring in with a shovel.

A plowman on his legs is higher than a gentleman on his knees.

As a tree falleth, so shall it lie.

A whistling girl and a crowing hen will always come to no good end.

Bad breath is better than none at all.

Better to have a tired arm than an empty stomach.

Candor breeds hatred.

Curses, like chickens, come home to roost.

Do a man a good deed and he'll never forgive you.

Do not call a man happy until you have seen the end of his days.

Don't dare to kiss an ugly girl; she'll tell the world about it.

Every old hen thinks her chick is the blackest.

Experience keeps a dear school, but fools will have no other.

Fear kills quicker than illness.

Fools think the same things at the same time.

Good courage breaks bad luck.

He's like a goose: he wakes up in a new world every morning.

He who lives in hope will die fasting.

Hope deferred makes the heart sick.

If you go barefoot, don't plant thorns.

If you sleep with dogs, you will wake up with fleas.

Industry makes all things easy.

Kissing don't last; cooking does.

Knaves and fools divide the world between them.

Let sleeping dogs lie.

Lies ride upon debt's back.

Little strokes fell great oaks.

Modest dogs miss much meat.

Nothing but money is sweeter than honey.

Nothing dries faster than a tear.

Only fools are sure.

Patch grief with proverbs.

Pity melts the mind to love.

Procrastination is the theft of time.

Quick stitches save the britches.

Ready money is ready medicine.

Sleep is the brother of death.

So late smart, so soon dead.

Sweep before your own door.

The person who always has an ax to grind doesn't chop much.

The sleeping fox catches no poultry.

They that touch pitch will be defiled.

Ugliness is the guardian of woman.

Useful burdens become light.

Warm hands, warm heart, cold feet, no sweetheart.

What can't be cured must be endured.

You never miss the water until the well goes dry.

Zeal is only for wise men, but is found mostly in fools.

Monroe Brannon

I don't know what will be our next blessing in disguise. In my ninety years of experience, I find that the last twenty-five years have been the most progressive. I hope that in the last quarter of the twentieth century our present and future generation will continue to carry on. For that is the purpose for which we are all created. That is, we are to go forth and multiply and subdue the earth. Good luck to you all.

—M. Brannon

Monroe Brannon was born in Louisiana, but he moved to the Gary area as a child. Not too long ago, he moved to nearby Carthage, where he is now living in a nursing home. He is still bright and alert to the affairs of the world around him.

Monroe was one of the very first persons ever interviewed for *Loblolly,* and the stories he shared with the Gary students appeared in the first issue. After that, he frequently gave his time to describe his remembrances of Gary past with the magazine staff members. All that he asked was a day's notice in order to collect his thoughts on the particular subject. Then he would be ready to talk when the interviewers appeared at his home.

Monroe shared with *Loblolly* his fantastic memory of events and people going back to the time he was two and a half years of age. Throughout his life, he was a keen observer of all that he saw and heard, and he forgot little. And so he was able to provide stories on a wide range of people and activities. He did so with kindness and wit. In the pages that follow, you are invited to share in the experiences of his long life.

—Loblolly

I was born in Choudrant, Louisiana, on May 7, 1886, in Lincoln Parish. Left there in 1895. Moved to Ford community, and got there Christmas morning, where I went to school in 1895. Lived there five years, and attended school at the Ingram schoolhouse; then for three years, we went to Tennessee church. Then, in 1900, in January, we moved down here two miles from town and bought the R. V. Cassity place, and attended school up the tracks. When they went to extend the rail lines from Gary to Center, that school was in the way. So my father, and two other men who were trustees, put that schoolhouse on long skidpoles, and moved it off down here, and bought an acre from right where your schoolhouse is located now, and the railroad gave them one hundred dollars for the house and moved it for them, and that was the first schoolhouse that was built here in town. Then later, they built this two-story house right down here where Miss Naomi Williams lives. That was the next schoolhouse they built.

The family consisted of my father, mother, three brothers, two sisters, and a hired hand. There were nine of us in all. We first located in what is now known as the Ford community, about five miles southwest of where Gary was to be. Farming was our occupation. We found the country sparsely settled with small farms. At most, about twenty percent of the land was in cultivation, with small farms round the house. The houses were made of logs, with stick and dirt chimneys. There were some better houses made of planks, but they all had the same kind of chimneys.

Farming was the only enterprise at that time. We had very few farm implements. In fact, plows were about the only tools we had, except for the hoes and axes. People lived in a way to make a living, supporting themselves on small farms. They planted gardens. They had potatoes, peanuts, corn, and a small amount of land in cotton for a money crop.

They usually canned or dried fruit and put away all the potatoes and everything else they possibly could for a home living. We could shuck corn and take it to the mill to be ground for our bread. We had milk and butter and most else, so there were very few things to buy. The main items were sugar, coffee, and flour. Of course, we had to buy soda and salt and a little black pepper. Outside of that, every farm was self-supporting.

There was about twenty percent of the land in cultivation then. The rest of it was forests of short-needle pine. The creek and the river bottoms were heavily timbered with large hardwood trees like oak. Having very limited farm implements, we had no way of clearing the land, because the timber was so heavy. And our farm tools were such that we couldn't cultivate very much land anyway.

The people that lived here were fine people. They were happy folks and made the best type of neighbors. They would help you in every way.

What did we do for fun? We'd cook up a great pot of syrup candy, then we'd grease our hands with tallow and go to pulling that candy. We'd get with a girl, and one would pull crossways, and one would pull the other way, until that candy would become real light. You know, it would be dark in the beginning.

Now, when we had a real candy drawing, we'd buy the candy—penny sticks of various colors. We'd write the girl's name on a piece of paper and put it in a box and the boys would draw names. If the colors matched, they'd get another draw, but if they mismatched, they's out, and you have to wait until they called your name again.

And in those days, we'd play River Bend and Ocean Wave, and that was just as near dancing as you could get! We'd take a little old brass lamp, with just a little bitty wick and a little handle, and put it on the mantel, and you know, it was really dark around in there. After we'd pull this candy, we'd all be eating that candy, and we'd drip that candy around on the floor, and you know, you could just hear it pulling loose. Those were great times.

And then when we'd have our valentines. You see, there was no store-made valentines in those days; they all had to be cut out and printed and made. We had what was called love cards, beautiful little cards. We'd cut out part of those cards and paste it on the valentine and write some verses under there, such as:

> As sure as the grass grows,
> Round the stump,
> You are my Valentine,
> Sugar lump,
> Sure as the grapes grow,
> On the vine,
> You are my sweet
> Valentine.

These'd all have to be drawn out, you know, and read! Oh, yeah! They were all deposited in a box, and we'd appoint someone to read them; the boys and girls would take turns. We'd always know who was going to get that valentine before it was read! And sometimes we'd write a valentine to a certain girl and put it in that box and it would just kill some of them old boys! Those were great days!

Playing those ring games, one of the main games was Snap. A boy and a girl would hold up and the third party would snap the girl (or a girl would snap a boy), and they'd run round and round that ring till they caught them. Then, whichever one got caught, well, they was out.

Monroe Brannon

Then we'd waltz, you know, hook up and march around, and that was called Irish Trot. Ocean Wave and River Bend was a lot like square dancing.

We usually had about one week for our holidays because our schools were from four to six months. We could not lose much time from farm work—everybody had to work, you know. We'd have a Fourth of July picnic and a great Christmastime. They'd have two great cedar trees and have each fixed so you could turn them, and the people would tie all of their presents and things on there, and they'd play the violin for a while. Then they'd have a number of the younger ones picked to deliver the presents. Then we'd have more music. We'd work till Christmas Eve at dinner. Then we'd go to town, little town like Gary or Carthage, and buy your candy 'n' apples 'n' oranges; it was stick candy then, wasn't any fancy candy in those days, fancy-made candy chocolate and stuff like that. We

had a variety of nuts, such as pecans and almonds and butternuts and chestnuts, and a coconut or two. Firecrackers, oh, that was it! These little five-cents-a-bunch China firecrackers, we'd buy those. We'd have to build up a fire to light them by. We didn't have too many matches, you know; we had no lighter. There was no such thing as a lighter. We'd build a fire up in front of the house in the neighborhood and the boys would gather, of course; girls never did run with the boys then. They were in the house with Christmas dolls and other things. They can't go out with the boys. No-o-o, that's too much fun! Anyhow, we'd build that fire up and all gather around and shoot those firecrackers and roman candles (we had those in those days) and skyrockets. You'd set it up in the ground and fire it and it'd go high and burst in the air. We had those things since 1900.

And after we'd finish all that, in those days people clearing the land would make "brushing," and nearly everybody cleared ten, fifteen, twenty acres each winter. Birds would roost in that. Well, we went to the lighted stumps and cut us some long-g-g splinters. Then went to the plum orchard and got up a little plum tree and had a good handle to it. Then we'd light those torches and all get around the brush and sort of shake it, and the little birds would come out. Then we'd kill the bird—that's called bird thrashing. Then, after the bird thrashing was over, we all gathered together and built up a fire, near a creek or the branch. We'd eat those birds. We'd cut us a little stick, just so long, and we carried salt along with us. We salted

The Loblolly Book

Monroe Brannon telling stories

those birds and stuck them on that and broiled them by the fire and sat around the fire. That was fun!

When we first came in here, we lived over yonder and there was no railroads anywhere. They first put in a hardwood mill down on Brushy Creek and built a little railroad out of Timpson down to the hardwood mill. Bunch of northern people from Akron, Ohio, cut that hardwood timber and shipped it up there to a furniture factory. That's when all the furniture was wood, you know. Then they decided they'd connect this railroad, and they branched off down here about two miles and came through our farm and came on to Gary with it and built it right in front of where Mable Bird lives. That was in 1898. They put in a big commissary and saloon just as you cross the railroad track to the right. They put in a big mill about two miles down the track to the right, and another mill about two miles down the track toward Timpson called the Wade Miller Mill. Then Ramsey and

Thomason put in a mill right down here where James Phillips lives. Then we had a big mill down here at Murvaul.

That was when whiskey was here, and it was plenty rough. Dr. Daniels and I worked together—I'd hold them and he'd sew them up. Charlie Boggs got ahold of a fellow over there one night in that saloon across the track with a handsaw, and he whipped him over the face with it, and we laid him out there on the counter and sewed him up and patched him up. We'd also amputate fingers and toes, and we had no way to do it but just cut it off! Had no anesthetics or anything like that when I was a druggist.

In 1898, when the railroad came through, it connected Timpson and Carthage. Gary sprang up and with it three large saloons. The first one up was Garrison and Avery in the east part of the town. They had a large general store and saloon combined. Then our next saloon was Davison and

Kyle, known as the Red Front. I knew Mr. Jeff Kyle real well, the saloon-keeper. They had an old Irishman named Dad, and he'd take a washpot out back of the saloon and make chili. All those old-timers would have a few drinks and get around that pot of chili and really have a time. The next saloon was owned by Tom Treadaway. It was where G&S grocery now sets. He had a saloon there and a hotel, rooming house upstairs.

Whiskey was brought in by train. I remember they'd put two- by twelve-inch planks right on the floor of the Garrison and Avery saloon up to the boxcar doors. They'd get the barrels down those and roll right into the saloon. They'd stop it and store it away.

At the time the Red Front saloon was in operation, it was the most popular place in town. There was a large sawmill north of town at Murvaul, another one mile east of Gary, and an extra large mill and planer two miles south of Gary, the Wade Miller Mill. When they laid off Saturday, at noon usually, all that sawmill crowd would come to town and they'd gather mostly at the old Red Front saloon.

Between Davison's store and the Red Front saloon was a half a lot with no building on, and that gave them a roadway to the back of the Red Front saloon. Well, old Dad, an old Irishman, they didn't know where he came from, set him up a chili joint to make chili. He bought him a forty-gallon washpot, those old cast-iron washpots, and two number-two tubs, and had a common table. He bought a bunch of bowls and spoons. On a Saturday morning, early, he would get about thirty pounds of beef and cut that in half-inch cubes, and he'd then get five pounds of beef fat and put that in the pot. Then he'd add a few gallons of water and get it to boiling, and then he would add two or three cans of cayenne pepper and about a cup or two of salt. With all that he'd have a day's supply of chili ready for his customers.

Dad had that forty-gallon pot of chili, and they'd sometimes pitch in and buy a gallon barrel of whiskey to put on the table out there. They'd all drink some whiskey, and then the wrestling matches would start up. They'd select three judges—we didn't know anything about referees then, they were called judges. There would be three judges, and the wrestlers that were to wrestle would put their knives and money, watch, or whatever they had into the judges' hats. The time limit was to be three minutes. It was "bear hug," no side wrestling, no sideholds in those days, just "bear hug." They would start with the bear hug and had two minutes in which to throw the man down. Then he had to hold him down one minute to win the match. Sometimes an opponent could throw the man down, but the man would get up. Then it would be a draw. Then they'd all drink a round or two apiece and have another bowl of chili, and they'd get pretty well steamed up. Then those wrestling matches really got rough.

They were mostly men of forty to sixty years old; a lot wore full beards. And we had right smart trouble later in the evening when they got all steamed with that liquor. The fights got rougher, and they might grab a handful of beard. Then they would get to fighting—black an eye or knock a tooth out. But the judges would stop them before it went too far. And that was exciting to a teen-ager standing on the side like Otto Bell, Oce Cassity, and myself. We stood way back, leaned back against the Davison general store, and let them have the entire wrestling ground. It was about an acre around there. And it would be one wrestling match after another and a few little fights in between. The longer the thing lasted, the rougher it got later in the evening.

Now the older set, sixty years and older, was across the tracks in front of the Henry Griffith Hotel playing marbles. Jesse McGee and John Smith were the notorious marble players. They were the best. And the younger teen-age boys had a croquet yard right in front of the Daniels drugstore on the square. And they'd play croquet and the old men would play marbles, and generally, the sawmill element was the one that put on the big show in back of the Red Front. It really grew rough sometimes, but those three judges would never let them go too far with the fight.

Saturday evening, the town, the square, was just covered with wagons and buggies and horseback riders. There'd be at least two hundred to three hundred people in town. We'd have a crowd of fifty to a hundred people in back of the Red Front saloon. It was a regular wrestling ground and chili stand. There was something going on to interest everyone. Life did quiet down afterwards when prohibition was voted in and when the sawmills moved on.

When I was nineteen years of age, I hired to the doctor, Z. L. Daniels, to work in the drugstore at Gary, Texas. On January 1, 1906, I moved into the home with the doctor and his good wife, Maude. They were good, hardworking, honest, Christian people. So, together, the three of us worked almost day and night.

The drugstore job consisted of a three-way proposition. His wife, Maude, was postmistress, and the post office was located in the drugstore. The only telephone in town was long-distance telephone, and it was also located in the drugstore. So between the three jobs of answering the phone, tending the post office, and selling drugs, I had quite a job.

Dr. Daniels practiced medicine at that time. We had no graded roads, and the sole transportation was by horseback. He would make his calls on horseback, carrying a little sack of medicine, and diagnose the case, dose out the medicine, and leave instructions for taking it. He'd say, "I'll see you tomorrow," and make off for the next house.

We had a lot of sickness during the summer months, such as typhoid fever, slow fever, malaria, and especially the killers—yellow fever and black jaundice. In the winter months, it wasn't much better. We had the flus, colds, and pneumonia.

I had access to the doctor's books, so I studied medicine at night and soon qualified to fill prescriptions under the old permit system. I had to take an examination for the license. It lessened the doctor's time with each case so he could have more time to visit more patients. He would write the prescriptions and send them in, and I would fill them.

In those days, all prescriptions and chemicals were sent in bulk. Everything was measured and weighed out. We used an apothecary scale. It was a scale which one measured drugs on. Apothecary weights are twelve ounces to a pound, whereas average scales are sixteen ounces. I could weigh small amounts to one-half grain. I would weigh out the medicine and then thoroughly compound it with a pestle and a mortar. Then I'd put it in a bottle and measure the liquid and granulates that measured from drops to cubic centimeters and ounces. I'd stir that in and add water in sufficient quantities to make the total amount of usually six to eight ounces. Then I'd find the cork, place it on the bottle, look at the directions, and write them on the label and paste it on the bottle. It was a long, drawn-out, time-taking operation.

I had to fill prescriptions day and night. I tell you, I had to go and fill prescriptions at the dead hour of night, and I would really be sleepy from working all day. The first thing I would do was to splash ice water on my face to wake me up. Then I would look carefully over the prescriptions, always, because there were five to six drugs. Then I would consult my medical book for maximum and minimum doses of all chemicals to see if there were any mistakes made.

In those days, there were no restrictions on the sales of poisonous medicines or narcotics. I was allowed to sell denatured alcohol, chloroform, carbonic acid, strychnine, also morphine. I sold that over the counter in the open market just like chill cure, aspirin, and other drugs.

When filling the prescriptions for my customers, I would sing them a little ditty. It goes like this: "When you get sick/Come in some time/Take a little turpentine." And sometimes I'd say to the customer when I was filling the prescription: "Take one every two hours until death comes as a sweet relief."

After filling prescriptions for ten years, I felt like I was the world renown. I could cure anything from ingrowing toenails, falling arches, to broken hearts.

One time, a little boy came in there and sat around on a little stool. He never did anything. I asked him, "What do you want?" He said, "I'm sorta looking around for the doctor." Well, I asked him if there was somebody sick. "Oh, no! There ain't somebody sick, only the baby is a-having spasms."

Another time, there was a great big boy. He came over to the drugstore one day. He lived with Uncle Cato, who was about a hundred years old. Everybody loved Uncle Cato. Well, the boy came over here when the doctor was out, and he told me that Uncle Cato was sick and that he wanted me to fix him up some medicine. I asked him what was the matter with Uncle Cato. He said, "Uncle Cato is constipated." Well, I went ahead and poured him three ounces of croton oil, and I put the directions on there.

It said, "Put three drops of oil on a teaspoon of sugar." He went home to give him the medicine. They couldn't read good, and they saw the three teaspoons, so they gave Uncle Cato three teaspoons full of that croton oil. The boy was back up there the next day, and I asked him about Uncle Cato. He said, "He is all right and he is resting well." I said, "Did the medicine work?" "Oh, yes, sir," was the reply. "He moved once before he died and twice after."

I had to get up many times in the middle of the night and fill prescriptions. We had no electric light, no rural-delivery mail service, no graded roads, and no local telephones. Many a time I had to deliver the medicine myself and also get out and call people into the long-distance telephones. I generally assisted the doctor in such cases as broken limbs and collarbones. We would set the bone in place and heavily wrap it with bandages and then use wooden splints to hold it in place for three to four weeks until it knitted back together. We had no hospital nearer than Shreveport, so people had to do their own doctoring at home as best as they could.

I had a lot of experience in the medicine business. We pulled teeth with no anesthetics. We just had the little hook instrument that goes right below the gum and gets the tooth loose. You didn't even cut around the tooth, but just yanked them out.

Oh, I pulled lots of teeth! They'd faint every time. I usually held their arm and hand down while the doctor went to work. There once was an old lady that hit me and knocked the breath out of me. We had mail sacks at the post office. We'd lay out the fainted person and later they'd come to. It was rough! Oh! We did the best we could for what we had.

Student Contributors

Chinquapin
Douglass School, Douglass, Texas (Adviser: Pauline Toumlin)

Carla Allen
Jack Allen
Leah Allen
Bonnie Baker
Carol Ball
Teresa Belyeu
Brenda Berry
Leonard Berry
Ike Blanton
Mike Bobo
Mickey Brandon
Denise Burkland
Richie Butler
Debbie Carroll
Dan Chumley
Dae Clayton
Dave Collier
Sherri Davis
Binford Deckard
Brenda Deckard
William Dolb
Lisa Fatherlee

Judy Fields
Demedia Flanagan
Rita Fox
Dennis Harber
Mitzi Harber
Phyllis Hayter
Bobby Hobson
Sheri Hobson
Dennis Johnson
Diana Johnson
Linda Johnson
Lisa Johnson
Tammie Johnson
Bambie Kerr
Mike Lowery
Darlene Lunsford
David Mayne
Mary Mayne
Raleigh McElroy
Robert McElroy
Frank McGowan
Steven Milstead

Susan Milstead
Rena Kay Parmley
Carl Perkins
Vickie Perkins
Sharon Pinkston
Susan Pitts
Susan Pruitt
Doris Scott
Pam Smith
Tammy Smith
Veronica Smith
Sandy Tackett
Joey Tarrant
Pam Tarrant
Susan Tarrant
Mavis Taylor
Lisa Tindall
Shelby Wages
Kelle Walters
La Jean Ward
Eloise Whitaker
Fred Wolfes
Tim Yates

Loblolly
Gary High School, Gary, Texas (Adviser: Lincoln King)

Geneva Adams
Sherry Adams
Billy Anderson
Johnny Arnold
Gaye Barton
James Barton
Jimmy Beasley
Brenda Beska
Emma Blair
Johnathan Chadwick
Valerie Clark
Rhonda Cockrell
Wesley Coleman
Margie Cranford
Tim Cranford
Brooksie Cross
Amelia Davis
Anita Davis
Annette Davis
Debra Davis
Scott Davis
Stuart Davis
Sylvia Davis
Nerissa Dill
Billy Downing
Peggy Downing
Terri Drewery
David Elliot
Tim Essery
Teena Fannin
Dee Fielder
Tom Fielder
Donna Frazier
Danny Garrison
Mary Garrison
Lauri Gauntt
Annette Gray
Darrel Griffith
Kay Griffith
Tonya Griffith
Vicki Griffith
Wanda Haberle
Glen Hall
Keith Hall
David Hammers
Rodney Hammers
Freda Hardin
Alene Harris
Timmy Harris
Sandra Harvey
Larry Hayles
Tammy Haynes
Belinda Hill
David Hodge
Tommy Hooper
Rhonda Hough

Student Contributors

Thomas Hughes
Keith Hulsey
Kevin Hulsey
Mark Hulsey
Greg Humber
Peggy Humber
Timmy Humber
Brenda Jones
Cindy Jones
Marvin Jordan
Bobby Kelly
Cynthia Korzeniewski
Norbert Korzeniewski
Valerie Korzeniewski
Geneva LaGrone
Beth Lake
Dwain Lake
Kathy Lenox
Regina Lenox
Jeff Lyons
Russell McCullough
Darla Marx
Henry Marx
Rhonda Mayo
Chris Morton
David Musick
Travis Nutt
Debbie O'Shields
David Pass
Myrtis Penn
Roger Penn
David Reider

Max Ritter
Terry Ritter
Mark Robinson
Jan Serwich
Sherry Serwich
Lisa Shaw
Gwenda Singletary
Donna Smith
Garland Smith
Bonnie Spence
Lisa Stephenson
Sally Stockwell
Cindy Storkstill
Steve Strain
Donna Thomas
Robin Thomas
Christine Tinkle
Fred Tinkle
Cheryl Williams
Darlene Womack
Jimmy Woodfin
Johnny Woodfin
Lester Wright
Valerie Wright
Bobbie Wyatt
Charles Wyatt
Connie Young
Sherry Young
Andy Youngblood
Lori Youngblood
Mike Youngblood

Old Timer
Albany High School, Albany, Texas (Advisers: Barney Nelson and Winifred Waller)

Candy Asbury
John Ayers
Larry Boone
John Caldwell
Ray Caldwell
Wade Caldwell
Jeri Cameron

Jamie Collinsworth
Nancy Durham
Tracie Edgar
Craig Estep
Gary Estep
Maryanna Green
Kris Groda

Mark Harris
Michelle Harris
Sallie Harrison
Karen Hill
Darla Holder
Charles Holson
Debbie Irvin
Alan Jones
Jonny Jones
Betty Key
Letha Key
Jim Law
James Lenamon
Renee McCoy
Karen Macgregor
Sharon Macgregor
Marshall Mitchell
Michelle Morgan
Deidra Newcomb

Becky Parker
Margaret Peacock
Lenaa Pickard
Paul Quesenberry
Liz Sazama
Karen Schkade
Tim Scott
Ray Seedig
Paul Stribling
Cathy Teinert
John Teinert
Rodney Wade
Lori Wafer
Jim Waller
Debbie Wilfong
Kay Williams
Deanna Wiloth
Tammy Wiloth